the best of
2006

TRAVEL
+LEISURE

the best of
2006
the world's greatest hotels, resorts, and spas

TRAVEL
+LEISURE
BOOKS

AMERICAN EXPRESS PUBLISHING CORPORATION
NEW YORK

TRAVEL + LEISURE THE BEST OF 2006

Editor Roy Finamore
Art Director Sandra Garcia
Photo Editor Malú Alvarez
Special Correspondent Jaime Gross
Copy Editor Marie Timell
Fact Checkers Meeghan Truelove, Alia Akkam
Production C. M. Wheeler
Editorial Intern Sarah Kantrowitz

TRAVEL + LEISURE MAGAZINE

Editor-in-Chief Nancy Novogrod
Executive Editor Jennifer Barr
Managing Editor Michael S. Cain
Design Director Emily Crawford
Features Editor Nathan Lump
Associate Managing Editor Jeffrey Bauman
Senior Copy Editor Jane Halsey
Associate Editor Amy Farley
Photo Editor Katie Dunn
Production Manager Ayad Sinawi

AMERICAN EXPRESS PUBLISHING CORPORATION

Senior Vice President, Chief Marketing Officer Mark V. Stanich
Vice President, Books and Products Marshall Corey
Senior Marketing Manager Bruce Spanier
Assistant Marketing Manager Sarah Ross
Corporate Production Manager Stuart Handleman
Senior Operations Manager Phil Black
Business Manager Tom Noonan

Cover design by Sandra Garcia
Front and back cover: Detail of a Sills Huniford–designed
room at the St. Regis Hotel, New York City.
Photograph by Andrea Fazzari.

Page 2: Murano Urban Resort in Paris, France.
Opposite: At Cuixmala, in Jalisco, Mexico.
Page 285: The Sleep Well room at Copenhagen's Hotel Fox.

ISBN 1-932624-12-0
ISSN 1559-0372

Published by American Express Publishing Corporation
1120 Avenue of the Americas, New York, New York 10036

Distributed by DK Publishing, Inc.
375 Hudson Street, New York, New York 10014

Manufactured in the United States of America

contents

Eagles Nest Luxury Villa Retreat, Russell, New Zealand, opposite.

how the book works

Rankings of the top hotels in the world (presented at the beginning of each chapter) are based on the 2005 results of *Travel+Leisure*'s annual readers' survey, the World's Best Awards. Subscribers to T+L were invited to take an on-line survey developed by the magazine's editors and monitored by the research firm Harris Interactive. Readers rated hotels they'd visited recently on a 1-to-5 scale for five characteristics: rooms/facilities, location, service, restaurants/food, and value. The ratings were then averaged, creating the overall scores given here. (A complete explanation of the methodology can be found on our Web site, www.travelandleisure.com.)

For the book, T+L editors have also selected new hotels, as well as existing hotels that have been redesigned or have added new features, to offer as the best new choices for travelers now. In addition, throughout the book you'll find "hotels we love"—editors' all-time favorites that stand out for their superlative features, whether it's the perfect hotel bar or a sublime spa.

introduction

BY NANCY NOVOGROD

What does it mean for a hotel, resort, or spa to be included in *The Best of 2006*? The first in a series of *Travel+Leisure* books, this volume takes as its starting point the results of our most recent World's Best Awards readers' survey, which ranks the top hotels based on the consistent level of quality in categories that include accommodations and service, great location, and outstanding cost/value ratio. To be sure, there are also less tangible attributes that propel a nominee to the top, whether it's the surprising juxtaposition of modern design with the rugged African bush, the sweeping panorama of a city skyline framed by a bathroom window, or the impossibly white sand of a perfect crescent beach. Because we know these are places that many of you will want to visit, we have included the World's Best Directory at the back of the book, with thumbnail reviews and essential contact information for the award winners.

But T+L is nothing if not forward-looking: along with useful travel insights and roundups of hotels we love for any number of reasons, from the perfect bar to the most helpful staff, we have gathered together our Editors' Picks of the new and newly redone properties that have appeared in the magazine's pages over the past year. Let's call them the World's Best Award contenders.

As U.S. travelers extend their reach into new and distant worlds, hotels have increasingly become destinations in and of themselves, embracing the regional style of their surroundings, highlighting the cuisine of their celebrated chefs, and providing the insider access of their expert concierges. The bar for excellence in travel keeps getting higher, both for the World's Best Award winners and for the favorites of the editors of *Travel+Leisure*. Rest assured that the best of 2006 are better than ever before.

united states
and
canada

world's best top 100
united states and canada

The Wheatleigh, in Lenox, Massachusetts,
right. Opposite, clockwise from top:
The Peninsula, Beverly Hills; a suite at the
Bellagio, Las Vegas; a junior suite
at the Wheatleigh.

1 **Rusty Parrot Lodge & Spa**
JACKSON HOLE, WYOMING **92.05**

2 **Blackberry Farm**
WALLAND, TENNESSEE **91.24**

3 **The Point** UPPER SARANAC LAKE,
NEW YORK **91.00**

4 **The Peninsula** BEVERLY HILLS **90.64**

5 **Aerie Resort** MALAHAT,
VANCOUVER ISLAND **89.77**

6 **Wickaninnish Inn** TOFINO,
VANCOUVER ISLAND **89.76**

7 **Post Ranch Inn** BIG SUR,
CALIFORNIA **89.44**

8 **Tu Tu' Tun Lodge** GOLD BEACH,
OREGON **89.34**

9 **Marquesa Hotel** KEY WEST,
FLORIDA **89.03**

10 **Monmouth Plantation** NATCHEZ,
MISSISSIPPI **88.32**

11 **Windsor Court Hotel**
NEW ORLEANS **87.97**

12 **The Peninsula** CHICAGO **87.84**

13 **Hotel Bel-Air** LOS ANGELES **87.74**

14 **Mandarin Oriental** MIAMI **87.70**

15 **XV Beacon** BOSTON **87.63**

16 **Ritz-Carlton Chicago
(A Four Seasons Hotel)** **87.39**

17 **Four Seasons Hotel** BOSTON **87.24**

18 **Auberge du Soleil**
RUTHERFORD, CALIFORNIA **87.16**

19 **St. Regis Hotel** NEW YORK CITY **87.05**

20 **Raffles L'Ermitage** BEVERLY HILLS **87.03**

21 **Four Seasons Hotel**
SAN FRANCISCO **87.02**

22 **Four Seasons Hotel**
NEW YORK CITY **86.91**

23 **Lodge at Pebble Beach**
CALIFORNIA **86.84**

24 **Four Seasons Hotel** LAS VEGAS **86.77**

25 **Inn at Spanish Bay**
PEBBLE BEACH, CALIFORNIA **86.74**

26 **Mansion on Turtle Creek,
A Rosewood Hotel** DALLAS **86.74**

27 **Inn at Little Washington**
WASHINGTON, VIRGINIA **86.50**

28 **Sooke Harbour House**
SOOKE, VANCOUVER ISLAND **86.46**

29 **Little Nell** ASPEN, COLORADO **86.45**

30 **The Wauwinet** NANTUCKET **86.40**

31 **Little Palm Island Resort & Spa**
LITTLE TORCH KEY, FLORIDA **86.40**

32 **Regent Beverly Wilshire**
BEVERLY HILLS **86.30**

33 **The Broadmoor** COLORADO
SPRINGS **86.16**

34 **Bellagio** LAS VEGAS **86.02**

key to the price icons   **$** under $250   **$$** $250 - 499   **$$$** $500 - 749   **$$$$** $750 - 999   **$$$$$** $1,000 - 1,999

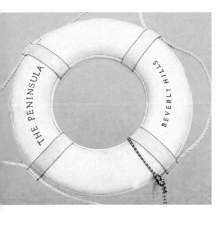

14

The Taipan Suite at the
Mandarin Oriental in New York,
above and right. Opposite:
The Four Seasons Resort, Maui.

world's best
top 25
hawaii

A guest room at
Chebeague Island
Inn. Opposite:
The hotel's exterior.

chebeague island inn

CHEBEAGUE ISLAND, MAINE

This Greek Revival–style building—a leisurely 1½-hour ferry ride from Portland, Maine—offers guests a trip back in time with simply styled, whitewashed rooms, cocktails on the veranda, and not a phone or a television in sight. Instead, guests can read by the large stone fireplace in the Great Room, play croquet on the lawn, or borrow one of the complimentary L.L. Bean bikes to explore the island. The dining room specializes in local cuisine—and by local, they really mean local. The seafood comes from island waters, and herbs and produce are procured from neighboring farms and the inn's own kitchen garden. There is one caveat: of the 21 rooms, five share bathrooms, so if you're seeking privacy (and no shower lines) be sure to request one en suite.

Chebeague Island Inn 61 South Rd., Chebeague Island, Maine; 207/846-5155; www.chebeagueislandinn.com; doubles from $$

twin farms

BARNARD, VERMONT

With its 1795 farmhouse, Twin Farms boasts what must be the 300 prettiest acres in New England, including wildflower meadows, apple orchards, pine forests, a lake, a private ski run—the works. It has two spanking-new buildings. Lost in the woods, the duplex Aviary is a freestanding shaft of glass and peeled white-cedar logs with a tiny footprint—just over 1,200 square feet. The Aviary has orange Douglas-fir paneling, an orange shag rug, and a bed with an orange buttoned-leather headboard and footboard. In the Farmhouse, a common space with library chairs in perforated apple-green leather with nail-head trim divides two pairs of stacked guest rooms. One set has a tailored, rather manly, barn subtext, with exposed framing, metal-corncob table lamps, and fieldstone fireplaces. The other, an amused riff on the classic all-American farm dwelling, has skip-troweled plaster walls, bead-board wainscoting, wing-backed sofas, and red-brick fireplaces.

Twin Farms 452 Royalton Turnpike, Barnard, Vermont; 800/894-6327 or 802/234-9999; www.twinfarms.com; Aviary from $$$$$, double, Farmhouse from $$$$$; rates include three meals, wine, and spirits

Exterior of the Aviary.
Opposite: Canoes on
Copper Pond, near the
Farmhouse.

bulfinch hotel

BOSTON, MASSACHUSETTS

A group of Boston real estate developers challenged Campion A. Platt (the designer responsible for New York's MercBar and the Park Avalon) to re-create this historic 1900 building in an up-and-coming neighborhood a few blocks from Beacon Hill. The resulting 80 small rooms (average: 250 square feet) have brown leather headboards, white-on-white striped damask sheets, sleek marble bathrooms, and user-friendly touches like cordless phones and free high-speed Internet—all at an affordable price. The triangular shape of the building (similar to New York's Flatiron Building) results in unique Nose Rooms, one on each floor, which have taller ceilings, larger windows, and an additional 100 square feet.

Bulfinch Hotel
107 Merrimac St.
Boston
Massachusetts
800/624-1486 or
617/624-0202
www.bulfinch
hotel.com
Doubles from $$

A Bulfinch Hotel guest room, opposite. Above: The hotel's flatiron–style exterior.

St. Regis Hotel
2 E. 55th St.
New York, New York
800/759-7550 or
212/753-4500

www.stregis.com
Doubles from $$$$

The St. Regis Hotel's Beaux Arts façade, opposite.
Above: The newly decorated Fifth Avenue Suite.

st. regis hotel

NEW YORK, NEW YORK

world's best The St. Regis, which had last been redone in 1991, was looking, to put it generously, triste. In making their case during the competition for the redesign, Stephen Sills and James Huniford envisioned tufted sofas, fringed ottomans, crystal column lamps, vases lifted from a Giorgio Morandi still life, velvet hopsack, straw cloth, and ticking stripes glamorously reimagined in taffeta. Their approach had the advantage of reconnecting the landmark to its past, to a time when people actually lived at the hotel. "For the architecture and quality of the craftsmanship, the St. Regis is the finest hotel in New York," says Sills. The refurbished rooms, completed in 2005, have a confidential, apartment-like feel that allows travelers to live in, if only for one night, that most enduring of fantasies: a Manhattan pied-à-terre of one's own. The rooms are filled with miles of sexy welting, luxurious trims, and—in place of the reproduction Chinese-export porcelain you see everywhere—things you might genuinely want to own, like one of those elegant buttoned sofas. The only shine in a lot of hotels these days is from the mirror on the inside of the closet door. Here, shine is built in to the design.

A second-floor guest lounge at the Hotel on Rivington.

hotel on rivington

NEW YORK, NEW YORK

Finding a hotel with luxury linens in a derelict-turned-trendy neighborhood can be tricky, but it needn't be with the opening of this 110-room property on Manhattan's thriving Lower East Side. It's the tallest structure in the neighborhood, offering a new perspective on the surrounding historic buildings. Minimalist interiors are invigorated by shots of color that vary from room to room (a buttery-yellow velvet couch here, an oxblood-red wall there). The bathrooms are a real treat, with tiny Bisazza mosaic tiles in tangerine or jet-black, a Japanese soaking tub or sexy shower-with-a-view, and amenities by Paul Labrecque. The cave-like entrance and airy atrium restaurant, Thor, were designed by Marcel Wanders. In the latter, Austrian chef Kurt Gutenbrunner turns out delicacies like slow-poached lobster with cherries, fava beans, and bearnaise sauce. Or, the concierge can secure reservations at perennially packed restaurants such as Balthazar or Pastis.

Hotel on Rivington 107 Rivington St., New York, New York; 800/915-1537 or 212/475-2600; www.hotelonrivington.com; doubles from $$

hotel qt

NEW YORK, NEW YORK

Hotel QT
125 W. 45th St.
New York, New York
212/354-2323

www.hotelqt.com
Singles from $
25% discount for
guests under 25

Hotel QT's lobby pool.

With this affordable boutique hotel, the eternally expensive city of New York puts out the welcome mat for stylish-but-budget-conscious travelers. André Balazs's innovative Hotel QT is happily out of sync with its Times Square address. The 140 small, ultramodern rooms are calming cocoons in a flesh-toned palette, with soft lights and platform beds (families can request bunk beds). Frugal frills are executed with whimsical flair: in place of room-service menus, there are take-out fliers from local restaurants; mini-bar items are sold at the kiosk-style front desk. But the hotel doesn't skimp on the essentials—the beds are surprisingly plush, the TV's are flat-screen and come complete with DVD players, and high-speed Internet access is complimentary. And—surprise!—there's a pool with a swim-up bar, and a coed sauna and steam room in the lobby.

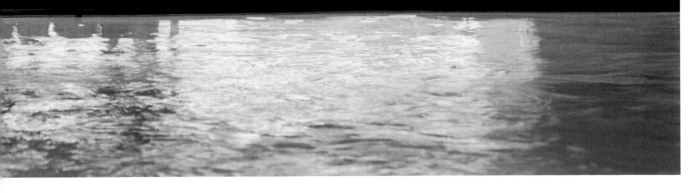

beyond room service

There's more to room service than just a basket of hard rolls dressed up as continental breakfast. ■ At New York's **Trump International Hotel & Tower** *(www.trumpintl.com)*, meals can be ordered from Jean Georges; for even more individualized service, someone will come to your room to prepare dinner. ■ The **Dar Ahlam** hotel in Skoura, Morocco *(www.darahlam. com)*, allows guests to enjoy clay-oven specialties anywhere on the property: in the desert, on the roof, or in the garden while they dangle their feet in the courtyard canals. ■ **Mollies**, the ultraluxe inn in Auckland, New Zealand *(www.mollies. co.nz)*, serves breakfast (with freshly baked pastries) on the porch overlooking Herne Bay. ■ We always come home from **Wheatleigh** *(www.wheatleigh.com)* raving as ecstatically about the resort's *pain au chocolat* as about the beauty of the Berkshires.

A dish from Jean Georges, delivered to a suite at the Trump International, above.

70 Park Avenue
New York, New York
877/707-2752 or
212/973-2400
www.70park
ave.com
Doubles from $$

Lefèvre House
14 Southside Ave.
New Paltz, New York
845/255-4747
www.lefevre
house.com
Doubles from $

70 Park Avenue

NEW YORK, NEW YORK

Kimpton's first venture in Manhattan, a 17-story limestone building four blocks from Grand Central Terminal, has a classical look—pale stone foyers, mahogany armoires, floor-to-ceiling mirrors—courtesy of renowned residential designer Jeffrey Bilhuber, whose clients include David Bowie and Anna Wintour. Enlivening the dark-wood and earth-tone interiors are playful touches such as busy-patterned pillows, logo-splashed bedspreads, and blobby Candela night-lights, which guests can move bathside for a romantic soak. Wine tastings are held in the hotel lobby and focus on a different region each month.

Lefèvre House

NEW PALTZ, NEW YORK

Don't let the frivolous pink façade of Lefèvre House fool you. Behind the Victorian frippery is a sleek, European-style inn. The 1870's farmhouse in New Paltz, New York, a funky mountain town 90 minutes north of Manhattan, puts a contemporary spin on the entire B&B stereotype. Grandmotherly antiques have been updated (a Regency love seat is covered in faux fur), starchy bed linens replaced with soft Versace sheets, and dark closets transformed into airy, walk-in showers. And forget blueberry muffins for breakfast—the morning menu now includes pears poached in pink champagne.

1804 inn at barboursville vineyards

BARBOURSVILLE, VIRGINIA

The restored interior of this intimate inn's Georgian villa, in Virginia's burgeoning wine region 20 miles from Charlottesville, is a refined mix of damask, oil paintings, four-poster beds, and claw-foot tubs. Three palatial suites have private balconies with views of the vineyards, lake, and majestic Blue Ridge Mountains; the Octagon Suite also overlooks the ruins of a historic Thomas Jefferson–designed mansion. For maximum seclusion, book one of the two cottage rooms, which are carved out of the brick 18th-century servant's quarters and screened from the rest of the property by a row of stately boxwood trees. Don't miss dinner at Palladio, the vineyard's elegant northern Italian restaurant.

**1804 Inn at
Barboursville
Vineyards**
17655 Winery Rd.
Barboursville,
Virginia
434/760-2212
www.the1804inn.com
Doubles from $

**Inn on
Biltmore Estate**
1 Antler Hill Rd.
Asheville
North Carolina
877/324-5866 or
828/225-1333
www.biltmore.com
Doubles from $

A veranda of the Inn on Biltmore Estate, opposite.

inn on biltmore estate

Hilly, humpbacked Asheville, which sits beside the French Broad River in a gap between two mountain ranges, is the cultural capital of the lower Appalachians, blending a spirit of rugged individualism with Nantucket-like sophistication. Typically, a visiting family finds a favorite hotel here and sticks with it through several generations, but a new spirit is in the air, as the old stone hotels spruce themselves up and add modern amenities to attract a younger clientele. The mammoth limestone Inn on Biltmore Estate overlooks the winery of the famous 8,000-acre Vanderbilt property. Its 213 rooms have a classic feel, like that of the manor itself.

southern
spas

Mint juleps and fried green tomatoes aren't
the only indulgences to be found below
the Mason-Dixon Line. Spas with an
antebellum twist are popping up like kudzu
at some of the South's finest resorts.
After all, even steel magnolias are entitled
to a little pampering now and then.

The open-air veranda of a
treatment room at the Inn at
Palmetto Bluff's spa. Opposite,
left: May River porch at the Inn
at Palmetto Bluff. Opposite, right:
Grand staircase at the
Sanctuary on Kiawah Island.

inn at
palmetto bluff

BLUFFTON, SOUTH CAROLINA

The Inn at Palmetto Bluff has 50 white clapboard cottages, most of which face the May River, just north of the Georgia state line. Each contains a gas-burning fireplace, Italian throws on downy beds, and a tiled bathroom scented with jasmine and pine. When housekeeping delivers the complimentary bottle of Merlot, you may want to sit tight for the rest of the day, but don't forget to wander over to the spa, which is next to a lagoon lined with oaks where snowy egrets roost at dusk. Some of the treatment rooms have old-fashioned claw-foot tubs, for soaking in frothy infusions of black cohosh, cypress, nettle, and bayberry—indigenous plants favored for centuries by low-country healers. *476 Mount Pelia Rd.; 866/706-6565 or 843/706-6500; www.palmettobluffresort.com; doubles from $.*

sanctuary on
kiawah island

KIAWAH ISLAND, SOUTH CAROLINA

Like a super-sized Tara, the Sanctuary at Kiawah Island belongs to a fictional plantation family. In the morning room, a portrait of the "Mistress" presides over moss-green brocades, floral drapes, and porcelain bibelots. The "Master" hangs his hat in the lobby bar. Tobacco-stained walnut planking creaks like the timeworn floors in an authentic antebellum mansion. Landscape architects transplanted 160 mature live oaks for the resort's entrance avenue, and Kiawah's beach glows pink at sunset as a shrimp trawler anchors in front of the resort. Treatments at the second-floor spa also have a distinctly Southern drawl: the Mint Julep Facial incorporates the Anakiri line's pure-peppermint essential oil. *1 Sanctuary Beach Dr.; 877/683-1234 or 843/768-6000; www.thesanctuary.com; doubles from $$.*

classic southern treatments

Farmhouse Spa
A fruit-infused body scrub and an herbal mask are the focus of hydrating Blackberry Mist treatment. *Walland, Tennessee; 800/273-6004 or 865/380-2260; wwwblackberryfarm.com; doubles from $$$.*

Greenbrier Spa
Named for a local mountain crop, Kate's Black Walnut Scrub is an exfoliating treatment that resurfaces dry skin. *White Sulphur Springs, West Virginia; 800/624-6070 or 304/536-1110; www.greenbrier.com; doubles from $$$.*

Sea Island Spa
The Georgia Mud Pie is a playful body wrap paired with a mineral bath. *Sea Island, Georgia; 800/732-4752 or 912/638-3611; www.seaisland.com; doubles from $$.*

Spa at Charleston Place
The spa's new Flavor of the Month sugar scrubs are made with iconic Southern infusions such as peach, magnolia, and peppermint. *Charleston, South Carolina; 800/611-5545 or 843/722-4900; www.charlestonplace.com; doubles from $$.*

old edwards inn & spa

HIGHLANDS, NORTH CAROLINA

Once a summer boardinghouse, the historic 30-room Old Edwards Inn & Spa spent three years shuttered during a makeover worthy of *The Swan.* In an annex to the original structure, the new spa is a frothy boudoir of silver, ice blue, and petal pink. The apothecary stocks Perle de Caviar creams. Vintage shoes adorn the pedicure stations. Crystal chandeliers glimmer in treatment rooms. Therapies are equally lavish: who can resist a salt scrub called Carolina Body Delight? The White Falls Facial uses a vitamin C–based whitening serum imported from Paris. A planned expansion includes rooms specifically for naps (ready in spring 2006). Nothing seems more decadent. *445 Main St.; 866/526-8008 or 828/526-8008; www.oldedwardsinn.com; doubles from $$.*

Paneled oval foyer between treatment rooms at the Old Edwards Inn & Spa, opposite. Above: Pedicure stations.

The iconic pool at the
Raleigh. Opposite:
exterior of the Setai.

miami beach redux

The little marzipan village—Miami as it used to be—is in the midst of an unprecedented real estate explosion, and new hotels are turning up all over. Beyond that, classics are being reborn, from the new tower at the Morris Lapidus–designed Fontainebleau to the revamped Raleigh, with its legendary pool. There is a bold new order—and a crowded field. Some of the standouts follow.

the standard

Sheltered from the riot of Collins Avenue, André Balazs's the Standard, Miami, riffs on the glories of the Lido's past with the inevitable dollop of irony. Every inch of the Standard plays with sin and redemption, excess and denial, in settings that alternately smack of Roman decadence and monastic purity. Next to a classic cedar sauna, private nooks are set aside for "self-exploration and indulgence." The heart of the hotel is the pool and hydrotherapy area, an ode to communal bathing as social sacrament. The outdoor aquacade encompasses a plunge pool, a hot tub, and a 12-foot-tall, three-inch-wide column of falling water. In the mud baths, guests can slather one another with "golden body mud." *40 Island Ave.; 305/673-1717; www.standardhotel.com; doubles from $.*

Denim sectional sofas in the lobby
of the Standard, Miami.

Rooftop bar area of the Sanctuary Hotel. Right: The Setai's Studio Suite. Opposite right: Spa hallway at the Hotel Victor.

fontainebleau resort miami beach

This crescent-shaped landmark hotel has a longstanding reputation for grandeur. Recently, more than $200 million was poured into an elaborate renovation, including the construction of a new entry and 36-story tower, with ocean views. Everything is done on a grand scale here, from the room count (1,338) to the humongous chandeliers to the elaborate pool—which has three whirlpools, a two-story waterfall, and a children's play area with a lazy river and giant water slide. Spring 2006 heralds the second phase of transformation. *4441 Collins Ave.; 800/548-8886 or 305/538-2000; www.fontainebleau. com; doubles from $.*

sanctuary hotel

A tasty little 30-room property that bills itself as South Beach's first female-friendly hotel, offering a year-round 25-percent discount for women traveling alone as well as more creative services such as cabana boys at the rooftop pool (specialty: suntan lotion application), and jogging and yoga companions. There's also a spa, salon, rooftop bar, and trendy Sugo restaurant. The 29 Zen-inspired suites offer all the comforts of home and then some: marble-countertop kitchens, 42-inch flat-screen plasma TV's, and steam showers or jetted Jacuzzi tubs in the bathrooms. *1745 James Ave.; 305/673-5455; www.sanctuarysobe.com; doubles from $$.*

the raleigh

The legend that is South Beach began at the Raleigh. The Art Deco star—designed by architect L. Murray Dixon in 1940—has been reborn under the eye of hotelier André Balazs. Turning up the volume of chic, Balazs has filled the lobby with vintage rattan furniture, replaced the outdoor gym with a cabana, and added thickets of palms. He has also revamped the iconic pool, where Esther Williams filmed her famous aquacades. In the kitchen, Eric Ripert of Le Bernardin is consulting chef. And this being Balazs-land, the social scene is abuzz with the glitterati. *1775 Collins Ave.; 305/534-6300; www.raleighhotel. com; doubles from $$.*

the setai

hotel victor

bentley beach hotel

The Setai, a much-anticipated condo-hotel combo, is plush as all get-out, with a Champagne-Crustacean-Caviar bar, three outdoor pools, and an opulent spa. Located at the tail end of South Beach, owned by GHM Ltd., and created by Adrian Zecha, the 125-suite oceanfront resort draws from both Miami's and Shanghai's Art Deco styles. The lobby is accented with Burmese teak, gray antique bricks from Shanghai, and a bronze fireplace. Guest rooms have black granite bathrooms and walls displaying jade pieces culled from the antique markets of China. *2001 Collins Ave.; 888/625-7500 or 305/520-6000; www.setai.com; doubles from $$$$.*

The L. Murray Dixon–built Hotel Victor has been restored in high sybaritic fashion by celebrated French designer Jacques Garcia. Inspired by the decadent 1930's, the interiors are opulent: the lobby has a dramatic see-through jellyfish tank; guest rooms have richly-hued satin headboards and ebony-lacquered furniture. The white-marble bathrooms are lovely places to linger, with rain showerheads and infinity soaking tubs. A tranquil spa features European treatments, with Anne Sémonin products, and a 500-square-foot Turkish hammam (South Beach's first). *1144 Ocean Dr.; 800/720-0051 or 305/428-1234; www.hotelvictor southbeach.com; doubles from $$.*

This 109-suite hotel at the southern tip of Ocean Drive (the quieter end of South Beach) couldn't be closer to the ocean. The sumptuous suites, only 10 per floor, come with kitchens or kitchenettes, marble bathrooms, and gilt-and-upholstered headboards. If you can swing it, spring for an oceanfront corner suite —the balcony is less than 60 feet from the water. Ideal for families, the Bentley offers milk-and-cookie turndown service, and the kid-friendly beach has water toys and pint-sized lounge chairs. *101 Ocean Dr.; 866/236-8539 or 305/938-4600; www.thebentley hotels.com; doubles from $$.*

site specifics

You've chosen your destination—now you just need to find a place to stay. We hit the Net to see which booking sites are doing the best job, based on usability, selection, prices, and more.

All-hotels.com
This site's first suggestion when we searched for New York "luxury hotels": a two-star motor inn in Queens. You can't search by neighborhood, only by price and name. And it doesn't give as many details on the properties compared with other sites.
Properties 100,000
Best feature The giant selection.

Expedia.com
You can sort results by price, name, class, and neighborhood; the site has great specifics on each property's location and features. The unique Virtual Tours option lets you browse through 360-degree views of guest rooms, restaurants, and lobbies.
Properties 70,000
Best feature Useful hotel descriptions.

Hotels.com
In Dallas alone, you can search for hotels near 22 attractions or neighborhoods. The site has good details on each property and a range of quality hotels. You may need to wade through sold-out properties, but at least no-vacancy status is mentioned up front.
Properties 20,000

Best feature Long lists of landmarks help you narrow your search.

Orbitz.com
You can search for hotels near a specific address or by neighborhood. We love the Matrix Display, which lets you quickly sort properties by three criteria: price, quality (from one to five stars), and distance from the city center.
Properties 50,000
Best feature Very user-friendly.

Quikbook.com
The selection may be small, but we found a decent range of hotels—each inspected and approved by Quikbook's staff. The search results page lists name, neighborhood, room type, and price. However, there are links to full descriptions, and photos of every property.
Properties 1,000
Best feature Only shows hotels with availability.

Travelocity.com
The Travelocity descriptions are helpful, but it's the write-ups from individual travelers that really give the site an insider edge. Travelocity also lets you search by any of 24 "amenities"—from swimming pools to on-site dry cleaning to all-suites properties.
Properties 55,000
Best feature Traveler reviews and AAA ratings.

amalfi hotel

CHICAGO, ILLINOIS

This small hotel brings a boutique sensibility to a slightly off-the-beaten-path (but still-convenient) location: a short hop west of Michigan Avenue, within walking distance of the Loop, and close to River North's restaurants, bars, and shops. Amalfi's colorful, sleek décor goes beyond the predictable (linens, for instance, are in soft creams rather than the ubiquitous white), and rooms are long on thoughtful touches, from good lighting and ottomans beside easy chairs to intriguing reading material. There's a great breakfast buffet set up on every floor each morning, so you can just throw on a robe and grab something to take back to your room. Nearby dinner options include the excellent Keefer's for steaks and seafood.

Amalfi Hotel
20 W. Kinzie St.
Chicago, Illinois
877/262-5341 or
312/395-9000
www.amalfihotel
chicago.com
Doubles from $$

Chicago's newest
boutique hotel, the Amalfi.

lake austin spa resort

AUSTIN, TEXAS

Just outside Austin's city limits, the Lake Austin Spa Resort has 40 ranch-style guest rooms facing a sparkling lake where tame geese paddle between rowing sculls. Granite gravel crunches underfoot as you climb a garden path to the limestone-and-cedar LakeHouse Spa, the evocation of an oil baron's Hill Country retreat. Make that an oil baron with a New Age sensibility: the slate-blue barn shelters a lap pool instead of livestock. On a screened-in treatment porch, therapist April Day administers a mind-bending craniosacral massage, which is followed by an equally impressive Tajii Moxa (Chinese heat therapy) session. But all this doesn't mean Lake Austin has lost its twang. An exfoliating scrub uses locally grown pecans, and the hallways are draped with quilts by a blue ribbon winner at the Texas State Fair. Meals are alcohol-free.

**Lake Austin
Spa Resort**
1705 S. Quinlan
Park Rd.
Austin, Texas
800/847-5637 or
512/372-7300

www.lakeaustin.com
Three-night
packages from $2760
per person, double

Lake Austin Spa Resort's
Pool House.
Opposite: JFK-style rockers
on the screened-in porch.

hotel paisano

The art-pilgrimage town of Marfa, Texas, was still very much a rancher's outpost in 1930 when the Hotel Paisano opened its doors. Designed by noted Southwest architect Henry Trost, who studied with Frank Lloyd Wright, the Spanish colonial–revival structure was based on Trost's design for the Hotel Valverde in Socorro, New Mexico, and is marked by a red-tile roof, delicate ironwork balconies, and an adobe-colored stucco exterior. A much-needed renovation by owner Joe Duncan tastefully updated—and, in many cases, enlarged—the 41 guestrooms, adding French doors that open onto small balconies, transforming the original radiators into bedside tables, and restoring the vintage bathroom fixtures.

thunderbird hotel

MARFA, TEXAS

Hotelier Liz Lambert has injected this formerly dilapidated 1950's motel with some quirky modern style, juxtaposing contemporary design with Western touches. The redesigned building, painted blue to match the desert sky, wraps around a central pool surrounded by shaded mesquite-topped tables and native ocotillo cactuses. The 24 rooms have pecanwood platform beds draped with handmade South American wool blankets, polished concrete floors with cowhide rugs, and walls hung with works by local artists. Harkening back to the hotel's vintage, guests can also borrow Polaroid cameras, record players, and old-school typewriters. The hotel is currently expanding into an adjacent building, which will add 16 rooms, a bar, and an additional pool.

Hotel Paisano
207 N. Highland Ave.
Marfa, Texas
866/729-3669 or
432/729-3669
www.hotel
paisano.com
Doubles from $

Thunderbird Hotel
601 W. San
Antonio St.
Marfa, Texas
432/729-1984
www.thunderbird
marfa.com
Doubles from $

A room where James Dean once stayed at the Hotel Paisano, opposite. Above: Spartan quarters at the Thunderbird Hotel.

Little Nell
675 East Durant Ave.
Aspen, Colorado
970/920-4600 or
888/843-6355
www.thelittle
nell.com
Doubles from $$$

Elk Mountain Resort
97 Elk Walk
Montrose, Colorado
877/355-9255 or
970/252-4900
www.elkmountain
resort.com
Doubles from $

little nell

ASPEN, COLORADO

world's best Interior designer David Easton has reimagined Aspen's only ski-in/ski-out property (located just 17 steps from the base of the Silver Queen Gondola). His organic style is reflected in the 92 guest rooms, which have sand-toned Belgian wool carpets, paintings by Santa Fe artists, gas fireplaces, and comfortable sofas stuffed with goose down. The Montagna restaurant specializes in "farmhouse" dishes; the Bar, a celebrity favorite, is one of Aspen's hottest après-ski scenes. The property specializes in pet-spoiling: upon check-in, your pooch receives a personalized brass identification tag stamped with the hotel's address and phone number, and the concierge knows all the best pet-friendly hiking trails, groomers, and pet-sitters.

elk mountain resort

MONTROSE, COLORADO

Surrounded by the 14,000-foot peaks of the San Juan Mountains and adjacent to more than 60,000 acres of national forest, Elk Mountain is like camp for grown-ups. It boasts a staggering assortment of adrenaline-pumping, glee-inducing activities: ATV riding, rock climbing on the property's 30-foot man-made boulder, and paintballing on a 4½-acre course. The resort also has a state-of-the-art shooting range and a helipad for heliskiing adventures. Luckily, no one sings "Kumbaya" here; instead, unwind in your soaking tub (big enough for two) or in your wrought-iron four-poster bed. There are also 18 secluded three-bedroom cottages, perfect for families.

galisteo inn

GALISTEO, NEW MEXICO

Rolling into the New Mexican village of Galisteo, 22 miles southeast of Santa Fe, is like traveling back in time. Dwarfed by high desert plains, the tiny town has dusty red dirt roads that wind their way among low-slung adobe houses, including the newly renovated Galisteo Inn. Each of its 11 affordable rooms is different, but all have rustic details such as soaring ceilings with raw vigas, handwoven cotton bedspreads, corner fireplaces, and well-worn floorboards. Shaded by cottonwood trees, the 300-year-old inn surrounds a grassy courtyard with a lap pool and a hot tub for those chilly desert nights. The cozy La Mancha Bar & Restaurant serves pineapple-infused vodka martinis, and in the restaurant, chef Enrique Guerrero whips up decadent portions of achiote-marinated shrimp and grilled honey-brine pork chops.

Galisteo Inn 9 La Vega, Galisteo, New Mexico; 866/404-8200 or 505/466-8200; www.galisteoinn.com; doubles from $, breakfast included

A guest room at Galisteo Inn.

western spas

Aspen's spa scene has been given a face-lift, and just when it seemed that Sin City couldn't get more decadent, two hotel spas in Las Vegas offer revelers a chance to recuperate.

The Ladies' Pool at THEhotel's Bathhouse spa. Opposite left: Massage room at the St. Regis Remède Spa. Opposite right: Watsu room at the Spa & Salon Bellagio.

the bathhouse at THEhotel

LAS VEGAS, NEVADA

The Bathhouse at THEhotel (the retreat within the expansive Mandalay Bay property) lives up to its name and gives pleasure seekers another way to indulge—away from the noisy casinos. The palette here is subtle, and the design features clean lines of stone and slate. Guests are encouraged to linger in the hot, cold, and warm pools before treatments or to sign on for one of the Bathhouse's signature soaks. Spend a good hour in a warm tub and those gambling losses will seem a little less painful.
3950 S. Las Vegas Blvd.; 877/632-7800 or 702/632-7777; www.thehotelatmandalay bay.com; doubles from $.

remède spa, at the st. regis resort

ASPEN, COLORADO

Built with locally sourced and imported timber and stone, the 15,000-square-foot Remède Spa, at the St. Regis Resort, takes its therapeutic cues from its surroundings: the coed soaking pool, which mimics Colorado hot springs, has cutouts along the river-rock wall for waterfall massages; treatment rooms come with down duvets and cashmere throws; the lounge has a fireplace and an oxygen bar (remember, Aspen is 7,900 feet up). Every therapy is based around the cultishly followed Remède product line, developed by Bliss founder Marcia Kilgore. *315 E. Dean St.; 888/454-9005 or 970/920-3300; www.stregis.com; doubles from $$.*

spa & salon bellagio

LAS VEGAS, NEVADA

world's best Located in part of the Bellagio's just-completed Spa Tower, the Spa & Salon Bellagio is a serene retreat two floors above the Strip. Accented with stone and wood, the 65,000-square-foot facility emphasizes the healing properties of water: reflecting pools are carved throughout the space, a meditation room is enclosed by waterfalls, and there's even a watsu (water shiatsu) room. Therapies draw upon international traditions, though some veer toward the bizarre—like the Egyptian Gold Treatment, during which gilded powder is sprinkled over the face and body. *3600 S. Las Vegas Blvd.; 888/987-3456 or 702/693-7111; www.bellagio.com; doubles from $$$.*

inspiring spaces

There's nothing better than a spa treatment in an inviting environment. ■ At **Enchantment Resort's** Mii Amo spa in Sedona, Arizona (*www.enchantment resort.com*), spiritual ceremonies are held in the Crystal Grotto, a gem-studded structure modeled on a Native American kiva. ■ The **Mauna Lani Resort** spa (*www.mauna lani.com*) offers aquatic bodywork treatments in its 1,000-square-foot watsu (water shiatsu) pool, set amid ancient lava tubes. ■ Listen to the river or the chatter of monkeys while getting a massage on your private terrace at **Singita Private Game Reserve**'s Ebony Lodge in South Africa (*www.singita.com*). ■ During the Thermal Suite treatment in the Samas spa at Ireland's **Park Hotel Kenmare** (*www.parkken mare.com*), guests relax on an "aquatic bench," while gazing at Kenmare Bay. ■ The Healing Waters Spa at **Silky Oaks Lodge,** in Australia (*www.silky oakslodge.com.au*), has a couples suite with a rain showerhead that pours into a sunken tub overlooking— what else?—a rain forest.

cal-a-vie

VISTA, CALIFORNIA

Cal-A-Vie
29402 Spa
Havens Way
Vista, California
866/772-4283
www.cal-a-vie.com
Doubles from $$$$$,
for three nights,
all-inclusive

 A grande dame among destination spas, this Provençal-style retreat 40 miles north of San Diego has just emerged from a head-to-toe renovation. Among the improvements are a full room redesign, a 17,000-square-foot state-of-the-art fitness center, and a new bathhouse complete with French antiques, and thalassotherapy and hydrotherapy rooms. A 4-to-1 staff-to-guest ratio guarantees that you'll always be the center of someone's attention, and all-inclusive stays ranging from three to seven nights ensure you'll leave loose-limbed and stress-free (notwithstanding your considerably lighter wallet). Your faux Mediterranean villa (terra-cotta tile roof, stucco façade, window boxes bursting with flowers) has a private terrace and carefully placed windows that open onto rolling hills framed by jasmine and oleander.

The Crystal Grotto at Enchantment Resort, in Sedona, Arizona, opposite.

ojai valley inn & spa

OJAI, CALIFORNIA

The 220-acre Ojai Valley Inn & Spa, situated in a mountain valley that aptly portrayed Shangri-la in the 1937 film *Lost Horizon*, has long been known for its classic 18-hole golf course and for its Native American–culture-inspired spa. Now it has upped the ante with a $70 million renovation, creating a new lobby, adding an additional 100 guest rooms, and refurbishing the existing 205 rooms with four-poster beds and decorative Mexican terra-cotta tiles. The style is Spanish colonial, but the substance is fully 21st century, including Wi-Fi and flat-screen TV's. In the spa, signature treatments incorporate locally grown organic ingredients (citrus, lavender), and a dedicated men's menu lures golfers with treatments such as the Gentleman's Luxury Facial and Golfer's Post-Round Massage, which can be administered, upon request, in a room outfitted with a fireplace.

Ojai Valley Inn & Spa
905 Country Club Rd.
Ojai, California
888/697-8780 or
805/646-1111
www.ojairesort.com
Doubles from $$

Poetry Inn
6380 Silverado Trail
Napa, California
707/944-0646

www.poetryinn.com
Doubles from $$$

poetry inn

NAPA, CALIFORNIA

With just three rooms, the Poetry Inn is one of the most tranquil spaces in the buzzing Napa Valley. Owned by the eponymous founder of the Cliff Lede Vineyards, this intimate inn gets everything right. Its hillside perch translates into jaw-dropping views from nearly every room; gigantic private balconies provide the perfect place from which to take it all in. The lobby and guest rooms are warm and modern, with dark woods, clean lines, and wood-burning fireplaces. Spa-style bathrooms, lined in marble and limestone, seem to be double the size of the guest rooms, with heated floors, deep soaking tubs, and both indoor and outdoor showers. Kick off the day with breakfast at a table overlooking the vineyards. If you get chilly, one of the three on-site innkeepers (yes, that's one per room) will materialize with a soft woolen throw.

The Robert Louis Stevenson room at the Poetry Inn, above.
Opposite: Ojai Valley Inn & Spa.

Designer Jonathan Adler in the library at Le Parker Meridien. Opposite top and bottom: A doorman at the hotel entrance; a guest room.

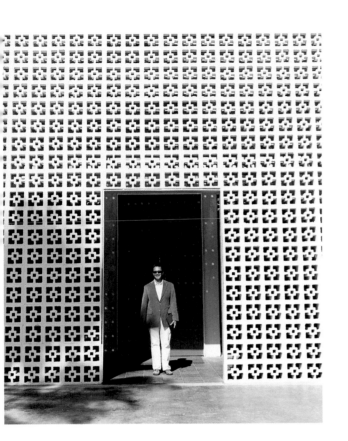

le parker meridien

Jonathan Adler's redesign of the 144-room Parker is perhaps the most ambitious recent attempt to restore the luster of Palm Springs—and the one that will likely be the benchmark for the luxury resorts that follow. Adler's approach embraces a world of influences. In the ambitious rooms, there are Peruvian weavings, an Edwardian chair, in which you can curl up and read, and a minimalist canopy bed inspired by the artist Sol Lewitt. From the lobby, decorated with suits of armor and wire-based Warren Platner chairs, to the Moroccan-inspired "hookah chill-out zone," everything in the Parker is just so. The hotel features many pieces of the pottery that made Adler a household design name; he also created the ceramic frieze that hangs below the concierge desk and reads: EAT DRINK AND BE MERRY FOR TOMORROW YOU SHALL CHECK OUT.

Le Parker Meridien 4200 E. Palm Canyon Dr., Palm Springs, California; 888/450-9488 or 760/770-5000; www.lemeridien.com; doubles from $$

hollywood roosevelt

LOS ANGELES, CALIFORNIA

Located along Hollywood Boulevard's Walk of Fame and across the street from Grauman's Chinese Theatre, this 12-story landmark recently rescued itself from seediness with a more than $25 million renovation. The Hollywood Roosevelt's 300 guest rooms now shine with a clean, modern look. Our favorites are the Cabana rooms, which have ebonized platform beds backed by Ultrasuede padded walls (designed to evoke old Hollywood sound stages), tinted-mirror bar areas, and triple-wide sliding doors which open to private flagstone patios. The most desirable rooms overlook either the sparkling Hollywood Hills or the David Hockney–painted pool.

shutters on the beach

SANTA MONICA, CALIFORNIA

When celebrity decorator Michael Smith took on Shutters on the Beach, Santa Monica's star-studded beachfront hotel, he retained the breezy, shingled building's laid-back, barefoot feel. The newly redone guest rooms have a chic, residential aesthetic, with plush sofas and hardwood floors—not to mention some luxuries you don't get at home (like packing services and preprinted boarding passes). All 198 rooms have private balconies; rooms ending in -47 or -22 have the most capacious ones. At turndown, instead of chocolates on your pillow, staff leave Post-its on your bathroom mirror listing options for the following day's activities, such as a ride on the Santa Monica pier Ferris wheel or a surf lesson with a local wave guru.

Hollywood Roosevelt
7000 Hollywood Blvd.
Los Angeles
California
800/950-7667 or
323/466-7000
www.hollywood
roosevelt.com
Doubles from $

Shutters on the Beach
1 Pico Blvd.
Santa Monica
California
310/458-0030 or
800/334-9000
www.shutterson
thebeach.com
Doubles from $$$

The Hollywood Roosevelt's iconic exterior, opposite.
Above: The Shutters on the Beach pool.

product placement

The luxurious amenities dressing up the best hotel bathrooms can inspire an upgrade of your own. ■ At the **Parker Palm Springs** (*www. parker meridien.com*), each bathroom is stocked with $150 worth of products, from Erno Laszlo body lotion to Peter Thomas Roth sunblock. ■ **Uma Paro** in Bhutan (*www.uma.como.bz*) introduces guests to the all-natural Como Shambhala company's peppermint-and-eucalyptus–based Invigorate line, which is said to clear the mind and relieve fatigue. ■ The **Cipriani** in Venice (*www.hotelcipriani.com*) uses aromatic Helleboro minis, produced by a small herbalist shop in Tirano. ■ At the **Burj Al Arab** resort in Dubai (*www.burj-al-arab.com*), guests find the entire range of Rocabar toiletries for men and the full Hemas line for women.

The vanity tray from the Parker Palm Springs, above. Opposite: In the Alderbrook Resort & Spa.

alderbrook
resort & spa

UNION, WASHINGTON

**Alderbrook
Resort & Spa**
10 E. Alderbrook Dr.
Union, Washington
800/622-9370 or
360/898-2200
www.alderbrook
resort.com
Doubles from $

The call of the wild meets upscale comfort at Alderbrook Resort & Spa, two hours west of Seattle. Spend the day hiking on trails lined with evergreens and cedars, or catch your dinner off the resort's 1,500-square-foot dock (the area is known for chinook and coho salmon, Hama Hama oysters, and Dungeness crabs). By night, retreat to the glassed-in pool, which has views of the Olympic Mountains, or to the outdoor bonfire, ringed with comfortable lawn chairs (marshmallows available upon request). There are 16 beachfront cottages; and most of the 77 guest rooms have cushioned daybeds in alcoves overlooking Puget Sound's Hood Canal fjord. Golfers can take advantage of advance tee-time reservations at the 18-hole Alderbrook Golf Club, whose par-72 course is peppered with massive fir trees.

A daisy-filled room
at the Jupiter Hotel.
Opposite: The hotel's
roadside exterior.

jupiter
hotel

PORTLAND, OREGON

Jupiter Hotel
800 E. Burnside St.
Portland, Oregon
877/800-0004
www.jupiter
hotel.com
Doubles from $

San Francisco has the Phoenix. Los Angeles has the Standard Hotel. Now Portland has the rock star–worthy Jupiter Hotel. Carved out of a 1960's motel and set around two courtyards, the hotel has 80 basic rooms (call them crash pads), outfitted with white platform beds and wallpapered in floor-to-ceiling nature scenes. Next door, in a Modernist log cabin, Doug Fir Lounge draws an eclectic crowd—artsy urbanites, bikers in black leather, aging hippies—for blackberry Cosmos and late-late-night comfort food (croque-monsieur at 4 A.M., anyone?). Cult rock acts such as Helmet and the Secret Machines play nightly. A word to the wise: the party rages on until the wee hours most nights, so if you want to get any sleep at all, be sure to ask for a room overlooking the "quiet courtyard."

moonlight lodge

This mountain escape has the traditional flair you'd expect at a Western lodge: inlaid stone floors, log beams, wrought-iron chandeliers, and a massive 40-foot rock fireplace that dominates the main lobby. To sleep in the company of all those Wild West accoutrements, you have to snag one of the four penthouse suites, each of which has vaulted ceilings, and some have picture windows overlooking the slopes of Moonlight Basin. For far less cash, you can rent one of the ski-in/ski-out two-bedroom log cabins; they have hand-braided rugs, gas-burning stoves, and outdoor hot tubs with great views of the Spanish Peaks. Not a lodge to miss out on a trend, Moonlight even has its own spa, where Rocky Mountain hot-stone massages and antioxidant-rich facials help skiers unwind after a competitive day of powder.

Moonlight Lodge 1 Mountain Loop Rd., Big Sky, Montana; 800/845-4428; www.eastwestbigsky.com; suites from $$$$$

The lobby at Moonlight Lodge. Opposite: A view of the Spanish Peaks at Moonlight Basin.

alive resort

BRITISH COLUMBIA, CANADA

**Alive Resort
for Wellness &
Longevity**
Lumby, British
Columbia, Canada
888/763-4744 or
250/763-4744

www.aliveresort.com
Five-day retreats
from $2514 per
person, double

Alive is not your average spa. Vic LeBouthillier, publisher of the health-obsessed *Alive* magazine, has a mission: to teach guests how to prolong life, increase physical health, and fight aging. Hidden in the forest high on a mountain outside of Lumby, the tiniest of towns in British Columbia, the resort is housed in what looks like a renovated lodge. From the first moment, you feel as if you're arriving at some relative or friend's house, one with no TV, no phone, and limited closet space. Outside the lodge, you find yourself nestled inside a healthy hush of glorious scenery, with vistas, waterfalls, and hiking trails to explore.

four seasons whistler

BRITISH COLUMBIA, CANADA

The Four Seasons' first Canadian ski resort hugs the base of Blackcomb Mountain, a short walk to the Whistler-Blackcomb lifts and the shops and restaurants of the quaint Whistler village. The 273 spacious and warm rooms are done up in ochre red, earthy green, and golden brown, and have cherrywood doors, roaring fireplaces, and trim, private balconies. Après-ski here means having the concierge arrange a dogsled ride through the forest to an alfresco dinner for two, served under a heated canopy. Or simply lounge in one of the outdoor hot tubs until the staff brings around shots of hot chocolate (or frozen blueberries on a skewer, depending on the season). During the winter months, don't miss the thrice-weekly "fireside chats" in the library, when local ski instructors dispense insider tips.

Four Seasons Whistler
Whistler, British Columbia, Canada
800/332-3442 or 604/935-3400
www.fourseasons.com/whistler
Doubles from $$

Alive Resort's main guest lodge, opposite. Above: The lobby of the Four Seasons Whistler.

The living room of a
W Montreal suite.
Opposite: The hotel's
Wunderbar.

w montreal

MONTREAL, CANADA

W Montreal
901 Victoria Square
Montreal, Canada
877/946-8357 or
514/395-3100
www.whotels.com
Doubles from $

Montreal's reputation as a city of style is getting another boost with the newly minted W Montreal. Housed in a formerly lackluster bank building on the border of historic Old Montreal, the hotel is a haven of singular design. The 152 rooms are kitted out with "peek-a-boo" bathrooms and glowing bedside tables. The three 1,000-square-foot Extreme WOW suites (note the skylight in one of the bathrooms) are already overbooked by visiting celebrities like Bruce Willis and Josh Hartnett. The colossal lobby, with two waterfalls and splashes of glossy red furniture, leads to a mezzanine drinking lounge, chef Franco Gioffre's Italian-fusion Otto restaurant, and Wunderbar, a space where out-of-towners can hobnob with the fashionable locals who line up nightly at the luminous acrylic bar.

A view from Isla Victoria, in northern Patagonia, Argentina.

mexico and central and south america

world's best top 25
mexico and central and south america

Clockwise, from top: La Casa Que Canta, in Zihuatanejo, Mexico; One & Only Palmilla, in Los Cabos; Cuernavaca's Las Mañanitas. Opposite: The Alvear Palace Hotel in Buenos Aires.

1 **La Casa Que Canta** ZIHUATANEJO, MEXICO **90.86**

2 **Four Seasons Hotel México, D.F.** MEXICO CITY **88.44**

3 **Ritz-Carlton** CANCÚN **87.40**

4 **Las Mañanitas** CUERNAVACA, MEXICO **87.22**

5 **Hotel Monasterio** CUZCO, PERU **86.91**

6 **Four Seasons Resort Punta Mita** MEXICO **86.67**

7 **Las Ventanas al Paraíso, A Rosewood Resort** LOS CABOS, MEXICO **86.55**

8 **Llao Llao Hotel & Resort** SAN CARLOS DE BARILOCHE, ARGENTINA **86.54**

9 **Blancaneaux Lodge** SAN IGNACIO, BELIZE **86.19**

10 **Hotel Villa del Sol** ZIHUATANEJO, MEXICO **85.48**

11 **Ritz-Carlton** SANTIAGO **85.18**

12 **Alvear Palace Hotel** BUENOS AIRES **85.12**

13 **Four Seasons Resort Costa Rica at Peninsula Papagayo** **85.00**

14 **One & Only Palmilla** LOS CABOS, MEXICO **84.96**

15 **Caesar Park** BUENOS AIRES **84.86**

16 **Turtle Inn** PLACENCIA, BELIZE **84.13**

17 **Maroma Resort & Spa** PUNTA BETE, MEXICO **83.75**

18 **Machu Picchu Sanctuary Lodge** PERU **82.98**

19 **Camino Real** OAXACA, MEXICO **82.82**

20 **JW Marriott Resort & Spa** CANCÚN **82.78**

21 **Le Méridien Cancún Resort & Spa** **82.23**

22 **Lodge at Chaa Creek** BELIZE **82.05**

23 **Las Brisas** ACAPULCO **81.64**

24 **Casa de Sierra Nevada** SAN MIGUEL DE ALLENDE, MEXICO **81.63**

25 **Machu Picchu Pueblo Hotel** PERU **81.51**

key to the price icons   **$** under $250   **$$** $250 - 499   **$$$** $500 - 749   **$$$$** $750 - 999   **$$$$$** $1,000 - 1,999

A restaurant at Aqua.
Opposite: One of the hotel's
seaside pools.

aqua

CANCÚN, MEXICO

Aqua
Km 12.5
Blvd. Kukulkán
Cancún, Mexico
800/343-7821 or
52-998/881-7600
www.fiesta
americana.com
Doubles from $$

A sizable resort with a boutique-hotel aesthetic, Fiesta Americana Grand Aqua Cancún opened in December 2004 on Cancún's last undeveloped beachfront plot. The hotel's Modernist shell was built in 2000 for Sofitel; then Fiesta Americana took over, bringing in crackerjack Mexico City–based residential designer Francisco Hanhausen. Hanhausen shopped globally: Spanish marble, Peruvian wood, Zimbabwean granite. He's big on comfort (there's a pillow menu in the room) and obsessive about details (artisanal soaps are made in Chiapas). He's also witty: a row of Felliniesque white canopied beds is spread out along the beach, and the spa is covered in blue tiles, giving it a subaqueous feel. Aqua sustained hurricane damage in October 2005. The hotel is being restored and will reopen in mid 2006.

dos casas

SAN MIGUEL DE ALLENDE, MEXICO

Urban Modernists have another reason to visit San Miguel de Allende: the five-room Dos Casas. Formerly two separate vacation houses (hence the name), the newly opened inn off the main square retains the colonial flair of the original buildings (a massive wooden front door, cozy fireplaces, and stone walls) but incorporates contemporary Mexican design elements,such as floor-to-ceiling leather headboards and Barcelona chairs. The Del Jardín room overlooks the garden, and Del Fuente opens to the patio courtyard with a running stone fountain, but La Terraza is the one to score—the top-floor suite has a private outdoor terrace, with a whirlpool, and the best views of the city. At breakfast, hang out with chef Lupita Rodríguez while she whips up her signature chilaquiles.

Dos Casas
101 Calle Quebrada
San Miguel de
Allende, Mexico
52-415/154-4073
www.livingdos
casas.com
Doubles from $

La Terraza guest room at Dos Casas, above.

turtle tracking

You've gone on a dino dig. You've watched the whales. The next creatures to zero in on: sea turtles! With scientists calling attention to their plight— all seven species are threatened or endangered —it seems every beach resort is rolling out a turtle program for guests. ■ At **Costa Azul Adventure Resort,** near Puerto Vallarta, in San Francisco, Mexico (*www.costaazul.com*), families help shepherd baby olive ridleys or leatherbacks into the water. Sadly, only one in a thousand hatchlings makes it to adulthood. ■ At **Four Seasons Resort Nevis** (*www.fourseasons.com*), kids can "adopt" a satellite-tracked animal to trace on-line back home. ■ Guests at Antigua's **Jumby Bay** (*www.rosewoodhotels.com*) take nighttime walks to watch hawksbills lay their eggs. The best resort programs are affiliated with conservation groups, ensuring that the turtles have the strongest possible chance of survival.

Hacienda Puerta Campeche
Calle 59
Campeche, Mexico
800/325-3589 or
52-981/816-7535
www.luxury
collection.com
Doubles from $$

hacienda puerta campeche

CAMPECHE, MEXICO

Crafted from a row of 17th-century houses, Hacienda Puerta Campeche brings a dose of urbane style to this historic colonial town. Most of the 15 guest rooms have 18-foot ceilings, a bathroom the size of a big-city apartment, and a sun-drenched daybed. Pools built between the red and yellow façades of the old manor houses flow through porticoes from room to room. It's the perfect base camp for day trips to nearby cultural sites, including the town of Becal, where you can watch local artisans, working in caves, as they stitch Panama hats. The hotel can even arrange private moonlit tours of the ruins of Edzna, a pyramid complex that dates from 600 to 300 B.C.

cuixmala

JALISCO, MEXICO

Alix Goldsmith Marcaccini has turned the former lair of her father, Sir James Goldsmith, in the Chamela-Cuixmala Biosphere Reserve, into a combination working farm, relentlessly hip eco-resort, colossal bed-and-breakfast, and politically correct watering hole for the neo-glitterati. Clifftop Casa La Loma is capped by an illuminated blue-and-yellow Moorish dome, which glows at night like a cheery, radioactive beacon. Included in La Loma's fee are seven guest cottages tucked into an overgrown knoll with views of the ocean. For mere mortals, a reasonably priced, nature-driven vacation can be had in one of the cute-as-a-button rental casitas.

Cuixmala Km 45, Carretera Barra de Navidad–Puerto Vallarta, Jalisco, Mexico; 866/516-2611 or 52-312/313-4310; www.cuixmala.com; casitas from $$; villas from $$$$$

The master bedroom at Casa La Loma.
Opposite: Cuixmala's Casa La Loma, perched on a cliff.

condesa df

MEXICO CITY, MEXICO

A trendy, artist-filled neighborhood in Mexico City now has a hip hotel to match. Surrounded by restaurants, bars, art galleries, and leafy tree-lined streets, Condesa DF is one of the most happening places in town. Paris-based interior designer India Mahdavi enlivened a triangular 1920's French Neoclassical building with floral patterns and vibrant turquoise walls in the public spaces. The 40 rooms, arrayed around a central courtyard, marry indigenous materials (stone floors, Oaxacan blankets, alpaca-wool carpets) with sculptural furniture, walnut paneling, and sleek couches with contrast piping. The place heats up at night, when the rooftop sushi bar and basement dance club pulse with house music and bright young things dancing till four in the morning.

Condesa DF
102 Avda. Veracruz
Colonia Condesa
Mexico City, Mexico
52-55/5241-2600
www.condesadf.com
Doubles from $

Restaurant El Patio at Condesa DF, opposite. Above top and bottom: The hotel's exterior; a guest room.

ponta dos ganchos

SANTA CATARINA, BRAZIL

Ponta dos Ganchos
Santa Catarina
Brazil
800/735-2478 or
55-48/3262-5000
www.pontados
ganchos.com.br
Doubles from $$,
including all meals

A beach walkway
at Ponta Dos
Ganchos, opposite.

A 20-bungalow retreat spread over 20 acres of Brazilian beachfront, Ponta dos Ganchos is picturesque to the extreme: a rain forest looms just beyond the shore; three tiny islands, which encircle a sandy bay, are reachable by canoe or kayak. The restaurant serves Brazilian and French fare, and romantic torchlit dinners can be arranged on one of the islands. For guests to take in all this beauty, the wood-and-stone clifftop cottages have glass walls and spacious decks with stellar views. The newest (and most luxurious) bungalows have private saunas, pools, and home cinemas for viewing any of the hotel's 200 DVD's.

faena hotel + universe

Faena Hotel + Universe
445 Calle Martha Salotti
Buenos Aires
Argentina
54-11/4010-9000
www.faenahotel
anduniverse.com
Doubles from $$

The lobby of Faena Hotel + Universe, opposite. Above: El Bistro.

BUENOS AIRES, ARGENTINA

Fashion-impresario Alan Faena and design "bad boy" Philippe Starck have transformed an abandoned century-old grain depository into the 105-room Faena Hotel + Universe. The outside may be prosaic, but the inside is pure Starck. A curtain-draped hallway lures guests to various corners of the "Universe," among them the Library Lounge, a clubby space outfitted with chesterfields and antique lamps, and El Cabaret, a late-night stop for local bands. Absent are reception and concierge desks. Instead, each guest is assigned three "experience managers" who are responsible for check-in, checkout, and fulfilling any wish.

argentine country hotels

More than a million square miles of spectacular terrain—ranging from cactus forests and subtropical jungles to crystalline lakes and colossal glaciers—offer visitors to Argentina the potential for unparalleled outdoor adventures. Traditional *estancias*, or rural estates, abound in the countryside, but many of these country refuges are uncomfortably outdated. Here, instead, are a handful of intimate escapes, including a fishing lodge for sybarites and a perfectly modern *estancia* with every 21st-century amenity. Even if hiking boots and wet suits are not your idea of relaxation, never fear—those who are after a luxurious leave of absence will feel right at home.

By the pool at Hostería Isla Victoria. Opposite left and right: The Isla Victoria library; Estancia el Rocío.

hostería isla victoria

NEUQUÉN PROVINCE

Imagine an all but uninhabited island, the size of Manhattan, in a glacial lake. There, place Hostería Isla Victoria, a reinvention of what was, from the early 1940's until a devastating fire in 1982, the ultimate romantic getaway for Buenos Aires's well-to-do. Reopened in 2001, with the same sheer-cliff perch and cypress-and-stone façade, the hotel's 22 spacious rooms are done up in jewel tones with a minimalist design, oversized windows, contemporary paintings, and traditional Mapuche woven rugs. There is also a library, a decadent spa, a screening room, and an ample wine cellar. Island expeditions are irresistible, whether taken by mountain bike, on horseback, or on foot. *Nahuel Huapi National Park; 54-11/4394-9605; www.islavictoria.com; doubles from $$$, minimum two-night stay, all-inclusive.*

estancia el rocío

BUENOS AIRES PROVINCE

It's hard to believe that just 60 miles outside the capital travelers can find this 400-acre property, located in the legendary Argentine pampas, where the horizon seems to stretch on forever.
The easy pace at El Rocío, a guesthouse and working ranch, makes it seem worlds away from the city. Days are spent riding the trails and eating authentic, cooked-over-an-open-fire *asado*, the country's barbecue. French owner Patrice Gravière and his Spanish-Argentine wife, Macarena Llambi, originally built this four-bedroom cottage as their personal residence, filling it with mementos from their travels throughout the world.
Km 102.5, Rte. 3, San Miguel del Monte; 54-2271/420-488; www.estanciaelrocio.com; doubles from $$, all-inclusive.

dos lunas

CÓRDOBA PROVINCE

Dos Lunas is a regeneration of a 96-year-old residence. Eight vintage country-house guest rooms are appointed with iron chandeliers and bed frames, charming floral-print bedspreads and lampshades, and sturdy wooden bureaus and tables. The pool, the barbecue hut (expect at least one extravagantly long cookout), and the broad wraparound porch all draw you outside. Guided excursions on one of the ranch's 80 *caballos criollos* (Argentine horses) take guests to the Moon Ravine to spy on condors or across velvety green hills and up red-rock formations. Overnights are spent high in the sierra listening to a guitar-strumming gaucho next to a roaring bonfire. *Alto Ongamira; 54-351/422-3012; www.doslunas.com.ar; doubles from $$, all-inclusive.*

pirá lodge

CORRIENTES PROVINCE

Back in 2000, Nervous Waters, outfitters specializing in ultraluxe boutique fishing lairs, hired Pablo Sánchez Eliá and Laura Orcoyen, a husband-and-wife design team, to create a luxuriously understated aesthetic for their new property, Pirá Lodge. The result: sienna-hued stones; raw acaciawood canopy supports; and heavy wooden furnishings. But Pirá Lodge is, first and foremost, a fishing destination, and guests have five multilingual Argentine guides and five speedy American skiffs at their service for no fewer than eight hours of angling a day from November through April. The rest of the year, Pirá is all about bird-watching and horseback rides. *Paraje Tacuaral, Mercedes, Esteros del Ibera; 877/637-8420 or 54-114/331-0444; www.nervouswaters.com; doubles from $$$$$, all-inclusive, for seven nights and six days.*

The pool at Pirá Lodge. Opposite,
left and right: Dos Lunas; Pirá Lodge.

Casas Rapa Nui at dusk, below.

casas rapa nui

EASTER ISLAND, CHILE

Easter Island, smack-dab in the middle of the Pacific, is an adventure lover's dream come true. Led by multilingual Explora guides, visitors can trek around volcanoes, dive among reefs, and examine the island's mysterious *moai*—giant basalt statues, origins unknown—up close. With a little advance notice, the guides can even pack a basket of snacks and pisco sours for a sunset happy hour beside the statues at Ahu Tahai, thought to be among the island's oldest. Casas Rapa Nui is a pair of comfortable houses in town, outfitted with nine bedrooms, whirlpool tubs, an expansive terrace, a barbecue, and (for better or worse) the latest technology to keep you plugged in.

Casas Rapa Nui
Easter Island, Chile
56-2/206-6060
www.explora.com
Doubles from $$$$$
for three nights

the caribbean, bermuda, and the bahamas

A stretch of beach on Canouan, St. Vincent and the Grenadines, opposite.

world's best top 25
the caribbean, bermuda, and the bahamas

At the Four Seasons Resort, in Nevis, above.
Opposite: Parrot Cay, in Turks and Caicos.

1 **Four Seasons Resort** NEVIS 88.94

2 **Curtain Bluff Resort** ANTIGUA 87.20

3 **Cap Juluca** ANGUILLA 86.44

4 **The Reefs** BERMUDA 86.40

5 **One & Only Ocean Club** PARADISE ISLAND, BAHAMAS 86.05

6 **Parrot Cay** TURKS AND CAICOS 85.65

7 **Horned Dorset Primavera** RINCÓN, PUERTO RICO 85.18

8 **Biras Creek Resort** VIRGIN GORDA 85.00

9 **Little Dix Bay Hotel, A Rosewood Resort** VIRGIN GORDA 84.35

10 **Four Seasons Resort Great Exuma at Emerald Bay** BAHAMAS 83.93

11 **Jamaica Inn** OCHO RIOS, JAMAICA 83.57

12 **Hôtel Guanahani & Spa** ST. BART'S 83.09

13 **Sandy Lane Hotel** ST. JAMES, BARBADOS 82.98

14 **Las Casitas Village & Golden Door Spa, A Wyndham Luxury Resort** FAJARDO, PUERTO RICO 82.50

15 **Peter Island Resort** PETER ISLAND 82.19

16 **Grace Bay Club** PROVIDENCIALES, TURKS AND CAICOS 81.97

17 **Ritz-Carlton** ST. THOMAS 81.80

18 **Anse Chastanet Resort** ST. LUCIA 81.77

19 **Jumby Bay, A Rosewood Resort** ANTIGUA 81.43

20 **Coral Reef Club** ST. JAMES, BARBADOS 81.34

21 **Sandals Grande Ocho Rios Beach & Villa Resort** JAMAICA 81.04

22 **La Samanna** ST. MARTIN 80.95

23 **Half Moon** ROSE HALL, JAMAICA 80.81

24 **CuisinArt Resort & Spa** ANGUILLA 80.71

25 **Ritz-Carlton Golf & Spa Resort** ROSE HALL, JAMAICA 80.35

key to the price icons **$** under $250 **$$** $250 - 499 **$$$** $500 - 749 **$$$$** $750 - 999 **$$$$$** $1,000 - 1,999

The living room of cottage 18 at Round Hill
Hotel & Villas, above. Right: Outside cottage 29.

round hill

MONTEGO BAY, JAMAICA

Thanks to fashion designer Ralph Lauren, the hotel at the iconic Round Hill has a fresh new look: white stone floors, whitewashed walls, four-poster bamboo beds stained a dark mahogany, and bright splashes of blue and pink. In addition, 27 privately owned villas are scattered throughout the former 110-acre pineapple and coconut plantation, and are available to rent when their owners are off-island. (Prices, which are steep, include a personal maid, cook, and gardener.) Set into an amphitheater-shaped hillside, they offer a perfectly composed view of the azure sea, scalloped coves rippling into the distance, framed by floppy banana leaves and latticed arches.

Round Hill Hotel & Villas Montego Bay, Jamaica; 800/972-2159 or 876/956-7050; www.roundhilljamaica.com; doubles from $$$

casa colonial beach & spa

PUERTO PLATA, DOMINICAN REPUBLIC

The absence of pink walls and plastic furniture isn't the only refreshing thing that sets Casa Colonial apart from other hotels in the Dominican Republic. Guests arriving at the 2½-acre retreat, on the northern coast, pass through the lobby's majestic white arches while Edith Piaf croons in the background. They're then led to one of just 50 suites, each an homage to colonial sophistication. Once settled, they can visit the low-density beach, one of the two restaurants, the rooftop infinity pool (with Atlantic views), or the 12,000-square-foot spa, which offers beachside Pilates and yoga classes.

Casa Colonial Beach & Spa
Puerto Plata
Dominican Republic
800/525-4800 or
809/320-3232
www.slh.com
Doubles from $$

The lobby lounge at Casa Colonial Beach & Spa, opposite. Above: Lucia II, one of the hotel's restaurants.

shore things

There's nothiing quite like an extraordinary beach to make a resort really stand out. ■ **Peter Island,** in the British Virgin Islands (*www.peterisland. com*), has five palm-lined, sugar-white strands. Have a massage beside the shallow waters of Deadman's Beach or a romantic moment on the cove at White Bay. ■ Quiet **Cocoa Island,** in the Maldives (*www.cocoa-island.com*), is surrounded by coral reefs, its warm waters filled with turtles and colorful fish, and its sandy strip of beach studded with deck chairs and white umbrellas. ■ The white-powder crescent at **Amanpuri** in Thailand (*www. amanresorts.com*) has sand, water, and sun, plus a cascading sweep of stone steps leading to the sea and beach boys ferrying fresh towels and cold drinks to guests. ■ The shore is just as lovely at the aptly named **Pink Sands,** on Harbour Island in the Bahamas (*www.islandoutpost.com*), which has three miles of, you guessed it, soft pink sand drifting into turquoise waters. ■ Heiresses dive the cobalt waters off Psarou, Mykonos's most elite shore, also home to the whitewashed **Grecotel Mykonos Blu** (*www.grecotel.com*).

the palms

TURKS AND CAICOS

The Palms
Turks and Caicos
866/877-7256 or
649/946-8666

www.thepalmstc.com
Doubles from $$$$,
including breakfast
and transfers

At the Palms resort, on Turks and Caicos' celebrated Grace Bay Beach, guests can visit the water gardens, relax beside the infinity pool, or choose from among traditional and high-tech treatments (silver ion mask, anyone?) administered in the 15,000-square-foot spa. All of the 72 suites—some of which have vaulted ceilings, marble floors, and whirlpool baths—overlook the ocean and come with private terraces, where couples can dine alfresco. For the last word in luxury, book one of the three-bedroom penthouse suites. They're accessible only by private elevator.

Cocoa Island's beach, in the Maldives, opposite.
Above: In the lobby of the Palms.

hôtel guanahani & spa

ST. BART'S

world's best Long before Diddy began chartering yachts here, St. Bart's was courting celebrities who basked in the glow of the flash-bulbs. It's surprising, then, to note that this ultrachic island has suffered the lack of a full-service spa. Thanks to the Hôtel Guanahani & Spa, the reign of spaless sun breaks is over. The hotel's 5,000-square-foot open-air space blends in with the pastel cottages—and caters to couples in search of corporeal indulgence. Here's a tip: Take a body scrub in tandem, then surrender to the island's laid-back rhythm in an Indonesian-style daybed for two, set beneath shady palms.

Hôtel Guanahani & Spa
St. Bart's
800/223-6800 or
590-590/276-660
www.leguana
hani.com
Doubles from $$$

The pool and sanctuary at the St. Regis Temenos Anguilla, opposite.
Above: A Hôtel Guanahani & Spa guest room.

st. regis temenos anguilla

LONG BAY, ANGUILLA

St. Regis Temenos Villas Anguilla
Long Bay, Anguilla
877/787-3447
www.temenos
villas.com
From $40,000
a week, including
personal butler

Each of the three two-story units at St. Regis Temenos Villas, a haven on the secluded western side of Anguilla, resembles a mini Aman resort, wraps around a spectacular infinity pool, and is set above a palmy beach. Architectural surprises abound—from Santorini-style terraces to secret alcoves, perfect for meditating or napping. The design is inspired by a beachy palette: the Sea Villa is done up in dark ocean blues; the Sand Villa, earth tones; and the Sky Villa, shades of light blue and green. All have marble floors, outdoor showers, capacious kitchens, and ocean-view offices, outfitted with laptops, printers, and fax machines.

carlisle bay

ST. MARY'S, ANTIGUA

When Gordon Campbell Gray assumed ownership of a half-built hotel in Antigua's rain forest, ripped out all vestiges of Caribbean kitsch and started from scratch. At first sight, Carlisle Bay's 80 guest suites seem too subdued for the tropics; then you realize that the décor's sneaky purpo is to draw your eye outside, to the blooming gardens and Crayola bays. Since going on vacatio doesn't have to mean shutting down your brain, the glass-adorned library contains a clev compendium of hardcovers. The evening entertainment is meticulously planned as well. Stilted hotel managers' parties have been abolished here in favor of films in the 45-seat cinema. At Ind on the Beach, an open-air bistro, the focus is on uncomplicated grills and organic salads.

la samanna

ST. MARTIN

world's best La Samanna is perfectly placed: equidistant to the nightlife on the Dutch side of St. Martin and the shopping and restaurants on the French side. Best of all, it's perched above Baie Longue, the island's most beautiful beach (made even more appealing by the recent addition of ipewood cabanas, outfitted with preprogrammed iPods and flat-screen TV's). The 81-room resort's Restaurant is also famous for its innovative French-Caribbean cuisine; reserve a table either on the terrace overlooking the ocean or in the expansive new wine cellar (for private dining, by prior arrangement), a cool respite from the tropical heat.

Carlisle Bay
Old Road Village
St. Mary's, Antigua
800/628-8929 or
268/484-0000;
www.carlisle-bay.com
Doubles from $$$$,
including breakfast

La Samanna
The Lowlands
St. Martin
590-590/876-400 or
800/854-2252
www.la
samanna.com
Doubles from $$$$

A Carlisle Bay suite, opposite. Above: The pool at La Samanna.

The cool
white
lounge at
the Beach
House.

the beach house

PALMETTO POINT, BARBUDA

The louvered front doors of the 21-room Beach House on Palmetto Point open to reveal the plein-air Club House, with its purple heartwood decking and white Italian-cotton slipcovered sofas facing an 18-mile arc of pink sand, laced with crushed pink coral. Apart from a flock of nesting terns, it's one of the western hemisphere's most vacant landscapes. The Beach House substantiates the "less is more" axiom and is ideal for anyone seeking refuge from clutter. Each guest room has the bare essentials: air-conditioning, a four-poster with silky Italian sheets, an espresso machine—and an ocean view. A guest's every whim is addressed by an SA (service ambassador) in a flowing outfit. Though there's a lack of armchair diversions, the hotel can arrange tours to nearby caves, lagoons, and frigate-bird sanctuaries. Horse trails wind along sandy lanes, ending at the resort's beachfront steps.

The Beach House Palmetto Point, Barbuda; 888/776-0333 or 268/725-4042; www.thebeachbarbuda.com; doubles from $$$$, including breakfast and two massages

These helpful souls are the gods of small things; it's their extra attention that can transform a run-of-the-mill vacation. ■ Milner Trottman, the grandmotherly babysitter available at **Ariel Sands** in Bermuda (*www.arielsands.com*), is so beloved by children, parents, and locals, her nickname is Sister. ■ The 15 butlers at the **Lanesborough** in London (*www.stregis.com*) will not only unpack suitcases but also track down favorite wines and even translate speeches for business travelers. ■ The **Park Hyatt Milan's** (*www.parkhyatt.com*) discreet concierge, Mario Eroico, secures hard-to-get tickets (La Scala—tonight!) and also sets the mood; he sent 100 roses to one guest's fiancée every day for a year. ■ Momoko, the chief concierge at the **Hotel Seiyo Ginza** in Tokyo (*www.seiyo-ginza.com*), is an expert at helping guests relax, by finding Reiki and shiatsu masters at a moment's notice. ■ The **Dorchester** in London (*www.dorchester hotel.com*) employs E-Butlers for guests' computer emergencies.

Overlooking the beach and lounge area of Laluna.

laluna

GRENADA

All 16 of the one- and two-bedroom cottages at Laluna, a celebrity hideout on lush Grenada, are up and running after 2004's Hurricane Ivan. Designed in an open style, with private decks and bathrooms en plein air, they offer spectacular views of one of the Caribbean's most intimate bays. Continue the sea gazing at dinner, which is served under a thatched roof on the beach.

Laluna Morne Rouge, St. George's, Grenada; 473/439-0001; www.laluna.com; doubles from $$$

STRATEGIES

vacation rentals made easy

The Internet has long been a great resource for listings, descriptions, and photos of properties that travelers can rent—from grand country estates to metropolitan apartments. But how do you know which of the many sites out there have the perfect villa in Provence or the quintessential Caribbean hideaway? Here, our picks for the best rental sites. Prices are for a seven-day rental.

AKVillas.com
This United Kingdom–based site, from Abercrombie & Kent, focuses on luxury properties—there are even a few castles on the list. Each rental is checked out by a company representative and rated on three points, from comfortable to ultraluxurious.

Properties 325, in Europe and the Caribbean
Prices $980–$53,000

Homesaway.com
Tons of information and pictures showcase the company's well-edited selection of luxury rentals. Staff members travel to Europe every year to inspect new acquisitions and review older inventory. The services of a local English-speaking host (up to 15 hours a week) are included.
Properties 65, in France, Italy, and Spain
Prices $6,500–$30,000

Rentvillas.com
Villas on this easy-to-use site are company inspected and given ratings (one to five stars) in seven categories—from ambience to location

to amenities. There are helpful reviews from previous guests in categories such as Enjoyed Most and Unpleasant Surprises.
Properties 1,706, throughout Europe
Prices $500–$75,000

Vacationspot.com
This site from Hotels.com has a wide range of villas and, more commonly, apartments and condos. Each property is examined and rated (one to five stars) on amenities, service, and location. The Vacation Ideas feature matches properties to your preferred activities.
Properties 2,500, worldwide, with an emphasis on the United States
Prices $450–$6,000

Villasoftheworld.com
Good photos and descriptions of these

rentals, one of which is Mick Jagger's six-bedroom beachside bungalow on Mustique (from $13,000 a week). You must first register with an e-mail address to check on availability.
Properties 3,000, worldwide
Prices $2,000–$200,000

Wimco.com
St. Bart's is a specialty of this 22-year-old company. Staff members visit each property before it's offered for rental. The search function allows prospective renters to choose villas by size and look for houses with a pool or kid-friendly facilities. E-mail registration is required to book.
Properties 1,200, in the Caribbean and Europe
Prices $1,200–$52,000

The reception area at Raffles Resort Canouan
Island. Opposite: The resort's fountain.

raffles resort canouan island

CANOUAN,
ST. VINCENT AND THE GRENADINES

Raffles Resort Canouan Island St. Vincent and the
Grenadines; 877/226-6826 or 784/458-8000;
www.raffles-canouanisland.com; doubles from $$$

The former Carenage Bay Beach & Golf
Club has been taken in hand by Singapore-
based Raffles International and given a
resonant new name, Raffles Resort Canouan
Island. The rebranding marks the arrival in the
Caribbean of a legendary hotel company that
helped make "invisible" Asian service the
industry's gold standard. Carenage's clunky
pastiche of tropical styles has been replaced
with something a whole lot sleeker and more
sophisticated. The color volume has been
turned way down—which does much kinder
things for the landscape. Among the catalogue
of enhancements is a spa with extravagant
cliffside treatment palapas, plus the next must-
have in hotel fitness centers: a boxing ring.

The Great Room at Cotton House, above. Opposite: A view from the hotel.

cotton house

MUSTIQUE, ST. VINCENT AND THE GRENADINES

Cotton House
Mustique, St. Vincent
and the Grenadines
877/240-9945 or
784/456-4777
www.cottonhouse.net
Doubles from $$$$$

This 20-room hotel on the private island of Mustique is always booked with boldface names, yet it retains a refreshingly laid-back vibe. At the Cotton House, casual elegance reigns; the interior is filled with loads of comfortable white-upholstered furniture, dark woods, and flowing curtains. Originally an 18th-century coral warehouse and sugar mill, it sits between two beaches and is just a "mule"-ride (island-speak for golf cart) away from five additional ones. The hotel recently upgraded most of its suites with private plunge pools and built a two-bedroom hilltop house, the Cotton Hill Residence, which has a dedicated staff and its own pool, with views to the sea.

Tower Bridge, London, England.

europe

world's best top 50 europe

1 **Château Les Crayères** REIMS, FRANCE **92.33**

2 **Four Seasons Hotel** ISTANBUL **91.74**

3 **Grand-Hôtel du Cap-Ferrat** ST.-JEAN-CAP-FERRAT, FRANCE **91.15**

4 **Hôtel de Paris** MONTE CARLO **89.88**

5 **Hotel Adlon Kempinski** BERLIN **89.86**

6 **Palazzo Sasso** RAVELLO, ITALY **89.80**

7 **Çiragan Palace Hotel Kempinski** ISTANBUL **89.62**

8 **Le Sirenuse** POSITANO, ITALY **89.48**

9 **Four Seasons Hotel** PRAGUE **89.24**

10 **Bauer Il Palazzo** VENICE **89.07**

11 **Four Seasons Hotel George V** PARIS **88.72**

12 **Il San Pietro** POSITANO, ITALY **88.71**

13 **Inverlochy Castle Hotel** FORT WILLIAM, SCOTLAND **88.69**

14 **Oustau de Baumanière** LES-BAUX-DE-PROVENCE, FRANCE **88.18**

15 **Domaine des Hauts de Loire** ONZAIN, FRANCE **87.74**

16 **La Bastide de Moustiers** MOUSTIERS-STE.-MARIE, FRANCE **87.68**

17 **Sheen Falls Lodge** KENMARE, IRELAND **87.62**

18 **Hotel Quinta do Lago** ALMANCIL, PORTUGAL **87.50**

19 **Chewton Glen** NEW MILTON, ENGLAND **87.39**

20 **The Goring** LONDON **87.30**

21 **Beau-Rivage Palace** LAUSANNE, SWITZERLAND **87.28**

22 **Raffles Le Montreux Palace** SWITZERLAND **87.13**

23 **Victoria-Jungfrau Grand Hotel & Spa** INTERLAKEN, SWITZERLAND **87.09**

key to the price icons   **$** under $250   **$$** $250 - 499   **$$$** $500 - 749   **$$$$** $750 - 999   **$$$$$** $1,000 - 1,999

Château Les Crayères, Reims, France, opposite left. Opposite right: Palazzo Sasso in Ravello, Italy. Left: A bar at Claridge's in London. Above: The Four Seasons Hotel, Istanbul.

chewton glen

HAMPSHIRE, ENGLAND

world's best When owners Martin and Brigitte Skan opened Chewton Glen in 1966, it was one of England's first country-house hotels. Over the years, they expanded the property, and now the Skans have finished work on the Poacher, a suite whose design departs from the staid floral curtains and Chippendale chairs in the other guest quarters. Its walls are paneled in grained, blond wood; the furniture is covered in tactile fabrics. Perhaps the main reason that Chewton Glen has been so successful, though, is that it has perfected the Jeeves-like ability to sweep you up and to deposit you in a bubble, untroubled by anything.

Chewton Glen
New Milton
Hampshire, England
44-1425/275-341
www.chewton
glen.com
Doubles from $$$

The ivy-covered patio at Chewton Glen, opposite.
Above: A view of the hotel's entry.

calcot manor

Calcot Manor
Near Tetbury
Gloucestershire
England
44-1666/890-391
www.calcot
manor.co.uk
Doubles from $$

GLOUCESTERSHIRE, ENGLAND

A collection of ancient stone buildings in the mellow Cotswold Hills, Calcot Manor originally began as a farm, constructed by Cistercian monks in the 14th century. The Ball family bought the property in 1984 and turned it into a seven-bedroom hotel. They continued to update it, converting barns and other outbuildings into additional guest rooms (there are now 30). During the past two years, the hotel has taken some big leaps forward with the opening of a 17,000-square-foot spa (try a spell in a flotation bed, followed by a juniper-and–pink grapefruit body polish) and an indoor recreation area for kids that has Sony PlayStations and a mini cinema.

The sauna at the
Calcot spa.
Opposite: Exterior of
the Four Seasons
Hotel Hampshire.

four seasons hotel hampshire

HAMPSHIRE, ENGLAND

Four Seasons Hotel Hampshire
Dogmersfield Park
Chalky Lane
Hampshire, England
800/332-3442
or 44-1252/853-010
www.four
seasons.com
Doubles from $$

The 133-room Four Seasons Hotel Hampshire, housed in an 18th-century Georgian manor house, is sure to please country and city mice alike. The former will be impressed by its urbane sophistication (the original stable block has been transformed into a destination spa and the lap pool is located in a conservatory-like glass structure), and the latter by its grounds (23 acres of English Heritage–registered gardens and more than 500 acres of tamed parkland). Spend the afternoon in the Zen meditation room or shooting clay pigeons. Hartley-Witney village, minutes from the property, boasts a quiet row of antique shops and the country's oldest cricket ground, but should you tire of rural bliss, the hustle and bustle of central London is an hour's train ride away.

lygon arms

WORCESTERSHIRE, ENGLAND

One could hardly get further from the chrome-and-wengewood minimalism of many contemporary hotels than the Lygon Arms (pronounced *liggin*). Furlong Hotels, the family-run firm that bought the place nearly two years ago, has taken on the task of bringing it into the 21st century. The Lygon today is a blend of ancient and modern. The public areas are a maze of small rooms with low, beamed ceilings, where patrons take tea with the daily papers, and most of the guest rooms, too, are archtraditional in style. However, a major refurbishment of one wing brought flat-screen TV's and futuristic shower fixtures to 19 of the hotel's 69 rooms.

Lygon Arms
Broadway
Worcestershire
England
44-1386/852-255
www.thelygon
arms.co.uk
Doubles from $$

The Great Hall at Lygon Arms, opposite. Above: A winding metal staircase at the hotel.

hotel endsleigh

DEVON, ENGLAND

In 1812, the Duchess of Bedford commissioned architect Sir Jeffry Wyattville to erect a rustic fishing lodge in a Devonshire valley above the river Tamar. Fashioned in the cottage-orné style—rough oak columns, Gothic gingerbread, shell grotto—this stone manor was recently acquired by another connoisseur of the good life. Designer Olga Polizzi, proprietor of the Hotel Tresanton in Cornwall, has turned the estate into the handsomely restrained, 16-room Hotel Endsleigh. Cream-hued guest rooms overlook a mossy bend in the trout-laden stream; fires crackle in the paneled library; and mosaic tables from Milan perk up the floral-wallpapered bar.

Hotel Endsleigh
Milton Abbot
Tavistock
Devon, England
44-1822/870-000
www.hotel
endsleigh.com
Doubles from $$

Summer Lodge
Evershot
Dorset, England
44-1935/482-000
www.summerlodge
hotel.com
Doubles from $$

A Hotel Endsleigh guest room, above. Opposite top and bottom: The bar at Summer Lodge; a private corner.

summer lodge

DORSET, ENGLAND

In the fall of 2003, the boutique-hotel chain Red Carnation bought an 18th-century manor house that dominates an out-of-the-way Dorset village. Beatrice Tollman, the company's colorful South African–born founder, added seven rooms to the original 17 and transformed every inch of the place, at a cost of some $9.5 million. Tollman has decorated each room with an attention to detail that makes visitors feel as though they were guests in an opulent private mansion. In 2004, a boutique spa with two treatment rooms opened next to the hotel's conservatory pool, and a smashing one-bedroom honeymoon suite recently came to life in an 18th-century cottage.

three london classics

THE BERKELEY

Three of London's most iconic hotels have duked it out— gloves off—for headlines. Digging deeply into their real estate, the Berkeley and the Savoy came up with ingenious ways of adding dozens of guest rooms. Countering the punch, the Dorchester spent $18.1 million on a bells-and-whistles renovation to woo a new generation of tradition-minded customers.

The ever-discreet Berkeley. Opposite left and right: A redecorated guest room at the Berkeley; arriving at the Dorchester.

the berkeley

The Berkeley looks like an expensive, elegantly poker-faced apartment house— the kind that breeds fantasies of a Belgravia pied-à-terre. Behind the discreet exterior, it turns out, is an old-school hotel that gives the genre a kick in the pants by also being blisteringly hip. With 49 recently coined guest rooms that blend old-fashioned and current notions of luxury, including mirrored bathing alcoves and heated marble floors, the Berkeley is the London hotel to beat these days. Decorator Alexandra Champalimaud has a light, tonic, insinuating touch everyone could learn from. Haute cuisine credibility is conferred by Marcus Wareing, who transplanted his one-Michelin-starred restaurant, Pétrus, to the Berkeley. *Wilton Place; 800/637-2869 or 44-20/7235-6000; www.the-berkeley.com; doubles from $$$.*

the dorchester

Not since Oliver Messel festooned the Dorchester's façade with coronation bunting in 1953 has the Dorchester looked so smart. In 2003, this 250-room Mayfair classic came off a refurbishment so complete it practically amounted to a rebranding. From room keys (fiber-optic) to desktop paraphernalia (handsome tented calendars), there's little at the Dorchester that hasn't been reexamined, rethought, or reinvented. Voluptuously swagged windows, sunburst bed canopies, and lacquer tray tables are the order of the day. And how refreshing that the Dorchester is happy simply to let the furniture and accessories speak for themselves. *Park Lane; 800/727-9820 or 44-20/7629-8888; www.dorchesterhotel.com; doubles from $$$$.*

the savoy

London is rich in historic hotels, but none feels more like a landmark than the Savoy, a Fairmont Hotel. Following the addition of 60 guest rooms by London's Lesley Knight, plus the intervention of Los Angeles decorator Barbara Barry in some of the public areas, the Savoy is still the Savoy. Barry transformed the front hall, and it now emits a low-voltage, present-day chic. And nobody would argue that the Grill isn't a younger and livelier place for Barry's attention. The new rooms bring the total to 263; some were carved out of offices and room-service staging areas, but most are in a recently built extension. And Knight's hardworking Savoy bathrooms get full marks. *The Strand; 800/441-1414 or 44-20/7836-4343; www.the-savoy.com; doubles from $$$.*

cocktail hour

Along with satisfying drinks and scintillating company, the perfect hotel bar offers a chance to take in the local scene. ■ In London, Sloane Rangers sip champagne at the **Berkeley**'s Blue Bar (*www.theberkeley.co.uk*), where everything from the leather chairs to the walls is Wedgwood-hued. ■ Caviar, vodka, and a view of the Bolshoi Theater—three of Moscow's most prized attractions—can be enjoyed at the Conservatory Lounge & Bar on the 10th floor of the **Ararat Park Hyatt** (*www.parkhyatt.com*). ■ One look at the cityscape from the rooftop bar, pool, and foosball deck at the **Standard** in downtown Los Angeles (*www.standardhotel.com*) tells us we've arrived in La La Land. ■ Argentinians don't cry for one another as they sample Cognac and live piano music under the chandeliers of the grand marble-and-mahogany lobby bar at the **Alvear Palace** in Buenos Aires (*www.alvearpalace.com*).

Banquette, the
Savoy's variation on
an American
diner. Opposite: The
Grill, revamped.

The Courthouse Hotel
Kempinski's 19th-century
prison doors. Opposite:
Looking into the hotel bar.

courthouse
hotel kempinski

**Courthouse
Hotel Kempinski**
19–21 Great
Marlborough St.
London, England
800/426-3135 or
44-20/7297-5555

www.kempinski.com
Doubles from $$

LONDON, ENGLAND

Many a rebellious lad, from Oscar Wilde to Keith Richards, has spent time within the confines of 19–21 Great Marlborough Street—the present-day site of the 116-room Courthouse Hotel Kempinski—not as hotel guests, but as defendants in what was the United Kingdom's second-oldest magistrate court. Book the Lalique Suite and unwind in the former residence of the metropolitan police commissioner; four other suites are situated in what once were the judges' robing rooms, and four more are in the clerks' chambers. Standard rooms are housed in a new wing built on the site of the old police station, including the holding cells and shooting range. Guests pass through salvaged prison gates to sip cocktails at the Bar and dine in the shadow of the judges' bench at Silk.

irish country hotels

The big news in Ireland today is hotels that reject the past and embrace the modern, modish—and mediocre. But this is not where the country excels. What Ireland does best is to hold on to tradition, as these joyously entrenched places—country houses in County Cork and on the Atlantic, a Ring of Kerry cottage, and a town house in the heart of Elizabeth Bowen country—attest. All are highly personalized, one-of-a-kind properties offering great value and an authentic Irish experience, including armfuls of hospitality.

Moy House, in County Clare.
Opposite left and right: Detail in the sitting room at
Iskeroon; a guest room at Moy House.

iskeroon

Hidden well below a coastal road at the bottom of a steep lane bedeviled with switchbacks, Iskeroon was built in 1936 to accommodate the overflow guests of the Earl of Dunraven and his American wife, Nancy. The house the earl built is a modest, low-slung, single-story cottage clad in stucco. The current color is a warm face-powder pink, set off rather daringly, but winningly, by navy trim. The blessedly un-twee interiors are colorful, casual, comfy, and forgiving. All guest rooms have dedicated baths, which are beguilingly adorned and two paces across the hall that slices through the house. Iskeroon is not luxurious and it's not meant to be. What it is is romantic, an elemental wind-tossed place that makes it easy to fall in love with nature, the sea, someone, yourself. *Caherdaniel, County Kerry; 353-66/947-5119; www.iskeroon.com; doubles from $.*

moy house

Built in the 18th century by a minor nobleman, Moy House may not be the loveliest house in County Clare from an architectural point of view, though you may find it impressive in a *Wuthering Heights* sort of way. Six of the nine accommodations give directly onto the water and are the ones you want. Carrowgar has two deep, cushioned window seats, beautifully worn original wide-plank floors, and a sumptuously curtained mahogany canopy bed. It will make you feel grand, if not like a grandee. The same cheerful ignorance of contemporary design extends to the drawing room, decorated with waffled chenille upholstery, a pair of dainty Waterford chandeliers, and orchids in footed brass cachepots. Sound grannyish? It's not. The effect is fresh and relevant. *Lahinch, County Clare; 800/323-5463 or 353-65/708-2800; www.moyhouse.com; doubles from $$.*

ballyvolane house

Drawing on his experience as general
manager of Babington House, Justin
Hall, who runs the six-room Ballyvolane
House with his wife, Jenny, is gently
taking the hotel to the next level.
He is planning on adding a swimming
pool and a tennis court. One thing
he knows enough never to change are
the guest rooms, which have the
loveliest, most peaceful garden views
and are enduringly furnished with
an organic assortment of wing chairs,
alabaster lamps, sofas that are
models of shabby chic, and Turkish
rugs layered over fitted carpets.
Dinner is a communal affair, served at
a double-pedestal table in mirror-
finish mahogany. The food is as true to
place as the floppy sofas.
Castlelyons, County Cork; 353-25/36349;
www.ballyvolanehouse.com;
doubles from $.

creagh house

Eight years after they moved in, Laura
O'Mahony and Michael O'Sullivan
continue their restoration of Creagh
House, an 1837 Regency building
celebrated for having perhaps the largest,
most elaborately embellished reception
rooms of any town house in Ireland outside
Dublin. Handmade custom molds were
commissioned to replace the dozens
of intricate components. They all look as
if they were piped on by a master pâtissier
armed with a canvas sleeve, a palette
of nozzles, and a million gallons of
buttercream. Happily for guests, no part
of Creagh, which sits squarely on
Doneraile's main street, is off-limits.
It's all as much for you as it is for the hosts
and their scampering, completely
precocious three-year-old daughter, Alice.
Main St., Doneraile, County Cork;
353-22/24433; www.creaghhouse.ie;
doubles from $.

A hall in Creagh House. Opposite left and right: The formal dining room of Ballyvolane House; a mahogany bed frame at Creagh.

Lute Suites
54–58 Amsteldijk Zuid
Ouderkerk
a/d Amstel,
The Netherlands
31-20/472-2462

www.lutesuites.com
Doubles from $$

A sitting area at Lute Suites, opposite. Above: The entrance
to the reception house.

lute
suites

OUDERKERK AAN DE AMSTEL,
THE NETHERLANDS

A temple of modern design
ensconced in a row of
18th-century working-class
homes, Lute Suites is the
brainchild of renowned Dutch
designer Marcel Wanders
and local chef Peter Lute. Each
of the seven duplex suites,
20 minutes outside Amsterdam,
has its own front door, and
there's no lobby. Wanders has
also given each of the rooms
distinct personalities. Suite One
is cheerfully modern, with
bright lamps and a 10-foot-high
window overlooking the Amstel
River. In stark contrast, Seven
is a contemporary take on Gothic
style, featuring an inlaid metal
floor and a spiral teak staircase.

murano
urban resort

PARIS, FRANCE

Folded into a stolid 19th-century building on a hectic Haussmann thoroughfare, the 51-room Murano Urban Resort offers itself up as a hipper-than-thou, early-21st-century alternative to the Parisian palace hotel. To woo a fast, pleasure-seeking crowd, the Murano deploys a freshly scrubbed Pop aesthetic. Christine Derory and Raymond Morel filled the hotel with Roy Lichtenstein–style lithographs of Bacall and Bardot, tulip chairs, and organdy curtains stitched into miles of rippling folds. Bathrooms are immaculate essays in chrome and slate. And did we mention the chesterfield sofa in the salon central? All 23 feet of it are covered in white leather.

hotel sezz

PARIS, FRANCE

Decorated by Philippe Starck–
trained Christophe Pillet,
the new, 27-*chambre* Hotel Sezz
is phonetically named after
the 16th Arrondissement it calls
home. The lobby, lit with
Murano-glass fixtures, doesn't
have a front desk—that's
been replaced by an itinerant
team of personal assistants,
one of whom remains at each
guest's beck and call—but
it does have La Grande Dame,
its Veuve Clicquot champagne
bar. Rooms are accented
with bright, acid colors that pop
against textured stone
walls and stainless steel
furniture, like the *lits de camp*,
or camp-style beds, fitted
with painted wooden drawers.

Murano Urban Resort
13 Blvd. du Temple
Paris, France
33-1/42-71-20-00
www.murano
resort.com
Doubles from $$$

Hotel Sezz
6 Ave. Frémiet
Paris, France
33-1/56-75-26-26
www.hotel
sezz.com
Doubles from $$

The lobby at the Murano Urban Resort, opposite.
Above: A Hotel Sezz guest room.

l'agapa hotel & spa

PERROS-GUIREC, FRANCE

Located in a seaside village, L'Agapa Hotel & Spa clings—like the agapanthus flower—to the rocks of the remote Granit Rose coast. The briny Atlantic permeates this 50-room resort, from the salt-and-algae body scrub in the spa to the tangy *pousse en claire* oysters at Le Belouga restaurant. Chef Franck Marchesi knows his bouillabaisse; a native of Corsica, he apprenticed with Michel Rostang at the maestro's Paris restaurant. Softly lit black-and-white interiors complement the hotel's Art Deco—era architecture, but the windows framing the ocean are the real draw. For the best views, stay in La Désirade, an adjacent 10-room villa where sea mist drifts along the balconies.

**L'Agapa
Hotel & Spa**
12 Rue des
Bons-Enfants
Perros-Guirec,
France
33-2/96-49-01-10
www.lagapa.com
Doubles from $

A view from Villa La Désirade at L'Agapa, above left.
Above right: A La Désirade guest room.

Le Manoir de Raynaudes
Monesties, France
33-5/63-36-91-90
www.raynaudes.com
Doubles from $

La Maison
Place de l'Église
Blauzac, France
33-4/66-81-25-15
www.chambres-provence.com
Doubles from $

le manoir de raynaudes

la maison

MONESTIES, FRANCE

BLAUZAC, FRANCE

When food editor Orlando Murrin and his partner, Peter Steggall, first visited the Tarn, outside Toulouse, they fell in love with the landscape and immediately relocated to the south of France. Soon after, the pair set about restoring a 19th-century estate, with a three-room guesthouse and four self-contained apartments. Though the contemporary flats come with fully stocked kitchens, few visitors will want to miss out on meals prepared by Murrin. He bases his authentic southwest French dishes on locally sourced produce and whatever is fresh from the garden.

With guesthouses in the south of France as common as snails after a rainfall, La Maison is giving the genre a stylish update. The 18th-century *maison de village*, just a few miles from the romantic market town of Uzès, has wide-open views of the surrounding garigue and Mont Ventoux and a walled swimming pool, fringed with olive trees and oleander. The inn's five rooms (Cuzco, with its own terrace, is the one to reserve) prove there is life in the French-country look yet.

hi

NICE, FRANCE

Situated in a posh residential
neighborhood and set back from the
water in Nice, the Hi was designed
by Matali Crasset, one of Philippe
Starck's protégés. The Hi is exactly
like a Starck hotel, only more so.
It is more toylike, has more gadgets,
and its underlying philosophy
is deeper. The Hi, Crasset has said,
is "a place for living an experience."
The experience does not include
porters, someone to show you
to your room, or bathroom Kleenex.
It does include plastic cups and
bathtubs in the middle of the
rooms, which are splashed with
acid colors. Crasset's design
for the Happy Bar—cleverly inspired
by the ribbed interior of a ship's
hull—is very tonic, very graphic.

Hi
3 Ave. des Fleurs
Nice, France
33-4/97-07-26-26
www.hi-hotel.net
Doubles from $

In the gadget-happy Hi, opposite and above.

hôtel metropole monte-carlo

MONTE CARLO, MONACO

When Fadi and Majid Boustany took the keys to their father's palatial Hôtel Metropole in 2001, the brothers knew the place needed some modern love. Despite its enviable location across from Monte Carlo's casino, the 1886 Italian Belle Époque building hadn't been lit up by a *Paris Match* flashbulb in decades. To bring the buzz back—and to lure a young clientele—the Boustanys hired Jacques Garcia, designer of Paris's nouveau-baroque Hôtel Costes. Tapestries and low-slung seating now sex up public spaces, while guest rooms mix Pierre Frey fabrics with ornamental columns and slate-and-wood bathrooms. Celebrity chef Joël Robuchon has installed a namesake restaurant, serving dishes such as crab atop citrus tabbouleh and grands crus by the glass. And to welcome those paparazzi back, the long, landscaped driveway ends at a 26-foot-high boxwood Arc de Triomphe.

**Hôtel Metropole
Monte-Carlo**
4 Ave. de la Madone
Monte Carlo,
Monaco
800/223-6800 or
377/93-15-15-15
www.metropole.com
Doubles from $$$

The grand entrance to the Hôtel Metropole Monte-Carlo, opposite. Above: Corridor from the hotel reception area.

The lobby of the Hotel Fox, in Copenhagen.

30 affordable european hotels

Travel + Leisure scoured 27 cities from Amsterdam to Athens and uncovered 30 modern hotels with rooms for under $300 a night where you don't have to forsake style for savings.

The Ecstasy room (No. 206) at Hotel Fox; the hotel's exterior, right. Opposite left and right: The rooftop of the Hotel Fox; inside London's B&B Belgravia.

vienna
AUSTRIA

At the 16th-century **Hotel König von Ungarn,** just a short walk from St. Stephen's Cathedral, gilded mirrors, boldly graphic wallpaper, and chandeliers ensure that no two rooms are alike. Sip coffee in the glass-covered courtyard atrium, steps away from where Mozart composed *The Marriage of Figaro,* or try a *sekt* (traditional sparkling wine) at the bar. *10 Schulerstr.; 43-1/515-840; www.kvu.at; breakfast included.*

antwerp
BELGIUM

The two charcoal-colored town houses of the **Hotel Julien** are surrounded by 17th-century churches, gabled mansions, and cobblestoned alleys. The pared-down interiors combine blond-wood surfaces with whitewashed furniture and handmade white porcelain vases. Freshly brewed coffee and Belgian chocolates are available around the clock in the library, which is filled with stacks of international magazines and art books. *24 Korte Nieuwstr.; 32-3/229-0600; www.hotel-julien.com; breakfast included.*

prague
CZECH REPUBLIC

The **Maximilian** is a welcoming spot near the Old Town Square. For a recent revamp, Czech-born and London-based Eva Jiricna (of Hotel Josef fame) ditched the hotel's cookie-cutter look in favor of light, geometric designs. The compact rooms have imposing dark-wood headboards that reach to the ceiling, and Philippe Starck bathroom fixtures. The on-site spa specializes in Thai massage. *14 Haštalská; 866/376-7831 or 420-2/2530-3118; www.maximilian hotel.com; breakfast included.*

copenhagen
DENMARK

To launch its latest car, Volkswagen commissioned 21 international graphic designers, graffiti artists, and illustrators to renovate the 61-room **Hotel Fox,** where the wildly fantastic décor is the draw. Brisbane-based design group Rinzen created the Sleep Seasons room (a pitched tent surrounded by a forest mural), and Friendswithyou, from Miami, covered the Harmony's Helm room with 25,000 powder-blue, bright-white, and canary-yellow mosaic tiles. *3 Jarmers Plads; 45/3313-3000; www.hotelfox.dk; breakfast included.*

copenhagen
DENMARK

Right next to Town Hall—and close to the Tivoli Gardens and the Strøget shops—the **Square** is emphatically unsquare, with scarlet Arne Jacobsen Egg chairs in the lobby and striking photographs lining the halls. As at many Scandinavian hotels, the feather duvet–topped beds are dressed in plain white linens. The sunny top-floor restaurant is open only for breakfast, a smorgasbord of hearty breads and cheeses. For dinner, try the nearby Det Lille Apotek. *14 Rådhuspladsen; 45/3338-1200; www. thesquare.dk.*

brighton
ENGLAND

In the middle of a grand sweep of wedding cake–style buildings known as the Regency Mile, the discreet sign for **Drakes** is easy to miss. But behind its scarlet lacquered door is a diminutive 20-room inn filled with objets d'art. Splurge on one of the circular sea-facing rooms, with a freestanding tub. The Gingerman, a modern British restaurant, which opened a year ago, is a local favorite. *44 Marine Parade; 44-1273/696-934; www.drakesof brighton.com.*

london
ENGLAND

Too often, bed-and-breakfast implies dingy paint and graying curtains. Enter Penny Brown, Colette Huck, and Lynne Reid, the owners of the 17-room **B&B Belgravia**. The trio went high style, gutting a Victorian town house in one of the city's most exclusive neighborhoods. Now, orange pansies brighten the entrance, an Ingo Maurer chandelier hangs in the foyer, and a Conran-style sofa sits in the front room, where guests take cappuccino by the fire. *64–66 Ebury St.; 44-20/7259-8570; www.bb-belgravia.com; breakfast included.*

london
ENGLAND

South Beach meets the East Village at London's cutting-edge **K West Hotel & Spa**. Noel Pierce, of Pierce Design International, fashioned 220 calm rooms, blending soft taupes, creams, and browns with stainless steel and sandblasted glass. Even cooler than the décor are the guests (mostly media mavens and touring musicians), who keep the scene at the K Lounge rocking all night long and recover the next day with holistic treatments at the Asian-inspired spa. *Richmond Way; 44-870/027-4343; www.k-west.co.uk.*

helsinki
FINLAND

The **Palace Hotel Linna**, a 1903 Finnish Art Nouveau fortress, was originally the local university's student union building. While historical details (stone arches, stained-glass windows) have been preserved in the public spaces, the 48 rooms have been spiffed up with leather headboards, suede chairs, and mod Diogenes lamps. Ask for No. 401, the only guest room in the imposing round tower and steps away from one of the hotel's three saunas. *29 Lönnrotinkatu; 358-10/344-4100; www.palace.fi; breakfast included.*

paris
FRANCE

The 47-room **Général Hotel,** just off the Place de la République, recently received a makeover by architect Jean-Philippe Nuel, who designed two other beloved, affordable Paris hotels: the Axial Beaubourg and the Lavoisier. His new touches include a sleek lobby and bar (low cocoa-colored suede sofas, walls covered in graphic floral images), rooms in neutral tones, all-white bathrooms, and a green apple on every pillow. *5–7 Rue Rampon; 33-1/47-00-41-57; www.legeneralhotel.com.*

Guest room at the Lloyd Hotel. Right: The entrance to the B&B Belgravia. Opposite: A lounge at the B&B Belgravia.

berlin
GERMANY

In the heart of the buzzing Mitte neighborhood, **Lux 11** is the latest creation from a dynamic minimalist duo, Claudio Silvestrin and his wife, Giuliana Salmaso. The 72 rooms (20 more are slated to open in early 2006), each a monolithic space, have open bathrooms finished in concrete and honey-colored wood. An Aveda spa occupies the ground floor, and a micro–department store, run by the former buyer for Quartier 206, one of Berlin's poshest fashion emporiums, is adjacent to the lobby. *9–13 Rosa-Luxemburg-Str.; 800/337-4685 or 49-30/936-2800; www.designhotels.com.*

hamburg
GERMANY

The 77-room **East Hotel,** in the city's rapidly gentrifying red-light district, was created by Jordan Mozer, the Chicago-based interior designer. Mozer opted for a Gaudí-goes–Far East feel, with nonlinear furnishings (undulating columns in the lobby and Asian-fusion restaurant) and molten-metal moldings (mirrored sculptures that appear to be dripping from the ceiling). On a sunny day, hit the rooftop terrace or the garden for a mai tai and a spicy salmon roll. *31 Simon von Utrecht Str.; 800/337-4685 or 49-40/309-930; www.designhotels.com.*

athens
GREECE

At **Fresh Hotel,** color is key: hot pinks, neon oranges, and cherry reds pop up everywhere, from the check-in desk to the bedside vases. The hotel's 133 rooms follow the standard minimalist guidelines—plastic furniture, Eames chairs, and Artemide bedside lighting. Fresh is quickly becoming a jet-set hangout thanks to the rooftop pool with views of the Acropolis and the nouvelle Greek cuisine at Orange Bar. *26 Sofokleous St.; 800/337-4685 or 30-210/524-8511; www.designhotels.com; breakfast included.*

budapest
HUNGARY

The **Art'otel Budapest** is part of a small, aesthetically minded chain that is considered the pioneer in the artists-designing-hotels trend. Art'otel invited American artist Donald Sultan to incorporate oversized images of needles, thread, and buttons into the hotel's carpets, wall hangings, even the flatware. Light-hued contemporary furniture makes no place for fluff and chintz in the spare riverfront rooms, which have floor-to-ceiling views of the neo-Gothic parliament building. *16–19 Bem Rakpart; 36-1/487-9487; www.artotels.com; breakfast included.*

florence
ITALY

The aristocratic **Casa Howard Guest House** is situated in a palazzo next to the Santa Maria Novella Pharmacy, which supplies the hotel's pomegranate and mint soaps. The 11 quirky accommodations have individual themes: the intellectual Library Room (wall-to-wall shelves filled with books); the sensual Hidden Room (erotic prints, a sunken bath); and the family-friendly Play Room (videos, a climbing wall). *18 Via della Scala; 39-06/6992-4555; www.casa howard-florence.com.*

milan
ITALY

rome
ITALY

venice
ITALY

amsterdam
THE NETHERLANDS

oslo
NORWAY

Opened in June 2004, **Alle Meraviglie** could not have a more appropriate name (roughly translated, it means "of wonders"). Its six airy rooms are just a five-minute walk from the Duomo and are outfitted with Baroque-style antique chairs, silk taffeta curtains, and surreal installations, such as a fringed sheet dipped in plaster. Each guest gets fresh flowers, Internet access, and a radio with short- and long-wave channels in English and Italian, but no TV's. *8 Via San Tomaso; 39-02/805-1023; www.allemeraviglie.it.*

Alessandro Bisceglie and Elyssa Bernard opened the three-room **Daphne Inn** in 2001. Since then, the chic guesthouse has expanded to 15 rooms in two palazzi near the Via Veneto. Details include Bisazza mosaics on the walls and offbeat artworks hanging above the beds. Each room comes with a cell phone for calling the staff. Although Nos. 222 and 223 are the most affordable rooms, they lack private bathrooms. *55 Via di San Basilio; 39-06/4544-9177; www.daphne-rome.com; breakfast included.*

At the ultraminimalist **Palazzo Soderini,** a three-room pension hidden in a 15th-century villa, everything is rigorously white, from the bed linens to the marble-chip terrazzo floors. Guests breakfast on croissants with organic honey in a walled garden amid perfumed jasmine, red roses, and white-blossomed pittosporum trees. During the high season, there's a minimum stay of two nights. *3611 Campo Bandiera e Moro; 39-041/296-082; www.palazzosoderini.it; breakfast included.*

More than 50 Dutch artists descended upon a 1921 gabled building in Amsterdam's trendy Eastern Docklands, transforming it from a defunct prison into the **Lloyd Hotel**. Cleverly furnished, rooms range from one-stars, which lack bathrooms but supply robes to wear down the hall, to spacious five-stars, like room No. 221, which has a piano. The restaurant, Snel, serves farm-fresh regional dishes, while the on-site Cultural Embassy advises on performances, festivals, and museums. *34 Oostelijke Handelskade; 31-20/561-3636; www.lloydhotel.com.*

In a country where "south of the border" means below the Arctic Circle, there's a hotel with a surprising Latin flavor, the **Radisson SAS Hotel Nydalen**. Urban rooms have a cosmopolitan feel, while the Chili quarters — with sculptures of red peppers mounted on the walls—need only a mariachi band to channel Mexico. At the restaurant, Circo, dishes such as roast pork rolled in Serrano ham add to the vibe. *33 Nydalsveien; 800/333-3333 or 47-23/263-000; www.radissonsas.com; breakfast included.*

A view from the rooftop pool at Las Casas del Rey de Baeza. Right: The lobby at the Général Hotel in Paris. Opposite left and right: The central patio at Las Casas del Rey de Baeza; breakfast at the Général Hotel.

warsaw
POLAND

Hotel Rialto is an ornate masterpiece in the heart of Warsaw. Polish firm DOM Architektury combed the antiques shops of Europe to secure authentic period pieces from the early 20th century. Most of the 44 rooms pay tribute to the work of figures such as designer Charles Rennie Mackintosh and artist William Morris, but for something a little different, try No. 13, which looks to Africa with its zebra-skin rug and warrior masks. *72 Ul. Wilcza; 800/323-7500 or 48-22/584-8777; www.rialto.pl.*

lisbon
PORTUGAL

The **NH Liberdade** portends a hip new Lisbon, with its rooftop swimming pool, black-and-cream motif, and provocative details (like the faux-fur lamp in the lobby). The centrally located hotel gives guests the personal treatment, down to a choice of pillows (firm, soft, feather). Stop by the restaurant, Do Teatro, for baked monkfish with mango. *180B Avda. da Liberdade; 888/726-0528 or 351-21/351-4060; www.nh-hotels.com.*

ljubljana
SLOVENIA

Touting itself as the world's most high-tech retreat, the 214-room **Royal Media Hotel & Casino** is a business and leisure traveler's dream, less than two miles from the city center. Plasma screens line the walls in corridors, conference rooms, and restaurants. The hotel's Grand Media Platform allows guests to access 42-inch satellite TV's, wireless Internet, and discounted international calls. Rejuvenate in the spa's Turkish bath or take a gamble at the casino. *154 Dunajska Cesta; 386-1/588-2500; www.dominagrandmedialjubljana.com.*

madrid
SPAIN

Service matters at **Bauzá Hotel**, where the young bellhops wear the words CAN I HELP YOU? embroidered in English on their uniforms. Rooms are monochromatic—save for a splash of red here and there—and have all the necessary amenities: Sony PlayStations; a CD, book, and pillow menu; and a top-notch sound system. Double-paned windows block the noise of the chic Salamanca shopping district below, without obstructing the view. *79 Calle Goya; 800/337-4685 or 34/91-435-7545; www.hotelbauza.com.*

madrid
SPAIN

The two flights of stairs (no elevator!) that lead to **7 Colors** might dissuade the unadventurous, but the hotel's bright, industrial rooms are worth the climb. Each one—down to the soap—is decorated in a single color. In the lobby you'll find a convivial breakfast room with a communal table; just outside are the popular bars of the trendy Plaza de Santa Ana. *14 Calle Huertas; 34/91-429-6935; www.7colorsrooms.com; breakfast included.*

san sebastian
SPAIN

In a city where even
the most luxurious
accommodations tend
toward the dowdy,
Villa Soro offers a much-
needed dose of
modern luxury. The
owners of this intimate
19th-century mansion
have preserved the 1898
manicured garden and
the stained-glass
windows, while
updating rooms with
a neutral color scheme,
wooden furniture,
and work from local
artists. Superior rooms—
$50 more than the
standards—are worth
the extra expense,
if only for the natural
light they receive.
*61 Avda. de Ategorrieta;
34/94-329-7970;
www.villasoro.com.*

seville
SPAIN

At first glance, **Las
Casas del Rey de Baeza**
might seem like just
another Andalusian
residence (whitewashed
façade, Moorish
courtyards), but inside,
everything is cool
sophistication. Leather
armchairs and birds
in antique cages fill the
inviting public areas;
the 41 cream-colored,
softly lit rooms have
stylized wicker furniture
and renovated
bathrooms. The larger
guest quarters are
outfitted with flat-screen
TV's and DVD players.
The more compact rooms
are more modestly priced.
*2 Plaza Jesús de la
Redención; 34/95-456-
1496; www.hospes.es.*

valencia
SPAIN

Swaggering onto
the scene, the **Hospes
Palau de la Mar**
announced Valencia's
coming of age. An
avant-garde group
of designers and
architects remodeled
two 18th-century
palaces near the Turia
River, balancing
original details (ornate
carved doors, a marble
staircase) with
contemporary touches,
such as a striking
glass-and-steel patio.
The 66 bedrooms have
dark parquet floors,
crisp white bed linens,
and free mini-bars.
*14 Navarro Reverter;
34/96-316-2884; www.
hospes.es.*

stockholm
SWEDEN

When he was
a photojournalist,
Per Hellsten dreaded
missing calls while
in the shower. Now as
owner of the **Rex Hotel,**
he has eliminated
that frustration by
installing phones—
along with heated floors
and towel racks—in
the gray Karystos-stone
bathrooms of this 1866
building on a quiet
street. The 32 bedrooms
combine original
details such as pine-
plank floors with
bright blue-and-
burgundy bedspreads
and Hellsten's own
photographs.
*73 Luntmakargt; 46-8/160-
040; www.rexhotel.se.*

istanbul
TURKEY

Local and international
trendsetters flock
to the bar at the 50-room
Bentley Hotel, where
on weekends lounge
music plays well into
the night. Milanese
architects Piero
Lissoni and Nicoletta
Canesi used large
windows, spare
dark-wood furniture,
and pale blue hues
to give guests a
calming respite just
five minutes from
Istanbul's hectic center
and bustling shopping
district.
*75 Halàskargazi St.;
800/337-4685 or
90-212/291-7730;
www.designhotels.com;
breakfast included.*

q!

Q!
67 Knesebeckstr.
Berlin, Germany
49-30/810-0660
www.loock-
hotels.com
Doubles from $

Despite being designed to within an inch of its life, the décor of Berlin's Q! hotel displays a coherence that's admirable. With sleek, *Clockwork Orange*–like white paneling and psychedelic angles and juxtapositions (bathtubs fused to beds, for example), the hotel makes a point of announcing its mod personality at every opportunity. The design (by the ultrahip Graft, known for its work for Brad Pitt) deploys lots of indirect lighting and beautiful bent-veneer accents that flow into benches and onto the floor, in an abundance of clean, curvy lines.

Studio room at Q!

Beau-Rivage Palace
17–19 Place du Port
Lausanne
Switzerland
800/223-1230 or
41-21/613-3333
www.brp.ch
Doubles from $$

The Hotel
14 Sempacherstr.
Lucerne
Switzerland
41-41/226-8686
www.the-hotel.ch
Doubles from $$

beau-rivage palace

LAUSANNE, SWITZERLAND

world's best

Known for its lakeside locale and award-winning service, the 169-room Beau-Rivage Palace in Lausanne has been catering to the whims of a diverse and prestigious clientele since 1861. The resort boasts a suite for every sensibility, whether decorated in the spirit of Le Corbusier or Napoleon III, and a newly Michelin-starred restaurant, La Rotonde. Plus, guests have their pick of playgrounds: the property's historic 10-acre park facing the Alps or the Cinq Mondes spa, which introduced Japanese cedar baths and Brazilian-coffee-bean soap scrubs to the shores of Lake Geneva.

the hotel

LUCERNE, SWITZERLAND

The Swiss are justifiably proud of their reputation for hospitality, and many in the broad range of Lucerne's hotels and restaurants are well worth visiting for their accommodating atmosphere alone. At the newer end of the spectrum is the Hotel, designed by Jean Nouvel, whose idea of luxury is ultraminimalist furnishings and bedroom ceilings decorated with fleshy scenes from the films of Pedro Almodóvar, Bernardo Bertolucci, David Lynch, and other titans of seriously salacious cinema.

palace luzern

LUCERNE, SWITZERLAND

Palace Luzern
10 Haldenstr.
Lucerne,
Switzerland
800/223-6800 or
41-41/416-1616
www.palace-
luzern.ch
Doubles from $$

Inside the sauna
at the Palace Luzern
spa, above.

world's best With architectural flourishes that include French balconies and Ionic columns, the 100-year-old Palace Luzern has clearly maintained its Belle Époque flair while cultivating a host of modern amenities—the most recent of which is an on-site spa with six serene treatment rooms for globally inspired therapies such as Balinese massage and Indian hot-stone chakra balancing. For those who prefer traditional European-style health coaching, the hotel now runs Swiss Clinics Checkup retreats, which focus on personal training and preventive health care. However, the resort's best therapeutic offering may be the five-minute stroll to town along the lakefront promenade with the Alps as your backdrop.

hotel caruso

RAVELLO, ITALY

Hotel Caruso
2 Piazza San
Giovanni del Toro
Ravello, Italy
39-089/858-801
www.hotelcaruso.com
Doubles from $$$

Once a hideaway for luminaries such as Greta Garbo, the Hotel Caruso, on Italy's Amalfi Coast, had all but faded into obscurity. That is, until Orient Express bought the 11th-century property six years ago and gave it a complete overhaul. Some $37 million later, the whitewashed structure, which sits atop a 1,150-foot limestone cliff in Ravello, has regained its luster. Interior designer Federico Forquet dressed up the 54 bedrooms with bronze lamps and Neapolitan-style furniture, while chef Franco Luise created a locally inspired menu (think: chilled zucchini soup with Parmesan ice cream) that's served outside, overlooking the Gulf of Salerno. The hotel's 45-foot fishing boat whisks guests off on day trips to Positano, but the real draw is the infinity pool, whose waters fade into the mountainous horizon.

The pool at Hotel Caruso.
Opposite: The exterior of Badia
a Coltibuono.

badia a coltibuono

Badia a Coltibuono
Gaiole in Chianti, Italy
39-0577/744-832
www.coltibuono.com
Doubles from $

GAIOLE IN CHIANTI, ITALY

Kick your cooking skills up a notch at Tuscany's "wine resort" Badia a Coltibuono, which means "abbey of the good harvest." The 1,000-year-old former abbey, outside Florence, has 10 surprisingly spacious guest rooms (eight were actually monks' cells), with furniture from the 16th century, white-marble bathrooms, and views over the classically landscaped garden. In the rustic kitchen, local chef Guido Stucchi Prinetti teaches aspiring cooks how to prepare a four-course Tuscan meal, then sends them off to olive-oil tastings or wine-appreciation courses at the property's nearby vineyard.

Hotel Puerta América
41 Avda. de América
Madrid, Spain
34/91-744-5400
www.hotel
puertamerica.com
Doubles from $$

Clockwise from above: A Zaha Hadid–designed floor lobby at Hotel Puerta América; a guest room on Gluckman Mayner's floor; the hotel's eye-popping façade. Opposite: A guest room by Ron Arad.

hotel puerta américa

MADRID, SPAIN

In an absurdly bold conceit, each of Puerta América's 12 guest floors, along with the restaurant, bar, and public areas, was conceived by a different architect or designer. The project's all-star cast included Norman Foster, creator of London's Millennium Bridge, and 2004 Pritzker Prize winner Zaha Hadid. The result is an architectural Tower of Babel where even the parking garage is compelling. Glass-cube elevators glide up and down the exterior, and at each floor the doors open to reveal a shocking new world. For the most part, the rooms live up to the hotel's five-star ambitions, treading the line between funkiness and function. For sheer bliss, it's hard to top Arata Isozaki's rooms, whose bedrooms, all rich black and charcoal gray, are masterpieces of understatement.

Clockwise from top: The Hotel Omm lobby; the building's distinctive façade; Moovida, one of the hotel's restaurants.

hotel omm

BARCELONA, SPAIN

Hotel Omm
265 Carrer Roselló
Barcelona, Spain
866/376-7831 or
34/93-445-4000
www.design
hotels.com
Doubles from $$

With its clean lines and unpretentious look, Juli Capella's Hotel Omm projects an incandescent warmth. The interiors, created by Sandra Tarruella and Isabel López, set pale woods in bright, airy rooms against moody, barely lit hallways and stylish lobby areas. The tour de force is the façade, a series of undulating limestone waves that peel back from the guest room windows—a daring echo of the nearby Casa Milà, designed by Antoni Gaudí almost a century ago. The exterior-wall curtain works as more than an artistic statement; it also effectively blocks traffic noise and adds an aura of intimacy to the rooms.

A guest room at Casa Camper. Opposite: Entering the hotel.

casa camper

BARCELONA, SPAIN

Casa Camper
11 Carrer Elisabets
Barcelona, Spain
34/93-342-6280
www.casa
camper.com
Doubles from $$

Fernando Amat, owner of Spain's housewares boutique Vinçon, and architect Jordi Tió created the 25-suite Casa Camper for the bohemian Spanish shoemaker. Whimsical touches like hammocks and fire engine–red walls temper strict minimalist interiors. Guest rooms—none of which face the street—are divided by a hallway into two spaces, one for sleeping and one for lounging. Complimentary healthy snacks and one of the city's only smoke-free zones (there's no smoking anywhere in the hotel) provide welcome respite from the lively Raval district, situated between the Ramblas and the contemporary art museum, MACB. With its foolproof design sensibility and recipe for stylish comfort, Camper proves that footwear and hotels have a lot in common.

almyra

PAPHOS, CYPRUS

Cyprus, a four-hour flight from London, has long been a favorite vacation spot of sun-seeking Europeans. And since the Greek part of the island joined the European Union, a flurry of stylish new hotels have opened. Among them is the recently revamped Almyra. Located in the western port town of Paphos and within walking distance of two of the most revered archaeological sites in the Mediterranean (the 13th-century Castle of Paphos and the intricately tiled House of Dionysus), the 158-room property has a minimalist décor, a slate-lined freshwater swimming pool, and a Mediterranean-Japanese fusion restaurant run by chef Rob Shipman, who was nabbed from London's Nobu. It's also a great place for families, proffering bedtime milk and cookies, children's books in four languages, a dedicated children's club and swimming pool, and even a selection of organic baby food.

Almyra
Paphos, Cyprus
800/337-4685 or
357/2693-3091
www.thanos
hotels.com
Doubles from $$

The lobby area at Almyra, opposite top, and the hotel's pool, opposite bottom. Above: A private terrace.

TRENDSPOTTING

hotel
in-flight
meals

With airlines downsizing wherever they can, some in-flight meals have landed on the chopping block. From champagne lunches à deux to portable bento boxes, these hotels are delivering well beyond checkout. ■ Thanks to the **Çiragan Palace Hotel Kempinski**, Istanbul (*www. ciragan-palace.com; $90 a person*), you can indulge your inner sultan with caviar, gold leaf–covered sushi, foie gras mousse, and baklava, all served in a sleek lacquer case and accompanied by a bottle of house wine. ■ The all-organic Air Sorrento menu, from the **Hotel Sorrento**, in Seattle (*www.hotel sorrento.com; $20 a person*), includes a grilled Niman Ranch–steak sandwich, wild Dungeness crab salad, heirloom potatoes, and fresh herbs. Call it Pike Place Market to go. ■ At select **Ritz-Carlton** hotels across the United States (*www.ritz-carlton. com; from $12 a person*), you can obtain Big Easy eats and SoCal snacks; these Flight Bites make you wonder how you ever survived with just a pack of Planters.

mykonos theoxenia hotel

MYKONOS, GREECE

**Mykonos
Theoxenia Hotel**
Mykonos, Greece
30-22890/22230
www.mykonos
theoxenia.com
Doubles from $

Standing between windmills and sand, blue crystal waters and the narrow, cobblestoned streets of Mykonos, the restored Mykonos Theoxenia Hotel is everything you wouldn't expect from a classic Greek hotel. Its 52 rooms revisit the sixties, with retro furniture playing off stark whitewashed buildings that glow in the afternoon sun. The glamorous free-form pool—with its four-poster "beds," curtained in white fabric—steals some thunder from the island's famed beaches, most of which are within a 10-minute drive. Romantics should hitch a ride to deserted Kapari Beach to watch the moon rise over the sacred island of Delos. The concierge will take care of all the details, even arranging for a speedboat to bring you back.

A room interior at EV.

ev

BODRUM, TURKEY

EV
Türkbükü,
Bodrum, Turkey
800/337-4685 or
90-252/377-6070
www.design
hotels.com
Doubles from $$$

Turkey's elite have long flocked to the southern Aegean resort town of Bodrum for its calm azure seas (great for snorkeling and sailing) and proximity to Lycian, Roman, and Ottoman ruins. The area's latest addition is EV, a hilltop hotel designed by Turkish architect Eren Talu. With 48 rooms and eight heated pools (you do the math), your privacy is just about guaranteed whether you take a dip outside or in the whirlpool in your ultramod, white-on-white room. Plasma-screen televisions and 24-hour butler service will please the most reclusive of travelers—true lovers of seclusion may even choose to skip the hotel's open-air restaurant and whip up dinner in their own fully equipped gourmet kitchens. But if you're ready to emerge once the sun sets, head down the hill for Bodrum's renowned hedonistic pursuits: the bars and clubs stay open till dawn.

africa and the middle east

Baobab trees outside
Pemba, Mozambique.

world's best top 25 africa and the middle east

Lebombo Lodge at Singita Private Game Reserve in South Africa, above. Opposite: Londolozi Private Game Reserve.

1 **Singita** SABI SAND, SOUTH AFRICA **94.57**

2 **Kichwa Tembo** MASAI MARA, KENYA **90.81**

3 **Cape Grace** CAPE TOWN **90.00**

4 **Sabi Sabi Private Game Reserve** SABI SAND, SOUTH AFRICA **89.41**

5 **Mount Kenya Safari Club** NANYUKI, KENYA **88.23**

6 **MalaMala Game Reserve** MPUMALANGA, SOUTH AFRICA **87.86**

7 **Table Bay Hotel** CAPE TOWN **87.29**

8 **Ngorongoro Crater Lodge** TANZANIA **86.95**

9 **Londolozi Private Game Reserve** MPUMALANGA, SOUTH AFRICA **86.34**

10 **Four Seasons Hotel Cairo at Nile Plaza 86.09**

11 **Ngorongoro Sopa Lodge** TANZANIA **85.00**

12 **Royal Livingstone** LIVINGSTONE, ZAMBIA **85.00**

13 **Serengeti Sopa Lodge** TANZANIA **84.23**

14 **Sweetwaters Tented Camp** SWEETWATERS GAME RESERVE, KENYA **83.85**

15 **Mount Nelson Hotel** CAPE TOWN **83.40**

16 **Ngorongoro Serena Safari Lodge** TANZANIA **83.33**

16 **Westcliff Hotel** JOHANNESBURG **83.33**

18 **Jumeirah Beach Hotel** DUBAI **83.13**

19 **Mara Serena Safari Lodge** MASAI MARA, KENYA **82.82**

20 **Samburu Serena Safari Lodge** SAMBURU NATIONAL RESERVE, KENYA **81.56**

21 **The Palace of the Lost City** SUN CITY, SOUTH AFRICA **81.41**

22 **Mena House Oberoi** CAIRO **81.19**

23 **La Mamounia** MARRAKESH **80.87**

24 **Sofitel Palais Jamaï** FEZ, MOROCCO **80.69**

25 **Park Hyatt** JOHANNESBURG **80.65**

key to the price icons $ under $250 $$ $250 - 499 $$$ $500 - 749 $$$$ $750 - 999 $$$$$ $1,000 - 1,999

The dining room at
Ksar Char-Bagh.
Opposite: The
hotel's swimming pool.

ksar char-bagh

Ksar Char-Bagh
Djnan Abiad,
Marrakesh,
Morocco
800/735-2478 or
212-44/329-244
www.ksarchar
bagh.com
Doubles from $$$

MARRAKESH, MOROCCO

Set on the edge of the Palmeraie, the exclusive palm-forested neighborhood outside Marrakesh, Ksar Char-Bagh combines Ottoman interiors with Andalusian courtyards, Moghul arches, and Persian gardens. Water is the most important element of the hotel's design. The rooms, called Harem Suites, are enormous—so big, in fact, that they swallow up rather than show off their handsome furnishings, which include sculpted fireplaces and Syrian chairs inlaid with camel bones. The sleeping areas (in alcoves behind Moorish arches) are cozier.

Inside Dar Ahlam.
Opposite: A guest room
in the hotel.

dar ahlam

Dar Ahlam
Casbah Madihi
Skoura, Morocco
800/735-2478 or
212-44/852-239

www.darahlam.com
Doubles from $$$$,
including meals
and drinks

SKOURA, MOROCCO

The palm-filled oasis town of Skoura—about a five-hour drive from Marrakesh—is surrounded by mud-walled casbahs, most of them in various states of disrepair. Dar Ahlam, which in Arabic means "House of Dreams," is a notable exception. This adobe palace was restored in 2002 by event organizer Thierry Teyssier. While guests have the ability to personalize much of their stay (from the scent of their shampoo to the wood in their room's fireplace), Dar Ahlam works hard to surprise. Meals, for example, are almost never served in the same place twice. Ultimately, what you remember about Dar Ahlam is a dreamlike quality—whether you're admiring the gardens from a hammock or wandering the silk-curtained corridors.

villa didon

TUNIS, TUNISIA

Villa Didon
Rue Mendès France
Tunis, Tunisia
216-71/733-433
www.villadidon.com
Doubles from $$

Here's one more reason to add Tunis, North Africa's most European capital, to your must-visit list: Villa Didon. The whitewashed hotel—which stands atop Byrsa Hill and has views of the ruins of Carthage, Queen Dido's city, below—is the work of French architect Philippe Boisselier. Each of his 10 pared-down suites (all named after figures from Greek and Roman mythology) is hidden behind a futuristic electronic sliding door. Inside, Portuguese linens are draped over whimsical Ron Arad–designed chairs; a tan marble floor leads to a center-of-the-room whirlpool bath, where you can soak while admiring the Gulf of Tunis through huge windows. A hammam, a lobby bar, with stone monochrome etchings and vibrant raw-silk banners by Algerian artist Rachid Koraïchi, and a sleek restaurant, with an open kitchen and views of the bay, turn the whole retreat into a modern classic.

Kasbah Tamadot's majestic setting. Opposite left and right: The lobby of the Villa Didon; the inn's exterior.

kasbah tamadot

ASNI, MOROCCO

Kasbah Tamadot
Asni, Morocco
800/225-4255
www.kasbah
tamadot.com
Doubles from $$

Seven years in the making, Richard Branson's Kasbah Tamadot has been one of the most eagerly awaited hotels in Morocco. A little less than an hour's drive south from Marrakesh, Tamadot was originally a Berber chieftain's private palace built in the casbah style. The grounds are covered in Zen-like cactus gardens, thick rose beds, and fragrant apple and cherry trees. The hotel's 18 guest rooms and suites mix Moroccan furnishings with Asian antiques. In addition to the accommodations in the main casbah building, a separate three-bedroom "master suite" with a private plunge pool can be rented as an individual villa. Despite its tranquil setting, Tamadot is not aimed at the kick-back-and-do-nothing crowd. Indeed, it is populated by type-A travelers who take full advantage of the resort's two tennis courts, well-equipped weight room, and large indoor lap pool.

al moudira

LUXOR, EGYPT

Al Moudira—a baroque hotel fit for royalty, just a few miles south of the Valley of the Queens—incorporates materials salvaged from the corners of Egypt: stained glass lines the ceilings; frescoes and latticework adorn the arched walls; and 100-year-old wooden columns surround the swimming pool. The air is fragrant with henna and jasmine, wafting from a 20-acre garden planted with lemon, mandarin, and guava trees. All 54 guest rooms are decked out with richly hued kilim rugs, desks inlaid with mother-of-pearl, and spacious bathrooms modeled after Turkish hammams.

A massage or scrub can do wonders, but when a spa pays attention to the smallest details, now that's transporting. ■ The Shiffa gem oils used by massage therapists at the Madinat Jumeirah resort's **Six Senses Spa,** in Dubai (*www.madinat jumeirah.com*), contain ground diamonds, rubies, and emeralds: their crystals are said to have healing properties. ■ At the **Canyon Ranch** locations in Tucson and the Berkshires (*www.canyon ranch.com*), guests have the use of heart monitors. ■ The women-only **Greenhouse Spa** in Texas provides an entire wardrobe to use during your stay (*www.the green housespa.net*). ■ The Zen bonuses at CHI, the spa at Shangri-La's **Mactan Island Resort & Spa,** in the Philippines (*www.shangri-la.com*), take mood alteration to an even higher plane: Tibetan cymbals summon deities, "singing bowls" create healing vibrations in the body, and hand-carved stones applied to pressure points balance stress and restore vitality.

emirates palace

ABU DHABI,
UNITED ARAB EMIRATES

Perhaps the best way to express the grandeur of the newly built, Kempinski-operated Emirates Palace—reportedly the most expensive hotel ever built—is to break it down by numbers. This sand-colored palace has 1,002 Swarovski chandeliers, 140 elevators, 114 domes covered in mosaic glass tiles, and a staff of 2,000. The 394 rooms are like mini palaces in themselves, with acres of gold leaf, marble, and silk, plus fresh-cut flowers and 24-hour butler service. Scattered throughout the 10.8 million–square-foot building are 30 interactive touch screens, with maps and directions, and an "overwhelming" number of signs. Overwhelming, indeed.

Al Moudira
West Bank
Luxor, Egypt
20-12/392-8332
www.moudira.com
Doubles from $

Emirates Palace
Abu Dhabi Corniche
Abu Dhabi, United
Arab Emirates
800/426-3135 or
971-2/690-8888
www.emirates
palace.com
Doubles from $$$

The grand Emirates Palace, above.

A lounge area at Baines' Camp, right.
Opposite left and right: A coming-of-
age ritual being performed near
Shompole Lodge; a lodge guest room.

baines' camp

Baines' Camp
Okavango Delta
Botswana
800/323-7308 or
27-11/781-1497
www.abercrombie
kent.com
Doubles from $$$$,
all-inclusive

OKAVANGO DELTA, BOTSWANA

Set along the Boro River in Botswana's Okavango Delta, Abercrombie & Kent's
intimate eco-lodge is built from plaster, burlap, and 150,000 aluminum cans
collected from the local community. Five elevated, balconied suites are connected
by suspension bridges; each has a mobile, mosquito net–draped four-poster
bed that can be wheeled outside for starlit slumbering. The camp is located in
the southern section of the famous Moremi Game Reserve (the "predator capital of
Africa") and offers a plethora of creative ways to view big game: paddling the
Boro River in a mokoro (dugout canoe), walking the grounds with the camp's trio of
adopted elephants, or even scouting wildlife from a helicopter.

shompole lodge

MAGADI, KENYA

Shompole Lodge
Magadi, Kenya
254-20/883-280
www.shompole.com
Doubles from $$$$,
including all meals
and activities

Overlooking Kenya's Great Rift Valley at the edge of the Nguruman Escarpment, Shompole Lodge is a successful alliance between a private safari company and those Masai who are employed as the hotel's staff and rangers. The Shompole Group Ranch community receives conservation fees and the opportunity to reinvest in increasing shares in the lodge; by 2018, they are expected to gain majority ownership. This gradual earn-in gives the Masai time to hone their operational skills while the safari company maintains a base in one of the world's most spectacular game reserves. The lodge is a lavish introduction to the African bush, with guided walks and game viewing in the private conservancy, which can be followed by a splash in the "cool pool" that's a feature of every suite.

quilálea island resort

QUILÁLEA ISLAND, MOZAMBIQUE

The only tenant of the island of Quilálea is the nine-room Quilálea Island Resort, the first high-end hotel in Mozambique's Quirimbas Archipelago. On a stone-and-mahogany deck overlooking the beach, a saltwater pool glistens in the sun. Quilálea's nine thatched-roof villas were hewn out of rock, teakwood, and mahogany and are furnished with ornate wooden carvings by the Makonde, a tribe from the northern mainland. The villas open onto a small private beach; from your sprawling king-sized bed, framed by flowing white-cotton curtains, you can gaze at the mirror-like surface of the bay.

Quilálea Island Resort
Quilálea Island
Mozambique
44-131/661-6000
www.quilalea.com
Doubles from $$$$,
including meals

A guest room at Quilálea Island Resort, opposite.
Above: Rock formations near the resort.

Inside one of the
Matemo Island Resort's
villas. Opposite:
Looking westward from
Matemo Island,
toward the mainland.

matemo island resort

Matemo Island Resort
Matemo Island
Mozambique
800/524-7979 or
258-1/303-618
www.matemo
resort.com
Doubles from $$,
including breakfast
and dinner

MATEMO ISLAND, MOZAMBIQUE

Approaching Matemo Island Resort—a 20-minute puddle-jumper flight from
Pemba—you drive past seaside villages of mud huts shaded by swaying palms.
A few minutes later you come upon the resort's entrance—a sweeping Moorish
arch framing a crescent-shaped beach and radiant ocean. The resort's man-made
elements are equally stunning, all Afro-Arab opulence: a thatched-roof lounge
is brightened by Zanzibari daybeds piled high with colorful Moroccan cushions;
stained-glass lanterns line the walls. The 24 wooden villas are set along a
private beach and outfitted with Persian rugs, teak four-poster beds, and sliding
glass doors that open onto private porches, equipped with sea-facing hammocks.

Some hotel bathrooms are so indulgent and lovely that they're practically a vacation in themselves. ■ The villas at **North Island** in the Seychelles (*www.north-island.com*) blend indoors with outdoors: the bathrooms, which include two-person Glasstone tubs, lead to outdoor showers and private massage decks. ■ The exceptionally large bath suites at Bangkok's **Sukhothai** hotel (*www. sukhothai.com*) are like personal minispas, with granite-tiled showers, teak floors, and spotlighted bathtubs. ■ At the **Losari Coffee Plantation** in Java (*www.losaricoffee plantation.com*), once you stop staring at the red marble and bamboo walls, bronze sinks, and deep stone tubs, you notice the views of the surrounding volcanoes. ■ From the windows of the expansive "wet rooms"—which hold egg-shaped bathtubs and rain showers— attached to the *baños* at Mexico's **One & Only Palmilla** resort (*www.one andonlypalmilla.com*), you can look out on the Sea of Cortés.

dugong beach lodge

VILANCULOS, MOZAMBIQUE

Dugong Beach Lodge
Vilanculos
Mozambique
258-82/306-4880
www.dugong
lodge.co.za
Doubles from $$,
including meals

Located on a white-sand peninsula within a marine and wildlife sanctuary, Dugong Beach Lodge, an eco-resort on the Mozambique coast, has just 10 "chalets"—framed canvas tents, with hardwood floors and outdoor showers, under Jekka grass–thatch canopies. Guests can sit by the pool and gaze past the jetty to the bay or else kayak, deep-sea fish, or snorkel, sharing the open Indian Ocean with manta rays, leatherback turtles, and the eponymous dugong (an endangered mammal that's something like a manatee). At sunset, head to the gazebo at the end of the jetty and order a cocktail to sip while nibbling baobab-fruit bar snacks.

A bathroom at North Island, opposite.
Above: Dugong Beach Lodge, with its jetty and gazebo.

cape town spas

In Cape Town, South Africa, Table Mountain rises behind the skyline, penguins pad along Boulder's Beach, and restaurants and shops rival those of any international city. With the opening of three spas at top hotels in the South African metropolis, travelers are also flocking to the sophisticated city for pampering, turning it into a destination for an urban spa safari.

altiraspa at the arabella sheraton grand hotel cape town

Half of the prime top-floor real estate at the city's newest luxury hotel is devoted to coddling. Altiraspa's 16 treatment rooms allow stressed-out travelers to surrender themselves to facials, body wraps, hydrotherapy-tub soaks, and 13 kinds of massages. As good as the therapies are (try the Cleopatra Body Treatment), however, it's the facilities that have guests lingering for hours on end. Spa-goers fresh from their scrubs recline on heated rubberized lounges in the shaded water-bed room. Everything, even the sauna, takes advantage of the panoramic vistas: the sky-high hothouse is glassed-in on two sides, with views across the waterfront to the ocean beyond. *Convention Square; 27-21/412-9999; www.starwoodhotels.com; doubles from $$.*

AltiraSpa's lap pool. Opposite left and right: A treatment room at the Spa at Cape Grace; the Sanctuary Spa's reception area.

spa at
cape grace

sanctuary spa at the
twelve apostles hotel

world's best Each treatment at the spa on the fourth floor of the 122-room Cape Grace hotel includes an African method or product, such as facial massages that use round Xhosa beads and a four-hand rub performed with a Zulu knopkerrie—a wooden walking stick with a smooth knob. Even the soothing motions used during the African Massage are inspired by the Khoisan tradition of dancing circles around a sick person in an effort to enhance healing. The treatment leaves your back loose and the rest of your senses pleasantly fuzzy. The Spa at Cape Grace is exclusive to hotel guests. *West Quay Rd., Victoria and Alfred Waterfront; 27-21/410-7100; www.capegrace.com; doubles from $$$.*

The Sanctuary Spa is fast becoming one of the most popular destinations in Cape Town. The lower level is dominated by three rough-hewn stone pools modeled on underground springs. The seven treatment rooms are outfitted with colored-light therapy equipment. The spa's signature treatment is a sea-salt exfoliation followed by a body wrap infused with buchu (a shrub known for its detoxifying properties). After a day of indulgent treatments and floating in pools, you pass from the dark, womblike enclosure of the spa to the dazzling sunlight of the Western Cape. *Victoria Rd., Oudekraal; 800/223-6800 or 27-21/437-9000; www.12apostleshotel. com; doubles from $$$.*

melrose arch hotel

Melrose Arch Hotel
1 Melrose Square
Johannesburg
South Africa
27-11/214-6666
www.africanpride
hotels.com
Doubles from $$

JOHANNESBURG, SOUTH AFRICA

Johannesburg's first design hotel has plenty of design-for-design's-sake touches: ficus trees planted in galvanized-steel buckets, mood lighting in the elevator, an underlit lobby "runway" that cycles through a spectrum of colors, and a café out back with tables set in a shallow swimming pool. Rooms are comfortable and well thought-out, with exposed brick walls, glass-topped work desks, free Internet, and safes large enough to stow laptops. Bath areas have rain showers, with gigantic showerheads ("the size of a manhole cover," promises the hotel), and an oversized, egg-shaped bathtub separated from the rest of the room by a flowing white curtain. Upon arrival, treat yourself to a glass of cognac in the über-trendy Library Bar, whose shelves are stocked with classics and the works of local authors.

madikwe safari lodge

MADIKWE GAME RESERVE,
SOUTH AFRICA

**Madikwe
Safari Lodge**
Madikwe
Game Reserve
South Africa
888/882-3742 or
27-11/809-4300

madikwe.safari.co.za
or www.ccafrica.com
Doubles from $$$$,
all-inclusive

Owned by safari company
CC Africa, Madikwe Safari
Lodge occupies the northwest
corner of the nearly 190,000-
acre malaria-free Madikwe
Game Reserve in South
Africa. The reserve is famous
for 2004's Operation Phoenix,
the world's largest game-
translocation exercise, in
which more than 8,000 native
animals were brought in to
restore the farmland to its
natural environment. It was
a great success, as witnessed
by the fantastic game- and
bird-watching there today. The
16 plush suites highlight design-
guru Chris Browne's natural
touch. Circular stone fireplaces,
outdoor showers, freestanding
copper tubs, and springbok-
fur comforters are sure to satisfy
even the most jaded sybarites.

Inside the Melrose Arch Hotel, opposite.
Above: A room at Madikwe Safari Lodge.

phinda zuka lodge

PHINDA PRIVATE GAME
RESERVE, SOUTH AFRICA

For families or other groups on safari, you can't do much better than CC Africa's outpost in the Phinda Private Game Reserve, a four-hour drive from Johannesburg. There are just four thatched bush cottages, which must be rented all together. Each has a cowhide rug and a wide deck that overlooks an active water hole, with lush valleys and thickly wooded hills just beyond. Plan the day's activities with your private ranger over breakfast, choosing from an eclectic menu, which includes canoeing on the Mzinene River, white-rhino tracking, rhino-darting, and game drives in your private 4 x 4 vehicle.

Phinda Zuka Lodge
Phinda Private
Game Reserve
South Africa
888/882-3742 or
27-11/809-4300

www.ccafrica.com
Entire lodge $2,264
per night for 8
adults, all-inclusive

A cottage interior at Phinda Zuka Lodge, opposite.
Above: A lounge deck overlooking the water hole.

asia

A view in the Kabuki-cho area of
Shinjuku, Tokyo, Japan, opposite.

world's best top 25
asia

The Four Seasons Resort Bali at Sayan, above. Right: The Oberoi Amarvilas, in Agra, India. Opposite: The Peninsula, in Bangkok.

1 **Four Seasons Resort Bali at Sayan** 95.00

2 **Oberoi Rajvilas** JAIPUR, INDIA 94.00

3 **Four Seasons Resort** CHIANG MAI, THAILAND 92.84

4 **The Peninsula** BANGKOK 92.10

5 **Four Seasons Resort Bali at Jimbaran Bay** 91.85

6 **The Oriental** BANGKOK 91.71

7 **Amandari** BALI 91.02

8 **Amankila** BALI 90.44

9 **Oberoi Amarvilas** AGRA, INDIA 90.11

10 **The Peninsula** HONG KONG 89.84

11 **Banyan Tree** PHUKET, THAILAND 89.00

12 **Four Seasons Hotel** SINGAPORE 88.89

13 **JW Marriott Phuket Resort & Spa** THAILAND 88.50

14 **The Sukhothai** BANGKOK 88.48

15 **Ritz-Carlton Bali Resort & Spa** 88.03

16 **Ritz-Carlton, Millenia** SINGAPORE 87.90

17 **Four Seasons Hotel** BANGKOK 87.30

18 **Amanpuri** PHUKET, THAILAND 87.26

19 **Raffles Hotel** SINGAPORE 86.92

20 **Shangri-La Hotel** BANGKOK 86.58

21 **Ritz-Carlton** OSAKA 86.25

22 **Raffles Grand Hotel d'Angkor** SIEM REAP, CAMBODIA 86.20

23 **Ana Mandara Resort & Spa** NHA TRANG, VIETNAM 86.09

24 **St. Regis** BEIJING 85.97

25 **Park Hyatt** TOKYO 85.94

key to the price icons   **$** under $250   **$$** $250 - 499   **$$$** $500 - 749   **$$$$** $750 - 999   **$$$$$** $1,000 - 1,999

**One & Only
Reethi Rah**
North Male
Maldives
960/664-8800
www.oneandonly
resorts.com
Doubles from $$$$

one & only reethi rah

MALDIVES

A definitive sign that the Maldives are on the road to recovery after the 2004 tsunami: the debut of One & Only Reethi Rah, the archipelago's newest retreat. The luxe experience begins at the airport, where custom yachts (which double as check-in desks) greet guests and whisk them to the North Male atoll. There, 130 villas—many of which have private lap pools or hover above the sapphire lagoon—have been crafted with tropical touches, such as coconut-shell sconces, sea grass thatch, and bamboo arches. Should you tire of sipping mango smoothies on any of the resort's 12 secluded beaches, there are dozens of diversions, including an orchid farm that supplies the property with freshly cut arrangements, a tennis academy, the 100,000-square-foot E'Spa with overwater treatment rooms, a PADI dive center, and pedal-boat rentals. The island chain may sit 300 miles from any major landmass, but dishes from every corner of the globe are presented in three restaurants —or on your villa's private teak deck, with no company other than the swaying palms.

Villas above the lagoon at
One & Only Reethi Rah.

The palatial Amanbagh.

amanbagh

ALWAR, INDIA

Situated in a Rajasthan oasis, the secluded Amanbagh is an attempt to re-create a maharajah's palace. Some of the 24 Haveli Rooms come with private balconies; all have courtyards shaded by centuries-old mango trees. The 16 Pool Pavilions have individual gardens and are linked by scalloped archways that evoke the area's Moghul past. Handwoven Indian silks swathe the interiors, bathtubs have been sculpted from solid blocks of green Udaipur marble, and colonnades of local pink sandstone are buffed using traditional techniques. The staff can arrange excursions to the surrounding Aravalli Hills and elephantback tours to the nearby temple.

Amanbagh Ajabgarh Alwar, India; 800/477-9180 or 91-1465/223-333; www.amanresorts.com; doubles from $$$

wildflower hall

SIMLA, INDIA

Wildflower Hall
Himachal Pradesh
Simla, India
800/562-3764 or 91-
177/264-8585
www.oberoi
hotels.com
Doubles from $$

Located in the foothills of the Himalayas and surrounded by cedar forests and snowcapped mountain ranges, Wildflower Hall was the former residence of Lord Kitchener, a commander of the British army. Though the original structure burned down in 1993, it has been faithfully reproduced (though on a grander scale) down to its many fairy tale–like balconies and turrets. Kitchener's adventurous spirit can still be felt: guests can raft on the surging Sutlej River, hike through oak forests dotted with colonial-era cottages, and ride on horseback through apple orchards and local villages. Two new Spa Pavilions offer more than 20 ways to loosen up, including the three-hour Spirit of Ayurveda package, an adventure in itself.

uma paro

PARO, BHUTAN

The newly opened Uma Paro is a 20-room, nine-villa retreat. With
an Australian chef, a spa manager from Portland, Oregon,
and bodywork practitioners imported from Thailand, Bali, India,
and New York, Uma Paro is a prototype of the new kind of
extremely high-end travel being cultivated in Bhutan, with the tacit
approval of the king. Built as a facsimile of a traditional Bhutanese
village on a site near the Paro Dzong monastery complex in the
town of Paro, the hotel owes much in style to the Beautiful Lobby
school of design. Serenity is the obvious message, and it is a
welcome one after the lifetimes of flying necessary to reach Bhutan.

Uma Paro
Paro, Bhutan
011-975/827-1597
www.uma.como.bz
Doubles from $$

The dining room of Uma Paro.
An interior courtyard, opposite.

An Amankora suite.
Opposite top and
bottom: In the dining
room; the hotel's exterior.

amankora

PARO, BHUTAN

Amanresorts opened Amankora in June 2004. Perched 7,400 feet above sea level, with views of snowcapped Mount Jhomolhari, this cluster of handsome rammed-earth villas is the company's first venture in Bhutan. The 24 large, two-room suites reflect Aman signature touches—wood-burning stoves, bathrooms constructed around tubs as big as sarcophagi—and general manager John Reed's determination to employ Bhutanese artisans: a bed cloth in a refined pattern rendered in nettle, tissue boxes crafted from pine.

Amankora Paro, Bhutan; 800/477-9180 or 011-975/827-2333; www.amanresorts.com; doubles from $$$$

hotel 1929

SINGAPORE

The tiny red lanterns and low-cost snack shops along Singapore's Keong Saik Road recall its red-light-district past, but since the opening of Hotel 1929, the area has earned a more sophisticated reputation. Built out of five landmark buildings, this 32-room property is colonial in style on the outside, pure mid-century modern within. The owner has filled the small rooms with big-name design details—from Verner Panton, Arne Jacobsen, and Eames furniture to Marimekko fabrics on the beds. Be forewarned: the rooms are extremely small (430 square feet on average), so be sure to request one with a balcony and outdoor bathtub for a little breathing room.

the fullerton

SINGAPORE

This stunning Palladian structure, a former British colonial post office, has been converted into an old world–style hotel. Don't expect to find colonial-era nostalgia. The Fullerton Singapore eschews glitz and focuses on the details—240-thread-count sheets, Donghia fabrics, discreet trapdoors for newspapers, and Philippe Starck bathroom fixtures. Original Italian-marble floors and coffered ceilings bespeak the building's past life, while sleekly modern interiors move things swiftly forward. To soak in the buzzing scene, sidle up to the underlit onyx bar for a blackberry caipiroska, a blend of vodka, fresh blackberry purée, and lime. The Friday and Saturday evening Chocolate Buffet, with its chocolate-fondue fountain, is not to be missed.

Hotel 1929
50 Keong Saik Rd.
Singapore
65/6347-1929
www.hotel
1929.com
Doubles from $

The Fullerton Singapore
1 Fullerton Square
Singapore
65/6733-8388
www.fullerton
hotel.com
Doubles from $$

Eames chairs in the lobby of Hotel 1929, opposite.
Above: The pool at the Fullerton Singapore.

The Dhara Dhevi rice terraces. Opposite: Paper shade umbrellas outside one of the Mandarin Oriental's restaurants.

mandarin oriental dhara dhevi

Mandarin Oriental Dhara Dhevi
51/4 Moo 1,
Chiang mai–
Sankampaeng Rd.
Chiang Mai
Thailand
800/526-6566 or
66-53/888-888;
www.mandarin
oriental.com;
doubles from $$

CHIANG MAI, THAILAND

Years in the making—and still not finished—the 60-acre Mandarin Oriental Dhara Dhevi quietly opened its doors in December 2004, with 40 guest rooms. An additional 183 villas will be added for the grand premiere. This is one of the most ambitious resorts Asia has ever seen: a teak fantasia modeled on a northern Thai village, with vegetable gardens, lotus ponds, moats and fortified walls, towering palaces, a marketplace, a town green, even a temple, all of it occupied by a veritable army of merchants, servants, farmers, weavers, cooks, woodcarvers, and massage therapists. If the property has a focal point, it must be the Dheva Spa, a magnificent re-creation of a 19th-century Burmese palace, fashioned entirely from burnished teak and capped by a 64-foot, seven-tier roof. The spa unfolds over 33,000 square feet, with no fewer than 25 treatment rooms.

Getting something that isn't charged to your room—like the thoughtful freebies at these hotels —is especially exciting. ■ Guests of the three **Amanresorts** on Bali (*www.aman resorts. com*) receive bedtime bookmarks handcrafted in nearby villages and bath oil spiked with frangipani. ■ The ever-generous **Cap Juluca** on Anguilla (*www. capjuluca.com*) welcomes visitors with a bottle of chilled champagne. ■ At the **Aleenta Resort & Spa** in Hua Hin, Thailand (*www.aleenta.com*), rice-filled sleeping masks scented with bergamot, lavender, and other aromatic oils help insomniacs fight jet lag. ■ Guests staying in terrace rooms at the **Lowell,** on Manhattan's Upper East Side (*www. lowellhotel.com*), receive sketch pads and watercolors. ■ Each room at **One Devonshire Gardens,** in Glasgow (*www.onedevonshire gardens.com*), comes complete with a putter and golf balls, giving you ample time to perfect your game.

trisara

PHUKET, THAILAND

Trisara
Bang Tao
Phuket, Thailand
66-76/310-100
www.trisara.com
Doubles from $$$

After a bumpy decade marred by the openings of beer bars and mediocre resorts, the southern Thai island of Phuket is regaining its sexy image. Heralding the new era is Trisara, an ultraprivate retreat conceived by Anthony Lark, the Australian general manager who helped launch Phuket's legendary Amanpuri. The sugary white swath of beach—with 50 acres of jungle behind it and its own bay in front—now houses 42 tropically modern villas. Outdoor showers have terra-cotta Buddhist reliefs, furniture is handcrafted from local teakwood, and luminescent Jim Thompson silks contrast with yellow travertine floors. Massage therapists who staff the six spa suites were handpicked from across the kingdom. And, reaching into the past, the restaurant serves dishes that pay homage to the island's place on the ancient spice route.

A private infinity pool outside one of Trisara's beachfront villas.

park hyatt seoul

SEOUL, KOREA

At the ultramodern Park Hyatt, in the heart of Seoul, floor-to-ceiling windows take in sparkling city views, and warm minimalist interiors and downy feather beds encourage nesting high above the action. Bathrooms are cavernous, with rough-hewn granite walls quarried from Japan and China, rain showers, flat-screen TV's, and miles of glass walls (press the button to lower the mechanized shades before stripping down). The place is a dream for business travelers; it is equipped with the city's largest deluxe guest rooms, safes that hold laptops, and wireless Internet everywhere. To settle in, head down to the cozy Timber House (modeled after a traditional Korean home) for a sake or soju cocktail.

Park Hyatt Seoul
995-14 Daechi
3-dong
Gangnam-gu
Seoul, Korea
888/591-1234 or
82-2/2016-1234

www.seoul.park.
hyatt.com
Doubles from $$

At the Park Hyatt Seoul, a Diplomatic Suite's living room, opposite, and bedroom, above.

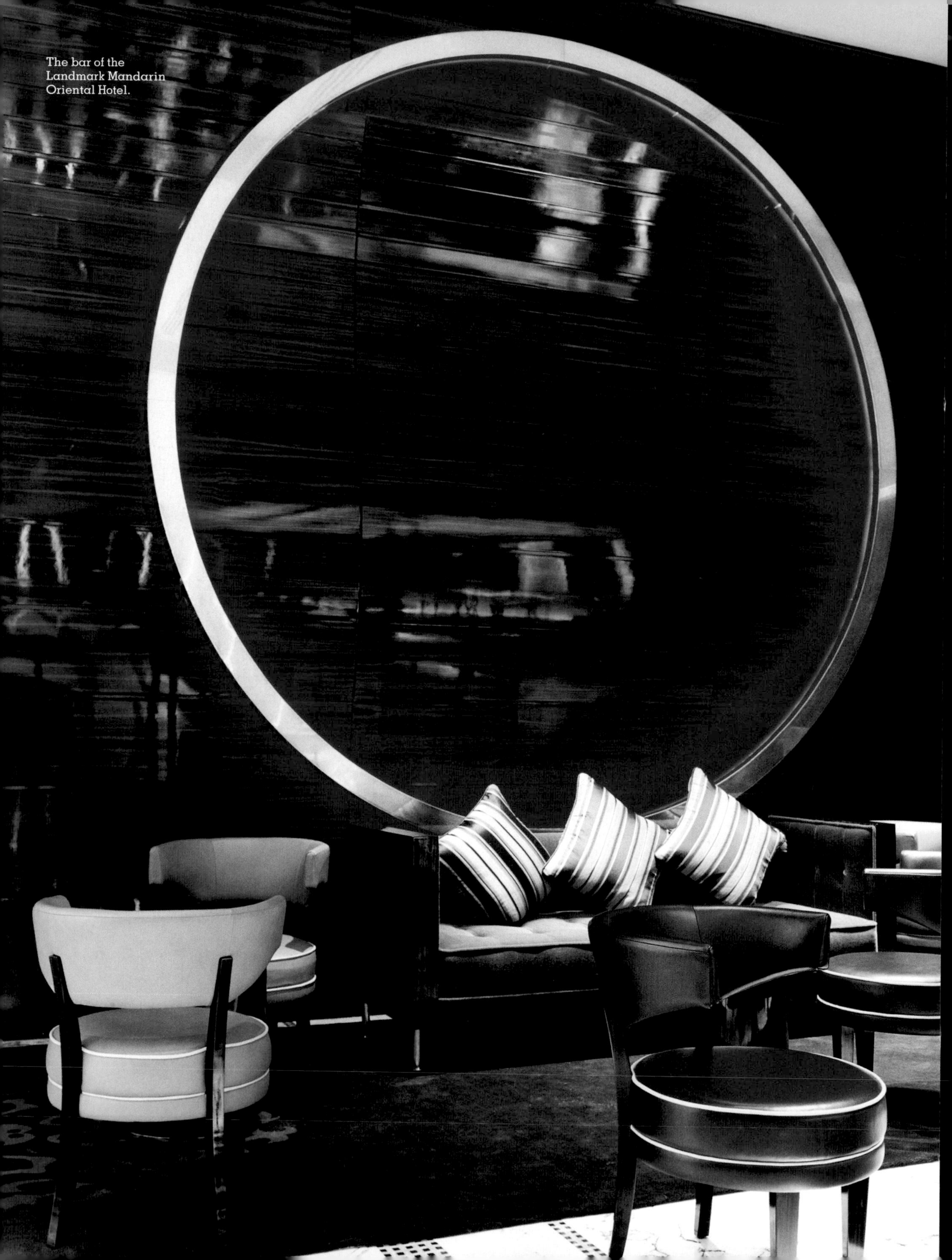

The bar of the Landmark Mandarin Oriental Hotel.

landmark mandarin oriental hotel

HONG KONG, CHINA

Named for the Central district complex it's built above, the glass-sheathed, 113-room Landmark Mandarin Oriental elevates hotel style both figuratively and literally. Masculine guest rooms (zebrano and ebony cabinetry, wengewood floors) are complemented by the understated spa with tropical-rain saunas, a Turkish hammam, and amethyst crystal–accented steam rooms. In the mahogany-paneled Amber restaurant, a free-form chandelier of 3,000 hanging golden rods creates a honey-hued ambience for dishes such as crisp chicken skin and sesame oil–seared tuna with soy reduction. The hotel's long list of services—highly connected concierges, in-room shopping from the likes of Chanel and Celine—make the new Harvey Nichols next door seem extraneous.

**Landmark Mandarin
Oriental Hotel**
15 Queen's Rd.
Hong Kong, China
852/2132-0188
www.mandarin
oriental.com
Doubles from $$$

Some hotel restaurants are so spectacular, in terms of both food and setting, they can make a meal the most memorable part of a vacation.
■ The outrageous design (courtesy of Philippe Starck) is just as dazzling as the Pacific Rim cuisine at the restaurant Felix, on the 28th floor of the **Peninsula,** Hong Kong (*www.peninsula.com*).
■ Under the jade flower–draped pergola at **Strawberry Hill,** in the Blue Mountains of Jamaica (*www.island outpost.com*), guests indulge themselves with pepperpot soup and the views of Kingston below. ■ Alfresco dinners on the Oak Grill terrace at California's **Ojai Valley Inn & Spa** (*www.ojairesort. com*) are prepared with herbs grown in the inn's gardens; 250-year-old oaks rise from the surrounding rolling hills. ■ At La Palapa at **Esperanza,** in Cabo San Lucas (*www. esperanzaresort.com*), the sight of a humpback whale surfacing in the Sea of Cortés might take your attention off the lime-marinated sea bass.

evason hideaway at ana mandara

Evason Hideaway at Ana Mandara Resort
Ninh Van Bay
Nha Trang
Vietnam
84-58/728-222

www.sixsenses.com
Doubles from $$

NINH VAN BAY, VIETNAM

On verdant hills that seem to tumble down to the sea, 54 thatched-roof villas face Ninh Van Bay's natural rock formations, which stand like sentries in the distance. The 2004-built Evason Hideaway at Ana Mandara Resort, sited on a pristine 600-acre lot on a peninsula that can be reached only by boat, takes its design cues from traditional Vietnamese architecture, with exposed, thatched ceilings and teak-and-bamboo four-poster beds. Even the construction methods are traditional: local craftsmen used only interlocking wood (no glue or nails) throughout the property. Rooms have private plunge pools carved into boulders, teak daybeds, and panoramic views (especially from the Hilltop villas). Competing with the view is the Six Senses Spa, where holistic remedies and yoga classes are performed beside the rhythmic sea.

red capital ranch

BEIJING, CHINA

There's not much at the arcadian Red Capital Ranch to disturb a weekend tryst—except, of course, its gaspingly close proximity to the Great Wall. There are just 10 Taoist-inspired stone cottages on the Ch'ing dynasty hunting grounds, linked by winding stone paths and ponds dotted with stepping stones; the most desirable have rooftop terraces. Ascend the wall at sunset to watch the surrounding hills, rustic villages, and crumbling watchtowers melt into the purple haze of northern China's twilight. Afterwards, feast on Manchurian mountain dishes (lamb roasted over an open fire with willow leaves), or simply cocoon in a corner of the Tibetan Tiger Lounge and soak up the serenity, yak-butter tea in hand.

Red Capital Ranch
Huairou District
Beijing, China
86-10/8401-8886
www.redcapital
club.com
Doubles from $

A beach villa living room at Evason Hideaway at Ana Mandara, opposite. Above: A small tea house at Red Capital Ranch.

これより先へのお立ち入りはご宿泊のお客様以外はご遠慮下さいませ
支配人

The walkway to the Baths at Gora Kadan. Opposite: The reflecting pool at the Niki Club.

japanese
onsen

Private *onsen* bathing at a *ryokan* (traditional Japanese inn) is a part of life for Japanese families, businessmen, and everyone in between. Now it's developing an international following. Three regions easily accessible from Tokyo—the Izu Peninsula, northern Honshu, and eastern Kyushu—are noted for the purity of their waters, and all have *ryokan* accustomed to initiating Westerners into the bathing process.

Ryokan rates include daily full breakfast (Western on request) and dinner.

Asaba
3450-1 Shuzenji
Izu-shi, Shizuoka
206/282-0727
www.luxuryryokan.com
Doubles from $$

Gora Kadan
1300 Gora
Hakone, Kanagawa
81-460/23331
www.gorakadan.com
Doubles from $$$

Hakone Ginyu
100-1 Miyashita
Hakone, Kanagawa

206/282-0727
www.luxuryryokan.com
Doubles from $$

Hiiragiya
Anekoji-agaru,
Fuyacho
Nakagyo-ku, Kyoto
206/282-0727
www.luxuryryokan.com
Doubles from $$$

Murata
1264-2 Kawakami-
Torigoe, Yufuin, Oita
206/282-0727
www.luxuryryokan.com
Doubles from $$$$

Niki Club
2301 TakakuOtsu
Nasu-machi

Nasu, Togichi
800/337-4685
www.designhotels.com
Doubles from $$

Yagyu-no-sho
1116-6 Syuzenji
Izu-shi, Shizuoka
206/282-0727
www.luxuryryokan.com
Doubles from $$

TOKYO SPAS
If you don't have time to explore an *onsen*, relax at one of these top hotel spas.

Grand Hyatt Tokyo
6-10-3 Roppongi
Minato-ku
800/233-1234 or

81-3/4333-1234
www.tokyo.grand.
hyatt.com
Doubles from $$

Four Seasons Tokyo at Marunouchi
1-11-1 Marunouchi
Chiyoda-ku
800/332-3442 or
81-3/5222-7222
www.fourseasons.com
Doubles from $$

Park Hyatt Tokyo
3-7-1-2 Nishi-Shinjuku
Shinjuku-ku
800/233-1234 or
81-3/5322-1234
www.parkhyatt.com
Doubles from $$

A super-heated tub for the *onsen* ritual
at Murata *ryokan*. Opposite, clockwise from
top left: Street clogs used at *onsen* across
Japan; the bamboo garden at Yagyu-no-sho;
relaxing outside the spa at the Niki Club.

four seasons resort langkawi

LANGKAWI, MALAYSIA

Four Seasons Resort Langkawi
Langkawi, Malaysia
800/332-3442 or 60-4/950-8888
www.four seasons.com
Doubles from $$

Ninety-one villas, teak-shingled in the traditional Malay style, overlook the turquoise Andaman Sea at Four Seasons Resort Langkawi; many have private garden paths, wooden patios, and private "spa rooms" with gold-hued Spanish-marble showers. The biggest attraction here is the sugar-sand beach, bordered by dramatic limestone formations that trail out to sea like a string of pearls. Coming in a close second is the main spa, an invitation to hedonism: six dark-wood pavilions floating above reflecting pools, with services that include Malaysian- and Indonesian-style massages, Ayurvedic treatments from India, and ancient Chinese remedies. To fully absorb the majesty of the surroundings, book a moonlit excursion in a *perahu* (a traditional Malaysian boat) and float beneath shadows cast by the granite cliffs that loom above the sea.

A Rajasthani-style dinner tent on the beach at the Four Seasons Resort Langkawi, opposite. Above: In a beach bungalow at the hotel.

The wood-and-stone
garden at Uma Ubud.

uma ubud

UBUD, BALI

Entering Uma Ubud requires passing between monolithic stone walls and a bench wrought from a centuries-old tree root. And that's just in the open-air lobby. The 29 rooms are in thatched-roof villas, which have reflective stone floors and private gardens. The suites come with plunge pools carved from jade-hued Batu Hijau stone. In Bali's cultural center of Ubud, this riverside hideaway is encircled by a lush patch of jungle and strewn with banana trees and plumeria. Activities director Phil Bowen can arrange temple visits and volcano ascents, both of which are just steps from the resort gates. But for guests who don't want to leave the grounds, there's an outpost of the famed Como Shambhala retreat, where yogis lead seminars.

Uma Ubud
Kedewatan
Ubud, Bali
62-361/972-448
www.uma.como.bz
Doubles from $

A good hotel shop disproves the cliché and says, Yes, you can take it with you. ■ If admiring local handicrafts was the high point of your Indonesian vacation, get some to go at the Boutique & Gallery at **Four Seasons Resort Bali at Jimbaran Bay** (*www.fourseasons.com*). ■ La Galería Que Canta, in the Mexican Riviera's **La Casa Que Canta** (*www.lacasaquecanta.com*), carries a handpicked selection of ceramics, jewelry, and folk pieces. ■ The gift shop at **Carlisle Bay**, on Antigua (*www. carlisle-bay.com*), offers Vilebrequin swim trunks, Babylone jewelry from Italy, and hand-embroidered Isabelle Fraysse clothes from London. ■ The **Vanessa Noel Hotel** on Nantucket stocks sought-after shoes created by the inn's designer-owner (*www. vanessanoel.com*). ■ Spa and fitness buffs rave about the shop at the **James Hotel** Scottsdale, in Arizona (*www.jameshotels.com*), which sells Aesop skin care and its own line of urbane T-shirts and gym wear.

Lake Wakatipu, Queenstown, New Zealand

australia, new zealand, and the south pacific

world's best top 25 australia, new zealand, and the south pacific

A guest room and the beach at Lizard Island, on Australia's Great Barrier Reef, top right and opposite. Right: Hayman Island, Great Barrier Reef.

1 **Lizard Island** GREAT BARRIER REEF, AUSTRALIA 91.82

2 **Huka Lodge** TAUPO, NEW ZEALAND 91.00

3 **Four Seasons Hotel** SYDNEY 86.28

4 **Observatory Hotel** SYDNEY 84.41

5 **Park Hyatt** MELBOURNE 83.95

6 **Hayman Island** GREAT BARRIER REEF, AUSTRALIA 83.71

7 **Hotel Bora Bora** FRENCH POLYNESIA 83.50

8 **Park Hyatt** SYDNEY 83.41

9 **Langham Hotel (formerly Sheraton Towers Southgate)** MELBOURNE 82.84

10 **Kewarra Beach Resort** CAIRNS, AUSTRALIA 82.58

11 **Bora Bora Lagoon Resort & Spa** FRENCH POLYNESIA 82.37

12 **Crown Towers** MELBOURNE 82.04

13 **InterContinental** SYDNEY 80.95

14 **Bora Bora Pearl Beach Resort** FRENCH POLYNESIA 80.87

15 **InterContinental Le Moana Resort** BORA-BORA, FRENCH POLYNESIA 80.24

16 **Sheraton on the Park** SYDNEY 79.91

17 **Lilianfels Blue Mountains Resort & Spa** KATOOMBA, AUSTRALIA 79.84

18 **Sofitel** MELBOURNE 79.39

19 **W** SYDNEY 78.89

20 **Crowne Plaza Darling Harbour** SYDNEY 77.86

21 **The Westin** SYDNEY 77.59

22 **Westin Denarau Island Resort & Spa** NADI, FIJI 77.58

23 **Sebel Reef House** PALM COVE, AUSTRALIA 77.32

24 **The George** CHRISTCHURCH, NEW ZEALAND 77.31

25 **Grand Hyatt** MELBOURNE 77.13

key to the price icons   **$** under $250   **$$** $250 - 499   **$$$** $500 - 749   **$$$$** $750 - 999   **$$$$$** $1,000 - 1,999

wrotham park lodge

QUEENSLAND, AUSTRALIA

**Voyages Wrotham
Park Lodge**
Queensland
Australia
800/225-9849 or
61-2/9364-8100
www.wrotham
park.com.au
Doubles from $$$$

Australia's most luxurious new hotel, Voyages Wrotham Park Lodge, sits in splendid isolation north of Cairns on a 1½ million–acre cattle station— isolated, that is, if you don't count the thousands of Brahman cattle, dingoes, emus, wallabies, and parrots that call the place home. A mere 20 guests stay in 10 hardwood bungalows, which reflect Australian vernacular architecture, with kangaroo-leather furnishings and oversized bathroom windows framing the paperbark-fringed Mitchell River. Outback traditions are preserved in the resort's endless activities, from horseback riding to cattle herding. After dinner— served communally if you like, and matched with local wines—you can relax under the stars in an Australian squatter's chair by the open fire.

The deck at Wrotham Park Lodge, opposite. Above: The entrance courtyard to Capella Lodge.

capella lodge

LORD HOWE ISLAND, AUSTRALIA

Capella Lodge
Lord Howe Island
Australia
61-2/9918-4355
www.lordhowe.com
Doubles from $$$

The maximum number of visitors permitted to this World Heritage–listed island, two hours from Sydney, is 400, ensuring that you'll always have a beach to yourself. The teak-clad nine-suite Capella Lodge—the most luxurious accommodation on the 10-mile island—has a relaxed beach-house feel and overlooks the rugged peaks of Mount Gower and Mount Lidgbird. Unspoiled nature is the prevailing theme of the island, 75 percent of which is preserved as a permanent park. A raised boardwalk passes through native kentia palms; walking paths meander through a virgin rain forest; and birdsong fills the air. Plan the next day's adventures from the open-air deck of Gower's Terrace, mango-lime-coconut daiquiri in hand. After surfing, sportfishing, or scuba diving, an Aboriginal-inspired treatment at the lodge's spa is the only way to end the day.

An Eagles Nest
bedroom. Opposite:
Eagle Spirit villa.

eagles nest luxury villa retreat

RUSSELL, NEW ZEALAND

All but unknown in America, Eagles Nest is famous in New Zealand for its setting (directly on the water in the placidly beautiful Bay of Islands), the scale of its five freestanding villas (the smallest is 1,107 square feet), and its aesthetic profile (brusquely modern and acres of glass). With villas sporting full up-to-the-minute kitchens and lap pools at four of the villas, Eagles Nest is an utterly private experience. The well-bred town of Russell is less than 10 minutes by foot from the retreat, at the bottom of a gentle hill edged in lush bush.

Eagles Nest Luxury Villa Retreat
60 Tapeka Rd.
Russell, New Zealand
64-9/403-8333
www.eagles nest.co.nz
Doubles from $$$$$

azur

Azur
23 Mackinnon
Terrace
Queenstown
New Zealand
64-3/409-0588

www.azur.co.nz
Doubles from $$$$

A sitting room in an Azur villa, opposite. Above: An
entranceway to one of the villas.

QUEENSTOWN, NEW ZEALAND

Azur consists of nine 800-square-foot freestanding villas on a steep cliff facing the alpine, Tolkienesque landscape surrounding Lake Wakatipu. Architect John Blair's designs are simple gabled forms, roofed in flint-colored corrugated steel and clad in Oregon red cedar and indigenous schist. The rooms are wildly plush without stealing attention from the views. Since Queenstown has many good restaurants and is only five minutes away, the owners made a pointed decision to offer only an exhaustive breakfast, plus all sorts of interesting nibbles throughout the day. Limited-edition Land Cruisers ferry guests into town around the clock at no charge.

otahuna lodge

CHRISTCHURCH, NEW ZEALAND

Set on 30 acres amid soft, sheep-speckled hills that look like the backdrop for a *Masterpiece Theatre* production of a Jane Austen heartbreaker, Otahuna Lodge is one of the finest examples of Queen Anne architecture in Australasia. The interiors celebrate the Arts and Crafts movement: embossed green-and-gold William Morris wallpaper in the grand dining room; cast-iron fireplace inserts, enclosed by glazed tiles patterned with sunflowers, in the guest rooms. The lodge's romantic, loosely stitched patchwork of arbors, drives, ponds, bridges, lawns, and woodlands so beloved by the colonialists was designed by a man who trained at Kew Gardens in London.

Otahuna Lodge
Rhodes Rd.
Tai Tapu
Christchurch
New Zealand
64-3/329-6333
www.otahuna.co.nz
Doubles from $$$$

Great Mercury Island
New Zealand
800/225-4255
www.seasonz.co.nz
Doubles from $20,000 per night

Inside Otahuna Lodge, above. Opposite: Overlooking the main compound on Great Mercury Island.

Through New Zealand's Seasonz Travel bespoke outfitters, you can rent a cloistered retreat on the privately owned 5,000-acre Great Mercury Island—25 minutes by helicopter from Auckland. Two clean-lined, Scandinavian-inspired residences are set into the hillside and have panoramic views of the Pacific. You won't feel isolated though: massage therapists, personal cooks, and expert guides are at your beck and call, and endless activities await—hiking, horseback riding, kayaking, motorcycling, and scuba diving off miles of pristine white beaches, just to name a few. If you want to get doubly remote, ask the staff to prepare a basket of picnic goodies and arrange for you to be transported by boat or helicopter to the secluded beach at Peach Grove, where you can play Robinson Crusoe.

great
mercury
island

NEW ZEALAND

Moorea Pearl Resort
beach bungalows.

**Moorea Pearl
Resort & Spa**
French Polynesia
68-9/55-17-50
www.pearl
resorts.com
Doubles from $$

moorea pearl resort & spa

FRENCH POLYNESIA

This resort will satisfy your every South Seas fantasy: an island dappled with pineapple plantations, pastel-painted cottages, and white-sand beaches; spectacular dive sites with bright fish and coral; thatched-roof bungalows on stilts over a crystalline lagoon; and French and Polynesian dishes served prior to a fire-dancing demonstration. When you're not being slathered with *umuhei* oil (a Tahitian love potion) at the resort's new holistic spa, you can spend time reconnecting with your partner in your over-water bungalow or tracing the shoreline as the sun sinks. Beyond the picture-perfect setting, the hotel also offers a menu of "romantic interludes," including a starlit dinner on your bungalow's terrace.

STRATEGIES
hotel experts

When you're in search of the perfect place to stay, need a reservation at a sold-out property, or just want a little extra attention at check-in, it often pays to work with a travel agent. Here are some of the industry's leading experts. For more, see T+L's A-List of super-agents at www.travelandleisure.com/alist.

Manny Beauregard
Years as Agent 34
Specialty Cruises (small-ship)
Consulting Fee $250
Valerie Wilson Travel, Atlanta; 800/762-2136; mannyb@vwti.com.

Jack Bloch
Years as Agent 29
Specialties Europe, Caribbean
Consulting Fee From $250
JB's World Travel Consultants, New York City; 800/232-8735; jackb@jbsworld.com.

Elayne Edelman
Years as Agent 35
Specialties Hawaii, cruises, family travel
Consulting Fee From $250
Regent Group Protravel International, Beverly Hills; 800/301-3993; elaynee@protravelinc.com.

Diane Hilliard
Years as Agent 34
Specialties Morocco, educational trips
Consulting Fee From $500
Hilliard & Olander, Stillwater, Minnesota; 800/229-8407; diane@hilliardolander.com.

Anne Morgan Scully
Years as Agent 26
Specialties Europe, Caribbean, cruises, villa rentals
Consulting Fee Varies
McCabe Bremer Travel, McLean, Virginia; 800/747-8401, ext. 5055; anne@mccabebremer.com.

Bob Watson
Years as Agent 22
Specialty Cruises
Consulting Fee $250
Watson & Watson, Ltd./ Protravel International, Scarsdale, New York; 800/892-8767; bob@watsonandwatson.com.

world's best directory

The 300 World's Best hotels all have excellence in common, but how do you know which one is right for you?

To help you choose the best place to stay for your next trip, T+L's editors and correspondents around the globe have created this easy-to-use directory, arranged by geographic location. In addition to basic information about these properties—from the number of rooms to the price range—you'll learn what distinguishes them from their competitors, which rooms to request, and how to make the most of your stay.

In short, the World's Best Directory is the ultimate guide to the most memorable hotels anywhere—and it's yours to use all year long.

key to the price icons
$ under $250   **$$** $250 - 499   **$$$** $500 - 749   **$$$$** $750 - 999   **$$$$$** $1,000 - 1,999

world's best top 100
united states and canada
plus top 25 hawaii

arizona

PHOENIX/SCOTTSDALE

■ Boulders Resort & Golden Door Spa (83.19) Lavish golf and spa resort with adobe casitas in the Sonoran Desert. An extensive renovation by Diller Scofidio + Renfro is planned for this year. **Stats** 215 rooms; 6 restaurants; 1 bar. **Competitive Edge** Modern architecture that blends seamlessly with surroundings. **Rooms to Book** South casitas have great golf course views. **Don't Miss** A session with the on-staff shaman, in a tepee. **Cost** Doubles from $$. *Carefree; 800/553-1717 or 480/488-9009; www.luxuryresorts.com*

PHOENIX/SCOTTSDALE

■ Royal Palms Resort & Spa (84.37) Intimate 1929 Spanish colonial–style mansion with plush interiors and extensive gardens, near Camelback Mountain. **Stats** 117 rooms; 2 restaurants; 1 bar. **Competitive Edge** One of the area's most romantic hotels. **Rooms to Book** Nos. 202–210 for their sunny patios. (Avoid 214–222, which get traffic noise.) **Don't Miss** The traditional paella at T. Cook's. **Cost** Doubles from $$. *Phoenix; 800/672-6011 or 602/840-3610; www.royalpalmsresortandspa.com*

SEDONA

■ Enchantment Resort (84.68) Family-friendly, adobe-style property with Native American influences, set inside a red-rock canyon. **Stats** 220 rooms; 3 restaurants; 1 bar. **Competitive Edge** An extraordinary range of activities (guided stargazing, pottery lessons). **Rooms to Book** Those off the main drive, with east-facing views of the canyon (Casita 11 has its own pool). **Don't Miss** Mii Amo spa's New Age treatments, such as Body Feng Shui, which starts with a psychic reading. **Cost** Doubles from $$. *800/826-4180 or 928/282-2900; www. enchantmentresort.com*

TUCSON

■ Arizona Inn (83.04) Collection of pink stucco houses and gardens on 14 acres in a quiet neighborhood. **Stats** 86 rooms; 2 restaurants; 1 bar. **Competitive Edge** An homage to 1930's Tucson, filled with antiques from the original owner, Arizona's first congresswoman. **Rooms to Book** Those on the east side overlooking the lush central garden. **Don't Miss** A Gibson martini at the Audubon Bar. **Cost** Doubles from $$. *800/933-1093 or 520/325-1541; www.arizonainn.com*

california

BIG SUR

■ Post Ranch Inn (89.44) Luxurious redwood-and-stone cottages on 100 secluded acres, with views of the Pacific. **Stats** 30 rooms; 1 restaurant. **Competitive Edge** Dramatic architecture that accentuates its cliffside setting. **Rooms to Book** Everyone wants an ocean view; we also like the treetop rooms (elevated on 9-foot stilts). **Don't Miss** A hot-rock massage with jade from nearby beaches. **Cost** Doubles from $$$, including breakfast. No guests under 18. *800/527-2200 or 831/667-2200; www.postranchinn.com*

BIG SUR

■ Ventana Inn & Spa (83.59) Contemporary resort of weathered cedar lodges on 243 acres bordering the ocean and the Ventana Wilderness area. **Stats** 62 rooms; 1 restaurant; 1 bar. **Competitive Edge** Summer camp for adults, with nature excursions, a clothing-optional pool, and a New Age spa. **Rooms to Book** Spa Suites, with outdoor hot tubs on private decks. **Don't Miss** Warm oyster gratin with caviar at Cielo. **Cost** Doubles from $$. No guests under 18. *800/628-6500 or 831/667-2331; www.ventanainn.com*

HALF MOON BAY

■ Ritz-Carlton (84.21) Dramatic manor-style spa and golf resort set on a bluff, 45 minutes south of San Francisco. **Stats** 261 rooms; 2 restaurants; 2 bars. **Competitive Edge** A pair of outstanding seaside courses, plus a range of amenities for non-golfers. **Rooms to Book** Two-thirds face the ocean, but be sure to ask for one with a balcony. **Don't Miss** A flight of New World vintages in the resort's Wine Room. **Cost** Doubles from $$$. *800/241-3333 or 650/712-7000; www.ritzcarlton.com*

LOS ANGELES AREA

■ Four Seasons Hotel Los Angeles at Beverly Hills (85.76) Contemporary 16-story tower, a few blocks from Rodeo Drive. **Stats** 285 rooms; 3 restaurants; 1 bar. **Competitive Edge** Four Seasons luxury combined with impeccable and discreet service. **Rooms to Book** Northwest Corner Deluxes have an extra window overlooking the hills. **Don't Miss** The pomegranate mojito at Windows Lounge. **Cost** Doubles from $$. *300 S. Doheny Dr., Los Angeles; 800/332-3442 or 310/786-2227; www.fourseasons.com*

LOS ANGELES AREA

■ Hotel Bel-Air (87.74) Pink Mission-style mansion with 12 acres of gardens in a residential neighborhood west of Beverly Hills. **Stats** 91 rooms; 1 restaurant; 1 bar. **Competitive Edge** A serene hideaway in a central location—Beverly Hills, Brentwood, Santa Monica, and downtown are all just 15 minutes away. **Rooms to Book** Suites in the south section are the largest. **Don't Miss** California bouillabaisse on the terrace. **Cost** Doubles from $$. *701 Stone Canyon Rd., Los Angeles; 800/648-4097 or 310/472-1211; www.hotelbelair.com*

LOS ANGELES AREA

■ Peninsula Beverly Hills (90.64) Polished and urbane hotel with a garden and a renovated spa, within walking distance of Rodeo Drive. **Stats** 196 rooms; 3 restaurants; 1 bar. **Competitive Edge** A balance of tranquil ambience and high-wattage bar and pool scenes. **Rooms to Book** Those in the west wing overlooking the gardens are the quietest. **Don't Miss** The Belvedere's famous mac and cheese topped with truffles. **Cost** Doubles from $$. *9882 S. Santa Monica Blvd., Beverly Hills; 800/462-7899 or 310/551-2888; www. peninsula.com*

LOS ANGELES AREA

■ Raffles L'Ermitage Beverly Hills (87.03) Asian-influenced 8-story hotel on a tree-lined boulevard minutes from Rodeo Drive. **Stats** 119 rooms; 1 restaurant; 1 bar. **Competitive Edge** Private pied-à-terre–style rooms averaging 675 square feet—they're among the largest in town. **Rooms to Book** Those ending in -9 have spectacular views of the Hollywood Hills. **Don't Miss** The rooftop pool overlooking Bel Air. **Cost** Doubles from $$$. *9291 Burton Way, Beverly Hills; 800/637-9477 or 310/278-3344; www. raffleslermitagehotel.com*

LOS ANGELES AREA

■ Regent Beverly Wilshire (86.30) Beverly Hills legend composed of the Neoclassical 1928 Wilshire Wing and the 1971 Beverly Wing. A Wolfgang Puck restaurant opens early this year. **Stats**

395 rooms; 2 restaurants; 1 bar. **Competitive Edge** An ideal location for shoppers, at the junction of Rodeo and Wilshire. **Rooms to Book** For Hollywood glamour, the roomier Premiers in the Wilshire Wing. **Don't Miss** Cocktails on the patio at the Blvd. (the $185 Baccaratini includes the crystal martini glass). **Cost** Doubles from $$. *9500 Wilshire Blvd., Beverly Hills; 800/332-3442 or 310/275-5200; www.fourseasons.com*

NAPA/SONOMA

■ **Auberge du Soleil** (87.16) Provençal-inspired hideaway set among olive groves and vineyards in mid–Napa Valley, well-sited for touring wineries. **Stats** 52 rooms; 1 restaurant; 1 bar. **Competitive Edge** Plush, private, and pampering, it's ideal for a romantic getaway. **Rooms to Book** Upper Valley Views have the most sweeping vistas. **Don't Miss** Plein air painting with the hotel's easels, oils, and brushes. **Cost** Doubles from $$$. No guests under 16. *Rutherford; 800/348-5406 or 707/963-1211; www.aubergedusoleil.com*

ORANGE COUNTY

■ **Ritz-Carlton, Laguna Niguel** (84.71) Family-friendly resort with an air of formality on a bluff above the Pacific, a short shuttle ride to the beach. **Stats** 393 rooms; 2 restaurants; 1 bar. **Competitive Edge** One of the oldest hotels in the area—and also one of the freshest, thanks to a recent $40 million overhaul. **Rooms to Book** It's worth spending the additional $100 for a west-facing room overlooking the ocean. **Don't Miss** Views from the floor-to-ceiling windows in the gym. **Cost** Doubles from $$. *Dana Point; 800/241-3333 or 949/240-2000; www.ritzcarlton.com*

PEBBLE BEACH

■ **Inn at Spanish Bay** (86.74) Scottish-style golf resort between the Pacific Coast and the Del Monte Forest on the Monterey Peninsula. **Stats** 270 rooms; 4 restaurants; 2 bars. **Competitive Edge** A younger vibe makes it the Tiger Woods to sister property the Lodge's Jack Nicklaus. **Rooms to Book** Those on the 1st fairway have the best views. **Don't Miss** A massage at the excellent 22,000-square-foot spa. **Cost** Doubles from $$$. *800/654-9300 or 831/647-7500; www. pebblebeach.com*

PEBBLE BEACH

■ **Lodge at Pebble Beach** (86.84) 1919 cream stucco buildings overlooking Carmel Bay, in the heart of the Pebble Beach community. **Stats** 161 rooms; 4 restaurants; 2 bars. **Competitive Edge** A classic golf-resort hotel, with a distinguished country-club feel. **Rooms to Book** Those facing Carmel Bay and the 18th hole, with fireplaces and balconies. **Don't Miss** Exploring the scenic oceanside bike path near the Lodge. **Cost** Doubles from $$$. *800/654-9300 or 831/624-3811; www. pebblebeach.com*

SAN DIEGO AREA

■ **La Valencia Hotel** (83.09) 1926 hotel with modern villas in the heart of La Jolla, across the street from the beach and 15 minutes from San Diego. **Stats** 115 rooms; 3 restaurants; 2 bars. **Competitive Edge** Old California atmosphere, thanks to original details (wrought-iron chandeliers, mosaic tiles). **Rooms to Book** Ocean-facing rooms have 180-degree views. **Don't Miss** A drink at the Whaling Bar, where Rey has bartended for the past 50 years. **Cost** Doubles from $$. *La Jolla; 800/451-0772 or 858/454-0771; www.lavalencia.com*

SAN FRANCISCO

■ **Campton Place Hotel** (84.42) Quiet, contemporary hotel with a residential feel, steps from Union Square, shopping, and the nearby financial district. Popular with business travelers. **Stats** 110 rooms; 1 restaurant; 1 bar. **Competitive Edge** A peaceful retreat in the heart of the city (thanks in part to soundproof windows). **Rooms to Book** Those ending in -01 are larger and overlook the lively square. **Don't Miss** Chef Daniel Humm's Provençal dishes paired with wine by sommelier John Ragan. **Cost** Doubles from $$. *340 Stockton St.; 800/235-4300 or 415/781-5555; www.camptonplace.com*

SAN FRANCISCO

■ **Four Seasons Hotel** (87.02) Sleek 41-story tower overlooking the Yerba Buena Gardens and arts district, 2 blocks from Union Square and the San Francisco Museum of Modern Art. **Stats** 277 rooms; 1 restaurant; 1 bar. **Competitive Edge** Ideal for culture-seekers: the hotel is home to one of the city's most extensive modern art collections and can arrange private tours of the nearby galleries. **Rooms to Book** Deluxe Views above the 10th floor on the Market Street side look out on Chinatown and North Beach. **Don't Miss** The 100,000-square-foot on-site Sports Club/LA. **Cost** Doubles from $$. *757 Market St.; 800/332-3442 or 415/633-3000; www.fourseasons.com*

SAN FRANCISCO

■ **Mandarin Oriental** (83.65) Asian-inspired property on the top 11 floors of a financial-district high-rise, 6 blocks from Union Square. Rooms currently undergoing a full renovation. **Stats** 158 rooms; 1 restaurant; 1 bar. **Competitive Edge** Bird's-eye views of the city for all guests. **Rooms to Book** Splurge on a Bridge to Bridge room for a 180-degree look at the Golden Gate and Bay bridges. **Don't Miss** Traditional Asian tea served in the lounge. **Cost** Doubles from $$. *222 Sansome St.; 800/526-6566 or 415/276-9888; www.mandarinoriental.com*

SAN FRANCISCO

■ **Ritz-Carlton** (85.21) Stately 1909 Neoclassical property near the financial district, Chinatown, Nob Hill, and Union Square. **Stats** 336 rooms; 2 restaurants; 3 bars. **Competitive Edge** The quintessential urban Ritz, and a magnet for local society and visiting celebrities. **Rooms to Book** Those above the 6th floor on the California Street side with views of Alcatraz. **Don't Miss** Made-to-order sushi in the Lobby Lounge. **Cost** Doubles from $$. *600 Stockton St.; 800/241-3333 or 415/296-7465; www.ritzcarlton.com*

SANTA BARBARA

■ **Four Seasons Resort Biltmore** (84.29) 1927 Spanish colonial–style estate on 22 beachfront acres in Montecito. Rooms are being renovated through March. **Stats** 207 rooms; 3 restaurants; 2 bars. **Competitive Edge** The gorgeous 79-year-old gardens, which are tended by 22 full-time gardeners and laced with paths to encourage walking. **Rooms to Book** Deluxe Cottage rooms with windows overlooking the gardens. **Don't Miss** Borrowing a bike for a leisurely ride to the harbor. **Cost** Doubles from $$$. *800/332-3442 or 805/969-2261; www.fourseasons.com*

SANTA BARBARA

■ **San Ysidro Ranch** (83.35) Former citrus ranch with bungalows on 500 acres in the Montecito foothills, 5 minutes from town. Full-property renovation ongoing throughout 2006. **Stats** 40 rooms; 2 restaurants (both closed until spring 2006). **Competitive Edge** A romantic retreat with discreet service and a tranquil ambience. **Rooms to Book** We like the newly redone cottages with stone fireplaces and outdoor showers. **Don't Miss** Exploring the ranch's 17 miles of trails. **Cost** Doubles from $$$. *800/368-6788 or 805/565-1700; www.sanysidroranch.com*

colorado

ASPEN

■ **Little Nell** (86.45) Contemporary ski lodge at the base of Aspen Mountain. A major redesign of the public spaces by David Easton has just been completed. **Stats** 92 rooms; 1 restaurant; 2 bars. **Competitive Edge** Aspen's only ski-in, ski-out resort, with a legendary après-ski scene. **Rooms to Book** Nos. 36, 38, and 40 have beautiful views of the interior courtyard and the mountain. **Don't Miss** Being the first down the mountain with the Little Nell's early-morning lift access privileges. **Cost** Doubles from $$. 888/843-6355 or 970/920-4600; www.littlenell.com

ASPEN

■ **St. Regis Resort, Aspen** (85.65) Sprawling red-brick resort, steps from 2 ski lifts and downtown. Fresh from a $37 million redo. **Stats** 179 rooms; 1 restaurant; 2 bars. **Competitive Edge** The area's most complete luxury resort, with full services and amenities, including a new 15,000-square-foot Remède Spa. **Rooms to Book** Those in the new Red Mountain wing have a more modern look; Deluxes are worth the extra $50 for their mountain views. **Don't Miss** Toddies and s'mores in the refurbished Shadow Mountain Lounge. **Cost** Doubles from $$. 888/454-9005 or 970/920-3300; www.stregis.com

COLORADO SPRINGS

■ **The Broadmoor** (86.16) 3,000-acre Italianate mega-resort on a lake in the Rockies, 20 minutes from Colorado Springs. **Stats** 700 rooms; 10 restaurants; 4 bars. **Competitive Edge** The family-friendly Western style, combined with loads of activities. **Rooms to Book** Deluxes in Broadmoor West have mountain views and private balconies. **Don't Miss** Dinner at the Summit, the Adam D. Tihany–designed restaurant. **Cost** Doubles from $$. 800/634-7711 or 719/577-5775; www.broadmoor.com

VAIL

■ **Sonnenalp Resort of Vail** (84.62) Bavarian-style ski resort in the village, near the Vista Bahn lift. A new $25 million wing opens this winter. **Stats** 127 suites; 3 restaurants; 1 bar. **Competitive Edge** Old-world hospitality from the 4th-generation hotelier and his staff, alongside some of the Rockies' top slopes. **Rooms to Book** We like those in the new addition—they're more modern but still European in feel. **Don't Miss** Raclette and Riesling at the new Swiss Chalet. **Cost** From $$$, including breakfast. 800/654-8312 or 970/476-5656; www.sonnenalp.com

connecticut

WASHINGTON

■ **Mayflower Inn** (85.00) Stately main building and cottages with English country house–style interiors, on 58 manicured acres near a nature preserve (great hiking and biking). **Stats** 30 rooms; 1 restaurant; 1 bar. **Competitive Edge** The inn's pastoral setting and new 20,000-square-foot spa make for a perfect romantic getaway. **Rooms to Book** The newer ones in the Allerton building have four-poster canopy beds and outstanding views. **Don't Miss** A trip into nearby Litchfield Hills for great antiquing. **Cost** Doubles from $$. No guests under 12. 860/868-9466; www.mayflowerinn.com

district of columbia

WASHINGTON, D.C.

■ **The Hay-Adams** (83.02) Italian Renaissance–inspired grande dame directly facing the White House. **Stats** 145 rooms; 2 restaurants; 1 bar. **Competitive Edge** As close as you can sleep to the Washington Monument (barring pitching a tent in protest). **Rooms to Book** Those on the 6th, 7th, and 8th floors face the White House lawn (note: tour buses can be noisy in the mornings). **Don't Miss** A martini at the classic Off the Record bar. **Cost** Doubles from $$. 16th and H Sts NW; 800/424-5054 or 202/638-6600; www.hayadams.com

florida

AMELIA ISLAND

■ **Ritz-Carlton** (84.65) 8-story beachfront tower set between dunes and fairways, 30 minutes from Jacksonville. **Stats** 444 rooms; 3 restaurants; 1 bar. **Competitive Edge** An unusual blend of family-friendly services with a sophisticated atmosphere. **Rooms to Book** It's worth the $50 upgrade to an Ocean View for a private balcony above the Atlantic. **Don't Miss** Kayaking through the marshes to spot pelicans and herons. **Cost** Doubles from $$. 800/241-3333 or 904/277-1100; www.ritzcarlton.com

FLORIDA KEYS

■ **Little Palm Island Resort & Spa** (86.40) Intimate South Seas–style getaway along a white-sand beach on a private 6-acre island. The resort is closing for 3 months this summer for a complete renovation. **Stats** 30 suites; 1 restaurant; 2 bars. **Competitive Edge** Florida's most ultra-private and ultra-romantic retreat. **Rooms to Book** For extra seclusion, the Mockingbird Suite; the Willet Suite is set between the pool and beach. **Don't Miss** A snorkeling trip to the Looe Key National Marine Sanctuary. **Cost** Doubles from $$$$$. No guests under 16. 800/343-8567 or 305/872-2524; www.littlepalmisland.com

FLORIDA KEYS

■ **Marquesa Hotel** (89.03) 4 interconnected clapboard houses with breezy interiors and a knowledgeable staff, set around pools and tropical gardens in the middle of Key West's historic district. **Stats** 27 rooms; 1 restaurant; 1 bar. **Competitive Edge** A remarkably calm oasis in the middle of town. **Rooms to Book** No. 10, for the private porch; No. 14, for dormers and a cozy writer's nook. **Don't Miss** Cooling off with a pitcher of iced tea by the pool. **Cost** Doubles from $$. 800/869-4631 or 305/292-1919; www.marquesa.com

FLORIDA KEYS

■ **Sunset Key Guest Cottages at Hilton Key West** (83.73) Pastel oceanfront cottages along a wide beach on a private island, 10 minutes by boat from the main resort. **Stats** 37 cottages; 2 restaurants; 2 bars. **Competitive Edge** A family-friendly fantasy island with hammocks and thatched-roof cabanas. **Rooms to Book** Manatee and Tamarind cottages are more secluded; Beachcomber and Osprey are near the beach. **Don't Miss** Taking advantage of the on-demand ferry service to Key West. **Cost** Doubles from $$$, including breakfast. 888/477-7786 or 305/292-5300; www.sunsetkeyisland.com

MIAMI AREA

■ **Mandarin Oriental, Miami** (87.70) Fan-shaped high-rise and private beach club, minutes from the business district. **Stats** 327 rooms; 2 restaurants; 3 bars. **Competitive Edge** A serene location away from the chockablock South Beach strip, with luxury perks, including a great 3-level spa. **Rooms to Book** Those ending in -25 or -26 have the biggest balconies. **Don't Miss** A martini at M-Bar, which overlooks the skyline. **Cost** Doubles from $$$. 866/888-6780 or 305/913-8288; www.mandarinoriental.com

MIAMI AREA

■ **Ritz-Carlton, South Beach** (83.52) 1953 Morris Lapidus–designed 11-story hotel flanked by two wings, in South Beach. Chef David Bouley's Evolution opened this winter. **Stats** 376 rooms; 3 restaurants; 3 bars. **Competitive Edge** All the sophistication of a Ritz-Carlton resort, in a South Beach setting. **Rooms to Book** Anything ending in -40 faces the ocean; the higher the better. **Don't Miss** A jet ski tour of the waterfront mansions in

Biscayne Bay. **Cost** Doubles from $$. *800/241-3333 or 786/276-4000; www. ritzcarlton.com*

NAPLES
■ **Ritz-Carlton** (85.28) The flagship Ritz-Carlton resort, a Mediterranean-inspired complex on a 3-mile beach; facilities at its sister property, the Golf Resort (see below), are available via shuttle. **Stats** 450 rooms; 7 restaurants; 4 bars. **Competitive Edge** An updated classic beach resort with superb service and access to some of the state's best golf. **Rooms to Book** South-facing Coastal rooms, for views past the pools to the Gulf. **Don't Miss** The 51,000-square-foot spa, the largest in the Ritz family. **Cost** Doubles from $$$. *800/241-3333 or 239/598-3300; www.ritzcarlton.com*

PALM BEACH
■ **The Breakers** (83.27) Oceanfront palazzo modeled after Rome's Villa Medici, on 140 acres, 5 minutes from Worth Avenue. **Stats** 560 rooms; 7 restaurants; 4 bars. **Competitive Edge** The grande dame of Palm Beach resorts has loosened up, but its aristocratic pedigree still shows. **Rooms to Book** Those overlooking the palm-lined main drive are more affordable than ocean views, and almost as nice. **Don't Miss** The soothing and rehydrating sunburn treatment at the excellent spa. **Cost** Doubles from $$. *888/273-2537 or 561/655-6611; www.thebreakers.com*

PALM BEACH
■ **Four Seasons Resort** (83.46) Contemporary low-rise with a tailored South Florida look, right on the ocean. **Stats** 210 rooms; 3 restaurants; 3 bars. **Competitive Edge** The most peaceful of Palm Beach's conveniently located resorts. **Rooms to Book** Those in the main building tend to be larger than those in the wings. **Don't Miss** A Palm Beach Massage (Swedish, deep-tissue, and reflexology) in a poolside cabana. **Cost** Doubles from $$. *800/332-3442 or 561/582-2800; www.fourseasons.com*

PONTE VEDRA
■ **Ponte Vedra Inn & Club** (84.55) Sprawling 300-acre resort with 2 golf courses on the Atlantic coastline. A new spa is being added and will open in the fall. **Stats** 250 rooms; 4 restaurants; 4 bars. **Competitive Edge** An expansive yet intimate-feeling family-friendly resort. **Rooms to Book** The 20 in the centrally located Atlantic House; No. 292, a corner room, has pool and

ocean views. **Don't Miss** Playing tennis at the club's new facilities. **Cost** Doubles from $$. *800/234-7842 or 904/285-1111; www.pvresorts.com $$*

SARASOTA
■ **Ritz-Carlton** (84.26) Family-friendly golf and beach resort at a downtown marina on Sarasota Bay. **Stats** 266 rooms; 3 restaurants; 3 bars. **Competitive Edge** Free shuttles to the new Tom Fazio–designed golf course and Lido Key beach club. **Rooms to Book** Deluxes above the 4th floor have the best skyline views. **Don't Miss** A round of golf: six tees for each hole ensure that the course plays well for all skill levels. **Cost** Doubles from $$. *800/241-3333 or 941/309-2000; www.ritzcarlton.com*

hawaii

BIG ISLAND
■ **Fairmont Orchid** (81.64) Pair of 6-floor oceanfront towers decorated with local touches on 32 landscaped acres. **Stats** 540 rooms; 5 restaurants; 5 bars. **Competitive Edge** The fantastic outdoor Spa Without Walls, plus the island's only concierge floor for those who want extra pampering. **Rooms to Book** Odd-numbered rooms, 2639 and above, on the north side of the North Tower face Kohala mountain and have ocean views. **Don't Miss** The green sea-turtles that come ashore in front of the Ocean Bar each afternoon. **Cost** Doubles from $$. *800/441-1414 or 808/885-2000; www.fairmont.com*

BIG ISLAND
■ **Four Seasons Resort Hualalai** (90.53) Four clusters of low-rise, crescent-shaped buildings carved into lava fields, steps from the rocky Kona coast. **Stats** 243 rooms; 3 restaurants; 3 bars. **Competitive Edge** The only hotel on the Big Island where every guest room has an ocean view. **Rooms to Book** Those in the Palm Grove crescent are more secluded; rooms on the second floor have the best views. **Don't Miss** Snorkeling in King's pond, the saltwater pool stocked with reef fish and spotted eagle rays. **Cost** Doubles from $$$. *800/332-3442 or 808/325-8000; www.fourseasons.com*

BIG ISLAND
■ **Hapuna Beach Prince Hotel** (82.94) Series of contemporary low-rises on a terraced bluff overlooking Hapuna Beach. **Stats** 350 rooms; 5 restaurants; 3 bars. **Competitive Edge** Set above one of the island's best beaches. **Rooms**

to Book Those in the Oceanfront Wing (floors 3 and above) are the closest to the ocean and also look out onto Maui and the Kohala mountains. **Don't Miss** Coast Grille & Oyster Bar's "island trio" entrée of 3 different fish prepared 3 different ways. **Cost** Doubles from $$. *866/774-6236 or 808/880-1111; www.princeresorts hawaii.com*

BIG ISLAND
■ **Mauna Kea Beach Hotel** (86.38) Open-air hideaway, built in the 1960's by Laurance S. Rockefeller. **Stats** 310 rooms; 4 restaurants; 2 bars. **Competitive Edge** The island's most authentic old-Hawaii ambience. **Rooms to Book** First-floor beachfront rooms, which have direct ocean access. **Don't Miss** Weekly tours of Rockefeller's 1,600-piece, museum-quality Asian and Pacific art collection, led by the hotel historian. **Cost** Doubles from $$. *866/774-6236 or 808/882-7222; www.maunakeabeachhotel.com*

BIG ISLAND
■ **Mauna Lani Bay Hotel & Bungalows** (84.99) Low-rise hotel and high-style bungalows between 2 beaches on the Kohala coast. **Stats** 338 rooms; 5 bungalows; 5 restaurants; 2 bars. **Competitive Edge** A high glamour quotient throughout, especially in the 40,000-square-foot spa. **Rooms to Book** Those at the tip of the L-shaped building have the best ocean views. **Don't Miss** Twilight at Kalahuipuaa, a cultural program with hula, Hawaiian music, and picnic dinners. **Cost** Doubles from $$. *800/367-2323 or 808/885-6622; www.maunalani.com*

KAUAI
■ **Grand Hyatt Resort & Spa** (84.38) Plantation-style resort (formerly the Hyatt Regency Kauai Resort & Spa) with a vintage Hawaiian feel set above Shipwreck Beach (best for surfers, not swimmers). **Stats** 602 rooms; 4 restaurants; 6 bars. **Competitive Edge** The island's best spa (soon to be 45,000 square feet) with more than 25 treatment rooms. **Rooms to Book** Those in the Poipu wing are away from the frenzied action at the pool. **Don't Miss** A concierge-arranged tour to Kahili Falls. **Cost** Doubles from $$. *800/554-9288 or 808/742-1234; www.hyatt.com*

KAUAI
■ **Kauai Marriott Resort & Beach Club** (81.55) Contemporary resort, surrounded by mountains on Kalapaki Bay. **Stats** 356 rooms; 4 restaurants; 2 bars.

Competitive Edge A convenient beachfront location near Lihue Airport—the perfect starting point for a Hawaiian vacation. **Rooms to Book** Those in the Kahili Tower have views of Kalapaki Beach. **Don't Miss** A round of golf on 1 of the 2 Jack Nicklaus–designed courses. **Cost** Doubles from $$. 800/220-2925 or 808/245-5050; www.marriott.com

KAUAI

■ **Princeville Resort** (81.46) 3 multiterraced buildings (with great views) that stretch down Puu Paoa Ridge to a stunning north-shore beach. **Stats** 252 rooms; 4 restaurants; 2 bars. **Competitive Edge** Kauai's premier golf course, the Prince, designed by Robert Trent Jones II. **Rooms to Book** Those ending in -01 to -12 on floors 8–11 have iconic Bali Hai views, made popular in the movie *South Pacific*. **Don't Miss** Toasting sunset from the glass-enclosed Living Room lounge. **Cost** Doubles from $$. 800/325-3589 or 808/826-9644; www.princeville.com

LANAI

■ **Four Seasons Resort Lana'i at Manele Bay** (84.78) Mediterranean-style resort (formerly the Manele Bay Hotel) with themed gardens, overlooking Hulopoe Bay. **Stats** 236 rooms; 4 restaurants; 1 bar. **Competitive Edge** It's the only beachfront hotel on this quiet island. **Rooms to Book** Those in the Red Ginger and Gardenia buildings are more secluded. **Don't Miss** A round of golf on a rugged course etched into a lava field. **Cost** Doubles from $$. 800/332-3442 or 808/565-2000; www.fourseasons.com

LANAI

■ **Lodge at Koele** (88.96) Intimate 2-story lodge in a tranquil upcountry location 8 miles above the ocean. Recently acquired by the Four Seasons, the hotel will be closed from January through June for extensive renovations. **Stats** 102 rooms; 3 restaurants; 2 bars. 800/332-3442 or 808/565-3800; www.fourseasons.com

MAUI

■ **Fairmont Kea Lani** (84.21) White 7-story landmark hotel on 22 acres fronting the secluded Polo Beach. **Stats** 413 suites; 37 villas; 4 restaurants; 3 bars. **Competitive Edge** The island's only all-suite (and villa) hotel, which means extra-large rooms. **Rooms to Book** Kilohana Suites, with unobstructed Pacific views from big wraparound balconies. **Don't Miss** An hour-long

traditional Hawaiian canoeing course. **Cost** Doubles from $$. 800/441-1414 or 808/875-4100; www.fairmont.com

MAUI

■ **Four Seasons Resort at Wailea** (89.05) 8-story, U-shaped resort with reflecting pools, fountains, and gardens, on a bluff overlooking one of Maui's best beaches. **Stats** 380 rooms; 3 restaurants; 3 bars. **Competitive Edge** Lots of included perks—parking, poolside cabanas, fitness classes, tennis—on an island where most resorts charge. **Rooms to Book** Oceanview Primes have the most expansive views. **Don't Miss** Kobe-beef burgers at the Pacific Grill. **Cost** Doubles from $$. 800/332-3442 or 808/874-8000; www.fourseasons.com

MAUI

■ **Grand Wailea Resort Hotel & Spa** (81.67) Family-friendly property with a multimillion-dollar art collection, on 40 acres fronting Wailea Beach. **Stats** 780 rooms; 5 restaurants; 7 bars. **Competitive Edge** A supersized resort with the biggest spa in the state (50,000 square feet) and its own 9-pool waterpark. **Rooms to Book** Those in the Napua Tower are centrally located, with easy access to the Botero Bar and main lobby. **Don't Miss** Watching the sunset from the floating restaurant in the hotel's lagoon. **Cost** Doubles from $$. 800/888-6100 or 808/875-1234; www.grandwailea.com

MAUI

■ **Hotel Hana-Maui & Honua Spa** (84.60) Small, peaceful plantation-style resort and cottages surrounded by nature with not another hotel in sight, 3 miles from Hamoa Beach on the island's eastern coast. **Stats** 69 cottages; 1 house; 2 restaurants; 2 bars. **Competitive Edge** Pure escapism: the resort prides itself on its lack of televisions, radios, or even clocks in the rooms. **Rooms to Book** Deluxe Ocean Views in the Sea Ranch Cottage with hot tubs on private decks. **Don't Miss** The Friday night Hula Buffet show, where locals perform traditional hulas. **Cost** Doubles from $$. 800/321-4262 or 808/248-8211; www.hotelhanamaui.com

MAUI

■ **Hyatt Regency Resort & Spa** (82.74) Massive resort of 3 connected towers on 40 acres along the white sands of Kaanapali Beach. **Stats** 806 rooms; 6 restaurants; 4 bars. **Competitive Edge** Activities a-go-go: catamaran cruises, luaus, golf, tennis—and even a Macy's for shoppers. **Rooms to Book** Ocean

Views in the Atrium Tower are the only ones with views of both the Pacific and the island of Lanai. **Don't Miss** Outdoor movie screenings every Sunday night during the summer. **Cost** Doubles from $$. 800/233-1234 or 808/661-1234; www.maui.hyatt.com

MAUI

■ **Kapalua Bay Hotel** (79.17) This hotel will close on April 6 as part of the Kapalua Resort redevelopment.

MAUI

■ **Marriott's Maui Ocean Club** (80.27) Since the World's Best readers' survey, this property is no longer operating as a hotel.

MAUI

■ **Renaissance Wailea Beach Resort** (81.86) 7-story contemporary resort on 15 palm-fringed acres along Mokapu Beach. **Stats** 345 rooms; 2 restaurants; 2 bars. **Competitive Edge** The smallest, most intimate hotel on the Wailea strip. **Rooms to Book** The freestanding Mokapu beachfront rooms, with private check-in and beach cabanas. **Don't Miss** Maui onion rings with hot-chile dip at the Maui Onion. **Cost** Doubles from $$. 800/992-4532 or 808/879-4900; www.marriott.com

MAUI

■ **Ritz-Carlton, Kapalua** (81.87) Terraced plantation-style building surrounded by 3 golf courses and a pineapple plantation, a short walk from the beach. **Stats** 548 rooms; 6 restaurants; 4 bars. **Competitive Edge** A more secluded and serene feel than most island properties. **Rooms to Book** Families should go for odd-numbered rooms in the Napili wing for easy access to a play area. **Don't Miss** The weekly Hawaiian slack-key guitar concerts hosted by George Kahumoku Jr. **Cost** Doubles from $$. 800/241-3333 or 808/669-6200; www.ritzcarlton.com

MAUI

■ **Sheraton Maui Resort** (78.17) Sprawling 1960's resort on a promontory above Kaanapali Beach. **Stats** 510 rooms; 2 restaurants; 3 bars. **Competitive Edge** A snorkeler's paradise, steps from Black Rock reef and the longest stretch of Kaanapali sand in the area. **Rooms to Book** Hale o Ka Moana (rooms 6101–6526), which are on a bluff overlooking the sea, have the best views and more privacy. **Don't Miss** Watching the nightly Cliff Diving ceremony, from the poolside Lagoon Bar. **Cost** Doubles from $$. 800/325-3535 or 808/611-0031; www.sheraton.com

MAUI
■ Wailea Marriott Resort & Spa (78.39)
8-story oceanfront resort (formerly the Outrigger Wailea) set between Wailea and Ulua Beaches. **Stats** 473 rooms; 3 restaurants; 1 bar. **Competitive Edge** The freshest rooms and facilities on the strip, thanks to a $65 million, full-property renovation that's scheduled to be complete in June 2006; the redo is adding a 10,000-square-foot Mandara spa and transforming the rooms with a sleek, Asian-inspired look. **Rooms to Book** Deluxe Ocean Fronts for the ultimate beach access: they're just 20 feet away. **Don't Miss** A traditional pohaku massage with hot lava rocks when the spa opens in June. **Cost** Doubles from $$. *888/236-2427 or 808/879-1922; www.marriott.com*

OAHU
■ Halekulani (90.02) 5 interlocking buildings with unfettered views of Diamond Head on the western side of Waikiki Beach. **Stats** 455 rooms; 3 restaurants; 3 bars. **Competitive Edge** The most luxurious hotel in Waikiki combines style, seclusion, and a central location. **Rooms to Book** 90 percent have ocean views; the Diamond Head Ocean View is the best of the best (but the most expensive). **Don't Miss** The crispy-skin Onaga (red snapper) at the South of France–meets–Pacific isles restaurant, La Mer. **Cost** Doubles from $$. *800/367-2343 or 808/923-2311; www.halekulani.com*

OAHU
■ JW Marriott Ihilani Resort & Spa (81.08) 17-story complex with a 35,000-square-foot spa on 15 waterfront acres at the southwest corner of the island. **Stats** 387 rooms; 3 restaurants; 2 bars. **Competitive Edge** A real tropical getaway: it's the island's only T+L 500–listed property located miles away from the tourist district. **Rooms to Book** We prefer west-facing rooms, which have great sunset views. **Don't Miss** The interactive Reef Safari, where guests head underwater to learn about everything from Medusa sea cucumbers to stingrays. **Cost** Doubles from $$. *800/626-4446 or 808/679-0079; www.ihilani.com*

OAHU
■ Kahala Mandarin Oriental (85.18) 12-story resort with plantation-style rooms, set on a quiet beach. **Stats** 364 rooms; 6 restaurants; 5 bars. **Competitive Edge** Peace and proximity: just 10 to 15 minutes from all of Honolulu's main attractions, yet it has the feel of being away from it all. **Rooms to Book** Corner

ocean-view rooms in the Koko Head Tower have panoramic vistas of both ocean and lagoon. **Don't Miss** A class in native cultural traditions, including Hawaiian quilting and how to play the ukulele. **Cost** Doubles from $$. *800/367-2525 or 808/739-8888; www.mandarinoriental.com*

OAHU
■ Royal Hawaiian (79.15) 1927 pink icon with Moorish-inspired architecture on a prime, 10-acre stretch of Waikiki Beach. **Stats** 528 rooms; 2 restaurants; 1 bar. **Competitive Edge** The feel of stepping back into old Hawaii, from the popular Mai Tai Bar to the resort's lush tropical grounds. **Rooms to Book** We like those in the 1927 wing for their historic details (rooms ending in -80, -81, and -82 on floors 3–6 have the best views); tower rooms are closest to the beach. **Don't Miss** Authentic Hawaiian cuisine (roasted Kalua pig) at the oceanfront luau. **Cost** Doubles from $$. *808/923-7311 or 800/325-3535; www.royal-hawaiian.com*

illinois
CHICAGO
■ Four Seasons Hotel (85.86) Floors 30–46 of a Michigan Avenue tower, above a high-end mall. **Stats** 343 rooms; 2 restaurants; 2 bars. **Competitive Edge** The tallest hotel in Chicago; dramatic city views are guaranteed from every room. **Rooms to Book** Those ending in -25 are on the southwest corner and have great lake and city views. **Don't Miss** The selection of regional farmstead cheeses at Seasons restaurant. **Cost** Doubles from $$. *120 E. Delaware Place; 800/332-3442 or 312/280-8800; www.fourseasons.com*

CHICAGO
■ Peninsula Chicago (87.84) Sleek 20-story tower with stylish interiors, close to Michigan Avenue shopping. **Stats** 339 rooms; 4 restaurants; 1 bar. **Competitive Edge** A local favorite, with 2 of the city's hottest restaurants: Avenues and the newly renovated Shanghai Terrace. **Rooms to Book** Those on the northeast side take in Michigan Avenue and the lake beyond. **Don't Miss** The green-tea body treatment at the 14,000-square-foot rooftop spa. **Cost** Doubles from $$. *108 E. Superior St.; 866/288-8889 or 312/337-2888; www.peninsula.com*

CHICAGO
■ Ritz-Carlton (87.39) Opulent, light-filled hotel occupying 21 floors of a high-rise next to the historic water tower. The hotel

was managed by Four Seasons at press time, but is expected to change management in early 2006. **Stats** 435 rooms; 3 restaurants; 1 bar. **Competitive Edge** Traditional style and exceptional service. **Rooms to Book** Deluxes on the southeast side have great views of the lake and Navy Pier. **Don't Miss** Doing a few laps in the tranquil, skylit pool. **Cost** Doubles from $$. *160 E. Pearson St.; 800/621-6906 or 312/266-1000; www.fourseasons.com*

louisiana
NEW ORLEANS
■ Windsor Court Hotel (87.97) 23-story building in the business district, close to the French Quarter. Emerged mostly unscathed from Hurricane Katrina. **Stats** 324 rooms; 1 restaurant; 2 bars. **Competitive Edge** An Anglophile's dream come true, filled with paintings of horses, jockeys, and gray-wigged gentlemen. **Rooms to Book** Those above the 15th floor for unobstructed views. **Don't Miss** The hotel's European art collection—one of the finest in the South. **Cost** Doubles from $$. *300 Gravier St.; 800/262-2662 or 504/523-6000; www.windsorcourthotel.com*

maine
KENNEBUNKPORT
■ White Barn Inn (83.03) 1860's clapboard inn and outlying cottages along the Kennebunkport River, a 5-minute stroll from the village. **Stats** 28 rooms; 1 restaurant; 1 bar. **Competitive Edge** Chef Jonathan Cartwright's inventive New England cuisine served in a gorgeous repurposed barn. **Rooms to Book** Those in the antiques-filled main house have more charm; in the winter, we like No. 8, which has a double-sided fireplace. **Don't Miss** A lunch cruise on the Inn's yacht. **Cost** Doubles from $$, including breakfast. *207/967-2321; www.whitebarninn.com*

massachusetts
BOSTON
■ XV Beacon (87.63) Beaux Arts building with comfortable, modern interiors on a quiet Beacon Hill street. **Stats** 60 rooms; 1 restaurant; 1 bar. **Competitive Edge** One of the most stylish hotels in the city, combined with a peaceful location. **Rooms to Book** Corner studios ending in -06 are light-filled and have Boston Common views. **Don't Miss** The guests-only rooftop deck, with panoramic views. **Cost** Doubles from $$. *15 Beacon St.; 877/982-3226 or 617/670-1500; www.xvbeacon.com*

BOSTON

■ **Four Seasons** (87.24) 16-story building opposite the Public Garden, a short walk from Newbury Street shopping. Currently in the midst of a head-to-toe renovation. **Stats** 273 rooms; 2 restaurants; 2 bars. **Competitive Edge** Extremely indulgent and attentive service. **Rooms to Book** Be sure to request one of the newly renovated rooms facing the Garden. **Don't Miss** Aujourd'hui's biweekly Epicurean Evenings (small plates paired with wines). **Cost** Doubles from $$. *200 Boylston St.; 800/332-3442 or 617/338-4400; www.fourseasons.com*

BOSTON

■ **Ritz-Carlton** (83.48) Landmark 1927 Beaux Arts building (the flagship Ritz) on the corner of Newbury Street, across from the Public Garden. **Stats** 273 rooms; 1 restaurant; 1 bar. **Competitive Edge** Boston's most old-world hotel (the choice of visiting royalty). **Rooms to Book** One of the four Deluxe rooms with a wood-burning fireplace (Nos. 404, 504, 604, and 704). **Don't Miss** A martini by the fireplace at the clubby bar. **Cost** Doubles from $$. *15 Arlington St.; 800/241-3333 or 617/536-5700; www.ritzcarlton.com*

LENOX

■ **Wheatleigh** (84.52) 19th-century Florentine-inspired villa with museum-quality art, walking distance from Tanglewood. **Stats** 19 rooms; 2 restaurants; 1 bar. **Competitive Edge** A refreshingly stylish and refined departure from the traditional country-house hotel. **Rooms to Book** Junior suites have romantic fireplaces; some have balconies with lake and mountain views. **Don't Miss** Roasted Maine lobster with orange milk chocolate emulsion at the excellent main restaurant. **Cost** Doubles from $$$. No guests under 9. *413/637-0610; www.wheatleigh.com*

NANTUCKET

■ **The Wauwinet** (86.40) Shingled inn and cottages, on a beach 9 miles from Nantucket Town and next to a wildlife sanctuary. **Stats** 34 rooms; 1 restaurant; 1 bar. **Competitive Edge** A serene setting, flanked by the bay and the ocean (with private access to both). **Rooms to Book** For sunsets and an extra 35 square feet (standards are a tiny 190 square feet), get a Bay View. **Don't Miss** Surf casting lessons, part of the eco-adventure program. **Cost** Doubles from $$$. No guests under 12, and those under 18 in cottages only. *800/426-8718 or 508/228-0145; www.wauwinet.com*

NANTUCKET

■ **White Elephant Hotel** (83.35) Sprawling inn with a classic island feel, a 10-minute walk from Jetties Beach. **Stats** 65 rooms; 1 restaurant; 1 bar. **Competitive Edge** A location right in the heart of the harbor and just a short stroll from galleries and boutiques in town. **Rooms to Book** Harbor Views are worth the additional $50–$75. **Don't Miss** Port-and-cheese hour in the well-stocked library. **Cost** Doubles from $$$. *800/445-6574 or 508/228-2500; www.whiteelephanthotel.com*

mississippi

NATCHEZ

■ **Monmouth Plantation** (88.32) Antiques-filled Greek Revival plantation on 26 acres, 5 minutes from downtown. **Stats** 30 rooms; 1 restaurant; 1 bar. **Competitive Edge** An atmospheric hotel—it's like stepping into the Old South. **Rooms to Book** Those in the 1818 main house have a more authentic antebellum feel; we like No. 22, for its canopy bed and desk of General John Anthony Quitman, Monmouth's most famous owner. **Don't Miss** Chef Lanny Brasher's 5-course menu of Southern dishes like quail grillades with savory grits. **Cost** Doubles from $. *800/828-4531 or 601/442-5852; www.monmouthplantation.com*

missouri

KANSAS CITY

■ **The Raphael** (83.17) 1927 former apartment complex, on historic Country Club Plaza, near shopping and entertainment. **Stats** 123 rooms; 1 restaurant; 1 bar. **Competitive Edge** Polished service in a town best known for down-home flavor. **Rooms to Book** Tech-savvy guests opt for Nos. 105 or 108—both good for piggybacking on the lobby's Wi-Fi hot spot. No. 606 is virtually a suite for the price of a standard. **Don't Miss** Fresh-baked cookies in the lobby every day at 5 P.M. **Cost** Doubles from $. *325 Ward Pkwy.; 800/821-5343 or 816/756-3800; www.raphaelkc.com*

nevada

LAS VEGAS

■ **Bellagio** (86.02) Italian-themed extravaganza on a man-made lake in the middle of the Strip. **Stats** 3,933 rooms; 16 restaurants; 7 bars. **Competitive Edge** The quintessential New Vegas hotel, complete with a palatial spa, top-notch dining, and dancing fountains. **Rooms to Book** Those in the newer Spa Tower for a more peaceful, off-the-Strip atmosphere. **Don't Miss** The fried mac and cheese at Fix restaurant. **Cost** Doubles from $. *3600 Las Vegas Blvd. S.; 888/987-6667 or 702/693-7111; www.bellagio.com*

LAS VEGAS

■ **Four Seasons Hotel** (86.77) Exclusive oasis on the Strip's south end, on floors 35–39 in a tower adjacent to Mandalay Bay. Rooms were recently redesigned. **Stats** 424 rooms; 2 restaurants; 2 bars. **Competitive Edge** The city's most refreshingly understated and elegant hotel, with no slots or tables in sight. **Rooms to Book** Strip Views, which look straight down the belly of the Strip. **Don't Miss** Dinner at the newly renovated Verandah restaurant and lounge. **Cost** Doubles from $$. *3960 Las Vegas Blvd. S.; 800/332-3442 or 702/632-5000; www.fourseasons.com*

LAS VEGAS

■ **The Venetian** (83.65) Colossal Italianate fantasy replete with faux Grand Canal. 3 new theaters are due to open mid 2006. **Stats** 4,027 suites; 19 restaurants; 6 bars. **Competitive Edge** At 650 square feet, the Venetian's standards are nearly double the size of average Strip digs. **Rooms to Book** Those in the newer Venezia Tower that come with a private concierge and evening cocktails. **Don't Miss** Chef Thomas Keller's braised pork roast with cabbage fondue and prunes at Bouchon. **Cost** Doubles from $$. *3355 Las Vegas Blvd. S.; 877/883-6423 or 702/414-1000; www.thevenetian.com*

new mexico

SANTA FE

■ **Inn of the Anasazi** (83.11) Pueblo-style hotel, full of regional art and Anasazi-inspired design, steps from the historic plaza. **Stats** 57 rooms; 1 restaurant; 1 bar. **Competitive Edge** The most regionally authentic luxe lodgings in town. **Rooms to Book** Nos. 306 and 320 are the largest and sunniest of the traditional standards. **Don't Miss** A guided hike through stunning red-rock canyons care of Santa Fe Mountain Adventures, the inn's activities partner. **Cost** Doubles from $$. *113 Washington Ave.; 800/688-8100 or 505/988-3030; www.rosewoodhotels.com*

new york

ADIRONDACKS

■ **Mirror Lake Inn Resort & Spa** (84.79) Laid-back, family-friendly lodge with Victorian details (stained-glass windows, polished walnut floors) on Mirror Lake. **Stats** 129 rooms; 3 restaurants; 1 bar. **Competitive Edge** The best of both worlds: surrounded by 7 secluded acres, but 2 blocks from Main Street. **Rooms to Book** A 4th-floor Marcy room, with a king-sized bed and unobstructed mountain views. **Don't Miss** An Adirondack Maple Sugar Body Scrub in the 11,000-square-foot spa. **Cost** Doubles from $$. *Lake Placid; 518/523-2544; www.mirrorlakeinn.com*

ADIRONDACKS

■ **The Point** (91.00) 1930's Great Camp built for William Avery Rockefeller on an isolated Saranac Lake peninsula. **Stats** 11 rooms; 1 restaurant. **Competitive Edge** The ultimate in country living: rustic-luxe décor, an ultra-exclusive vibe, and as much (or as little) to do as you'd like. **Rooms to Book** Roomy, light-filled Morningside has a cathedral ceiling; Lookout has a private deck and spacious steam shower. **Don't Miss** In winter, snuggling under a fur throw in the lodge's ice-fishing shack, to catch trout that the chef will prepare. **Cost** Doubles from $$$$$, including all meals, liquor, and activities. No guests under 18. *Saranac Lake; 800/255-3530 or 518/891-5674; www.thepointresort.com*

NEW YORK CITY

■ **Four Seasons Hotel** (86.91) Sleek 52-story I. M. Pei–designed tower, in midtown. The restaurant L'Atelier de Joël Robuchon opens this spring. **Stats** 368 rooms; 2 restaurants; 2 bars. **Competitive Edge** The luxury of space (guest rooms average 600 square feet) on one of Manhattan's busiest and most central blocks. **Rooms to Book** South-facing rooms on the 29th floor, which get lots of natural light. **Don't Miss** A cocktail in the see-and-be-seen Fifty Seven Fifty Seven Bar. **Cost** Doubles from $$$. *57 E. 57th St.; 800/487-3769 or 212/758-5700; www.fourseasons.com*

NEW YORK CITY

■ **Mandarin Oriental** (83.49) 2-year-old Asian-influenced hotel with sweeping Central Park views on floors 35–54 of the Time Warner Center, steps from Central Park. **Stats** 251 rooms; 1 restaurant; 2 bars. **Competitive Edge** The newest of the T+L 500 hotels in New York City, it has fresh, state-of-the-art facilities, including a fantastic spa. **Rooms to Book** Those overlooking the Hudson River have glorious sunset views, but we prefer rooms looking northeast onto the park. **Don't Miss** The 24/7 Thomas Pink room service, for forgotten cuff links or shirts. **Cost** Doubles from $$$. *80 Columbus Circle; 866/801-8880 or 212/805-8800; www.mandarinoriental.com*

NEW YORK CITY

■ **Peninsula New York** (83.16) 1905 Beaux-Arts building near Rockefeller Center and convenient to Fifth Avenue shops and Central Park. **Stats** 239 rooms; 1 restaurant; 3 bars. **Competitive Edge** Exceptional rooftop spa and glitzy Pen-Top Bar, which capture the city's glamour. **Rooms to Book** A well-priced Grand Luxe overlooking the busy 5th Avenue. **Don't Miss** A swim in the stunning glass-enclosed pool. **Cost** Doubles from $$$. *700 Fifth Ave.; 800/262-9467 or 212/956-2888; www.peninsula.com*

NEW YORK CITY

■ **The Pierre** (85.97) Commanding 1930's landmark with a hushed atmosphere and an attentive staff, across from Central Park. Now owned by Taj Hotels, Resorts & Palaces, the hotel will undergo renovations this year. **Stats** 201 rooms; 2 restaurants; 1 bar. **Competitive Edge** Posh residential feel and ornate public rooms make it one of the city's choice social addresses. **Rooms to Book** Parkviews on the 39th floor are worth it for their panoramas. **Don't Miss** The whimsical 1967 Edward Melcarth murals in the Rotunda, with mythological trompe l'oeil scenes. **Cost** Doubles from $$$. *2 E. 61st St.; 800/743-7734 or 212/838-8000; www.tajhotels.com*

NEW YORK CITY

■ **Ritz-Carlton Battery Park** (83.62) Sleek 2002 hotel with sophisticated Art Deco–inspired interiors on the first 14 floors of a downtown high-rise. **Stats** 298 rooms; 1 restaurant; 2 bars. **Competitive Edge** Manhattan's only luxury waterfront hotel, and the best in the financial district. **Rooms to Book** Harbor Views are worth the premium (about $100) for vistas of Ellis Island and the Statue of Liberty. **Don't Miss** A Libertini at sunset in the 14th-floor Rise bar, which has floor-to-ceiling windows. **Cost** Doubles from $. *2 West St.; 800/241-3333 or 212/344-0800; www.ritzcarlton.com*

NEW YORK CITY

■ **Ritz-Carlton Central Park** (85.91) 33-story limestone building with a luxurious town-house feel at the southern edge of Central Park. **Stats** 261 rooms; 1 restaurant; 1 bar. **Competitive Edge** Exceptional service and amenities, with all of Central Park at your door. **Rooms to Book** Those on the north side have tabletop telescopes and face the park. **Don't Miss** Complimentary in-town transport

in the hotel's ultra-swank Maybach. **Cost** Doubles from $$. *50 Central Park S.; 800/241-3333 or 212/308-9100; www.ritzcarlton.com*

NEW YORK CITY

■ **St. Regis Hotel** (87.05) 1904 Beaux-Arts landmark convenient to Central Park, Carnegie Hall, and Fifth Avenue. **Stats** 256 rooms; 1 restaurant; 1 bar. **Competitive Edge** A new renovation, which has given the rooms a fresher, more luxurious look while honoring its grande-dame past—plus top-notch service. **Rooms to Book** Deluxes ending in -28 (an extra $50) are large and quiet. **Don't Miss** A custom facial in the new Remède spa. **Cost** Doubles from $$$. *2 E. 55th St.; 800/759-7550 or 212/753-4500; www.stregis.com*

NEW YORK CITY

■ **Trump International Hotel & Tower** (83.08) Contemporary hotel on the first 17 floors of a Philip Johnson–designed tower, on Columbus Circle directly across from Central Park. **Stats** 167 rooms; 2 restaurants; 1 bar. **Competitive Edge** Easy access to the attractions of Columbus Circle, combined with a parkside address. **Rooms to Book** Those on the higher floors ending in -04 have great light and park views; No. 1704 is the best. **Don't Miss** Dinner at Jean-Georges Vongerichten's informal Nougatine. **Cost** Doubles from $$$. *1 Central Park W.; 888/448-7867 or 212/299-1000; www.trumpintl.com*

north carolina
PITTSBORO

■ **Fearrington House Country Inn & Restaurant** (84.84) Stately inn with gardens on the site of an 18th-century dairy farm near Raleigh-Durham and Chapel Hill. **Stats** 33 rooms; 1 restaurant; 1 bar. **Competitive Edge** Cow-dotted pastures and a re-created country village make this an idyllic rural retreat. **Room to Book** The renovated No. 9, which looks onto the White Garden. **Don't Miss** The restaurant's renowned chocolate desserts. **Cost** Doubles from $. *800/277-0130 or 919/542-2121; www.fearringtonhouse.com*

oregon
GOLD BEACH

■ **Tu Tu' Tun Lodge** (89.34) Eclectic backcountry lodge with an Asian-influenced Arts and Crafts aesthetic and a fantastic fly-fishing program, on the banks of the Rogue River, 7 miles from the Pacific. **Stats** 20 rooms; 1 restaurant;

1 bar. **Competitive Edge** Abundant wilderness activities (hiking, kayaking, boating) combined with all the creature comforts you could need. **Rooms to Book** Great views are standard; we prefer those with fireplaces and outdoor tubs. **Don't Miss** A massage in the new Tututni Waters riverside treatment cabana. **Cost** Doubles from $. 800/864-6357 or 541/247-6664; www.tututun.com

PORTLAND
■ **Hotel Vintage Plaza** (83.29) 1894 red-brick building with fanciful interiors near Pioneer Square. **Stats** 107 rooms; 1 restaurant; 1 bar. **Competitive Edge** Polished service and a casual, relaxed atmosphere commensurate with the décor. **Rooms to Book** King Deluxe corner rooms have larger windows and great views of downtown; we especially like No. 315. **Don't Miss** Italian pastries at the Pazzoria Bakery. **Cost** Doubles from $. 422 S.W. Broadway; 800/243-0555 or 503/228-1212; www.vintageplaza.com

pennsylvania
PHILADELPHIA
■ **Four Seasons Hotel** (84.85) Granite-clad 8-story hotel with Federal-inspired interiors and a courtyard, on Logan Square. **Stats** 364 rooms; 2 restaurants; 1 bar. **Competitive Edge** A location right in the city's cultural heart, near the museums. **Rooms to Book** Those on the 7th floor with private balconies overlooking the grand boulevard. **Don't Miss** An haute Philly cheesesteak in the Swann Lounge. **Cost** Doubles from $$. 1 Logan Square; 800/332-3442 or 215/963-1500; www.fourseasons.com

PHILADELPHIA
■ **Rittenhouse Hotel** (83.88) Floors 1–9 of a modern 33-story building with private garden on Rittenhouse Square. **Stats** 98 rooms; 2 restaurants; 2 bars. **Competitive Edge** An intimately scaled hotel in a revitalized downtown neighborhood, steps from restaurants and shopping. **Rooms to Book** 9th-floor Superiors have great views onto the parklike historic square. **Don't Miss** Proper afternoon tea, with scones, clotted cream, and homemade lemon curd. **Cost** Doubles from $$. 210 W. Rittenhouse Square; 800/635-1042 or 215/546-9000; www.rittenhousehotel.com

rhode island
NEWPORT
■ **Castle Hill Inn & Resort** (83.08) 1874 Victorian inn and newer oceanside cottages on a peninsula overlooking Narragansett Bay. **Stats** 25 rooms; 1 restaurant; 2 bars. **Competitive Edge** Privileged seclusion just off Newport's famed Ocean Drive. **Rooms to Book** The BeachHouse cottages have a private beach, heated floors, and fireplaces; in the main inn, the Turret Suite has 360-degree vistas. **Don't Miss** Chef Casey Riley's creative New England cuisine. **Cost** Doubles from $$. 888/466-1355 or 401/849-3800; www.castlehillinn.com

south carolina
CHARLESTON
■ **Planters Inn** (83.72) 19th-century Georgian building (with newer addition) on the edge of the City Market in the historic district. **Stats** 62 rooms; 1 restaurant; 1 bar. **Competitive Edge** An intimate retreat right in the center of town. **Rooms to Book** Nos. 214 and 215 in the new wing have large living areas and overlook the courtyard; in the atmospheric old wing, we like those with gas fireplaces. **Don't Miss** Chef Robert Carter's famous grilled bourbon shrimp at the excellent Peninsula Grill. **Cost** Doubles from $$. 112 N. Market St.; 800/845-7082 or 843/722-2345; www.plantersinn.com

tennessee
WALLAND
■ **Blackberry Farm** (91.24) Appalachian country estate popular with fly fishermen, on 4,200 acres in the foothills of the Great Smoky Mountains outside Knoxville. **Stats** 44 rooms; 1 restaurant; 1 bar. **Competitive Edge** Discerning service and plush quarters in a gorgeous rural setting. **Rooms to Book** Those in the main house (especially Queen Deluxes) tend to be bigger. **Don't Miss** An afternoon horseback ride through the foothills. **Cost** Doubles from $$$$, including meals. 800/273-6004 or 865/984-8166; www.blackberryfarm.com

texas
DALLAS
■ **Mansion on Turtle Creek** (86.74) Refined 1920's residence (and modern 9-story tower), 5 minutes from downtown. **Stats** 143 rooms; 1 restaurant; 1 bar. **Competitive Edge** All the amenities of a grand hotel combined with a residential feel. **Rooms to Book** Odd-numbered rooms on the south side have pleasant pool views; Nos. 101,103, and 105 open onto the deck. **Don't Miss** Tortilla soup, Chef Dean Fearing's signature dish. **Cost** Doubles from $$. 2821 Turtle Creek Blvd.; 888/767-3966 or 214/559-2100; www.rosewoodhotels.com

utah
PARK CITY
■ **Stein Eriksen Lodge** (84.38) Norwegian-style ski chalet halfway up the mountain in Deer Valley Resort. **Stats** 175 rooms; 1 restaurant; 1 bar. **Competitive Edge** Impeccable service and a European ambience in a ski-in, ski-out setting. **Rooms to Book** West Wing rooms have the best views of the Rockies. **Don't Miss** Wild game (elk, buffalo, wild boar) chile at Glitretind's Sunday brunch. **Cost** Doubles from $$$. 800/453-1302 or 435/649-3700; www.steinlodge.com

virginia
CHARLOTTESVILLE
■ **Keswick Hall at Monticello** (83.11) Tuscan-style 1912 villa and golf club on a hilly 600-acre estate, near vineyards and thoroughbred horse farms, 10 minutes from Monticello. **Stats** 48 rooms; 2 restaurants; 2 bars. **Competitive Edge** A full-service golf resort (with lots to do away from the course) in a beautiful bucolic setting. **Rooms to Book** Nos. 9 and 15–29 have spectacular views; Nos. 19 and 27 have large private balconies. **Don't Miss** An early-morning walk with the foxhounds and hound master. **Cost** Doubles from $$. 800/274-5391 or 434/979-3440; www.keswick.com

WASHINGTON
■ **Inn at Little Washington** (86.50) Romantic early-20th-century house— a theatrical riot of fabrics and wallpapers—with a 1-bedroom cottage down the road, near Shenandoah Valley, 90 minutes from D.C. The restaurant is being redone this month. **Stats** 16 rooms; 1 restaurant; 1 bar. **Competitive Edge** The eclectic New American cuisine of one of the country's best-loved chefs, Patrick O'Connell. **Rooms to Book** All are unique; we like No. 12 for its bi-level loft and the balcony that overlooks the village and surrounding mountains. **Don't Miss** A hike through the nearby White Oak Canyon. **Cost** Doubles from $$$. 540/675-3800; www.theinnatlittlewashington.com

washington
SEATTLE
■ **Inn at the Market** (83.23) Ivy-covered brick building at the entrance to the Pike Place Public Market. **Stats** 70 rooms; 3 restaurants; 2 bars. **Competitive Edge** A peaceful retreat in the midst of the city's most vibrant shopping area. **Rooms to Book** Southeast corner rooms on floors 6–8 for glittering city views; No. 419

for a glimpse of the Market and Puget Sound. **Don't Miss** The guests-only rooftop deck, which offers a bird's-eye view of the city. **Cost** Doubles from $. *86 Pine St.; 800/446-4484 or 206/443-3600; www.innatthemarket.com*

SNOQUALMIE
■ **Salish Lodge & Spa** (83.50) Modern chalet dramatically set on the edge of Snoqualmie Falls in the Cascade Mountains, 35 minutes from Seattle. **Stats** 91 rooms; 3 restaurants; 1 bar. **Competitive Edge** Fantastic outdoor activities in a dramatic mountain setting. **Rooms to Book** We prefer those with river views on the 4th floor. (Avoid 3rd-floor ones near the main entrance—too much traffic.) **Don't Miss** A massage with hot river rocks in the lovely spa. **Cost** Doubles from $$. *6501 Railroad Ave. S.E.; 800/272-5474 or 425/888-2556; www.salishlodge.com*

west virginia
WHITE SULPHUR SPRINGS
■ **The Greenbrier** (85.10) Stately Georgian-style resort with an endless supply of activities on 6,500 acres in the Allegheny Mountains. **Stats** 803 rooms; 4 restaurants; 4 bars. **Competitive Edge** All the amenities of a great American resort with a slightly more adult atmosphere. **Rooms to Book** Those near the north entrance overlooking the formal gardens. **Don't Miss** The resort's Cold War bunker, built to house the U.S. Congress in case of a nuclear attack. **Cost** Doubles from $$$, including breakfast and dinner. *800/624-6070 or 304/536-1110; www.greenbrier.com*

wisconsin
KOHLER
■ **American Club at Destination Kohler** (84.84) Tudor-style resort (with fixtures from its parent company, Kohler), 1 hour north of Milwaukee. **Stats** 240 rooms; 3 restaurants; 3 bars. **Competitive Edge** World-class golf paired with an excellent, newly expanded 21,000-square-foot spa. **Rooms to Book** We like those in the Carriage House, which have free spa access. **Don't Miss** Wisconsin cheese flights at the Winery Bar. **Cost** Doubles from $$. *800/344-2838 or 920/457-8000; www.destinationkohler.com*

wyoming
JACKSON HOLE
■ **Four Seasons Resort** (83.79) 2-year-old Western-style lodge with an 11,000-square-foot spa at the base of the mountain. **Stats** 124 rooms; 2 restaurants; 1 bar. **Competitive Edge** A ski-in, ski-out

location and year-round outdoor concierge services. **Rooms to Book** In the summer, Standards with terraces; in the winter, those with gas fireplaces. **Don't Miss** A soak in the hotel's hot springs–like pools, set among aspen trees. **Cost** Doubles from $$$. *800/332-3442 or 307/732-5000; www.fourseasons.com*

JACKSON HOLE
■ **Rusty Parrot Lodge & Spa** (92.05) Gabled lodgepole-pine inn, on Miller Park surrounded by Jackson's shopping and dining options. **Stats** 31 rooms; 1 restaurant. **Competitive Edge** The intimate scale and pitch-perfect service create a low-key (yet supremely elegant) Western experience. **Rooms to Book** Those ending in -11 with wood-burning fireplaces and oversized Jacuzzis. **Don't Miss** The bison strip loin at the excellent Wild Sage. **Cost** Doubles from $$, including breakfast. *800/458-2004 or 307/733-2000; www.rustyparrot.com*

canada

alberta
BANFF
■ **Fairmont Banff Springs** (83.40) Baronial Scottish-style castle at the confluence of the Bow and Spray rivers, a shuttle ride from skiing and town. **Stats** 770 rooms; 12 restaurants; 3 bars. **Competitive Edge** Banff's most historic property, with an excellent private golf course and easy access to skiing. **Rooms to Book** Room sizes vary; avoid tiny Fairmonts. East-facing Valley Views look onto the Fairholm Range. **Don't Miss** Apple strudel in the Bavarian-inspired Waldhaus. **Cost** Doubles from $$$. *800/441-1414 or 403/762-2211; www.fairmont.com*

BANFF
■ **Rimrock Resort Hotel** (83.02) Contemporary lodge built into the hillside, 700 feet up Sulphur Mountain. **Stats** 346 rooms; 2 restaurants; 2 bars. **Competitive Edge** An elevated location that offers extraordinary views of the park, and is steps from the natural Upper Hot Springs. **Rooms to Book** Deluxes have unobstructed views of Mt. Rundle. **Don't Miss** Pepper-crusted caribou at the French-influenced Eden. **Cost** Doubles from $$. *888/746-7625 or 403/762-3356; www.rimrockresort.com*

LAKE LOUISE
■ **Fairmont Chateau Lake Louise** (85.91) Imposing 19th-century resort on the lake, in Banff National Park. **Stats** 550 rooms; 8

restaurants; 2 bars. **Competitive Edge** One of the world's most magical settings—surrounded by snowcapped peaks above a glacial blue lake. **Rooms to Book** With Standards measuring just 165 square feet, Fairmont Golds are worth the $100 upgrade for nearly twice the space. **Don't Miss** A guided hike on the Lake Agnes trail. **Cost** Doubles from $$. *800/441-1414 or 403/522-3511; www.fairmont.com*

LAKE LOUISE
■ **Post Hotel & Spa** (85.61) Quiet luxe lodge and cabins on the Pipestone River, five minutes from Lake Louise. **Stats** 97 rooms; 2 restaurants; 1 bar. **Competitive Edge** More intimate in feel than the region's large resorts. **Rooms to Book** Standards face west over a parking lot; we recommend the quieter, east-facing ones. **Don't Miss** A mandarin-orange–and-honey body scrub in the new spa. **Cost** Doubles from $$. *800/661-1586 or 403/522-3989; www.posthotel.com*

british columbia
VANCOUVER
■ **Wedgewood Hotel & Spa** (83.99) Intimate downtown hotel with the feel of a private residence, across from the courthouse and Robson Square. **Stats** 83 rooms; 1 restaurant. **Competitive Edge** Genteel ambience that's more old-world than Northwest. **Rooms to Book** Newly redesigned Deluxe Executives have marble steam showers and bedside tubs—worth the extra $33. **Don't Miss** A chance to sample the 1950 Marcel Trépout Bas-Armagnac in the library. **Cost** Doubles from $$. *845 Hornby St.; 800/663-0666 or 604/689-7777; www.wedgewoodhotel.com*

VANCOUVER ISLAND
■ **Aerie Resort** (89.77) Mediterranean-style villa set high in the island's southern mountains. **Stats** 35 rooms; 1 restaurant. **Competitive Edge** A stunning, secluded location that delivers 180-degree views of the Cascades and the Olympics. **Rooms to Book** Nos. 2 and 3 both have a balcony and queen-sized sleigh bed. **Don't Miss** The excellent seasonal cuisine, such as lamb with fennel tempura and lavender jus. **Cost** Doubles from $$. *Malahat; 800/518-1933 or 250/743-7115; www.aerie.bc.ca*

VANCOUVER ISLAND
■ **Sooke Harbour House** (86.46) Charming clapboard inn overlooking a dramatic Pacific beach and the Olympic Mountains, 45 minutes from Victoria. **Stats** 28 rooms; 1 restaurant. **Competitive Edge** Chef Edward Tuson's inventive Pacific Northwest cuisine has made this a

legendary food and wine destination. **Room to Book** Blue Heron, for its large balcony and panoramic ocean views. **Don't Miss** Bald eagle–spotting on the nearby protected Whiffen Spit. **Cost** Doubles from $$. Sooke; 800/889-9688 or 250/642-3421; www.sookeharbourhouse.com

VANCOUVER ISLAND

■ **Wickaninnish Inn** (89.76) Casually luxurious cedar inn atop a rocky promontory on the island's remote western coast. **Stats** 75 rooms; 1 restaurant; 1 bar. **Competitive Edge** A magnificent setting, surrounded by a rain forest and the Pacific shore. **Rooms to Book** In winter, those ending in -09, which face west and south and overlook the wild Pacific storms. **Don't Miss** The Dungeness crab cookout on stunning Chesterman Beach. **Cost** Doubles from $$. Tofino; 800/333-4604 or 250/725-3100; www.wickinn.com

WHISTLER

■ **Fairmont Chateau Whistler** (83.78) Grand château-style ski-in, ski-out resort with a private golf course at the foot of Blackcomb Mountain. **Stats** 550 rooms; 2 restaurants; 1 bar. **Competitive Edge** A quiet setting outside the hubbub of the village, but still within walking distance. **Rooms to Book** Slopeside Fairmont rooms have views of Whistler and Blackcomb. **Don't Miss** An après-ski toddy and a soak in one of the heated pools that face the mountain. **Cost** Doubles from $$$. 800/441-1414 or 604/938-8000; www.fairmont.com

WHISTLER

■ **Four Seasons Resort** (85.71) Luxe rustic-style lodge (opened 2004) in the woods, 5 minutes via shuttle from the base of Blackcomb. **Stats** 273 rooms; 1 restaurant; 1 bar. **Competitive Edge** The freshest, most amenity-rich rooms in town. **Rooms to Book** 7th-floor Superiors for views of the courtyard, with the Rainbow and Sprout mountains in the distance. **Don't Miss** Indulging in a B.C. Glacial Clay Wrap in the stellar spa. **Cost** Doubles from $$. 800/332-3442 or 604/935-3400; www.fourseasons.com

nova scotia
INGONISH BEACH
■ **Keltic Lodge Resort & Spa** (83.40) Scottish-inspired retreat and inn on a rocky Atlantic promontory in Cape Breton Highlands National Park. **Stats** 105 rooms; 2 restaurants; 1 bar. **Competitive Edge** Seclusion in the coastal headlands with astonishing ocean views. **Rooms to Book** Those in the main lodge, though smaller,

have the most charm. **Don't Miss** A seaweed treatment at the new Aveda spa. **Cost** Doubles from $$, including meals. Open late May–late Oct. 800/565-0444 or 902/285-2880; www.signatureresorts.com

ontario
OTTAWA
■ **Fairmont Château Laurier** (83.88) 1912 mansion, next to the National Gallery and Parliament. **Stats** 428 rooms; 2 restaurants; 1 bar. **Competitive Edge** Convenient location in the heart of the city's political epicenter, a short stroll from area attractions. **Rooms to Book** Fairmont View rooms in the original building that overlook Parliament and the Rideau Canal. **Don't Miss** Scones and clotted cream at the afternoon tea. **Cost** Doubles from $. 1 Rideau St.; 800/441-1414 or 613/241-1414; www.fairmont.com

TORONTO
■ **Four Seasons Hotel** (83.80) Modern 32-story high-rise in a fashionable neighborhood. **Stats** 380 rooms; 3 restaurants; 2 bars. **Competitive Edge** Quintessential Four Seasons service on the company's home turf. **Rooms to Book** Ask for a Standard Queen above the 5th floor for a balcony with skyline views. **Don't Miss** Lemon ricotta pancakes at Studio Café. **Cost** Doubles from $$. 21 Avenue Rd.; 800/332-3442 or 416/964-0411; www.fourseasons.com

quebec
QUEBEC CITY
■ **Fairmont Le Château Frontenac** (84.99) Historic turreted castle overlooking the river in the heart of the Old Town. **Stats** 618 rooms; 3 restaurants; 2 bars. **Competitive Edge** The city's grandest and most atmospheric hotel, right where you want to be. **Rooms to Book** We prefer odd-numbered rooms, which have river views. **Don't Miss** The Sunday brunch at Le Champlain restaurant. **Cost** Doubles from $$. 1 Rue De Carrières; 800/441-1414 or 418/692-3861; www.fairmont.com

TREMBLANT
■ **Fairmont Tremblant** (83.88) Modern slope-side château at the foot of the Laurentian Mountains. **Stats** 314 rooms; 2 restaurants; 1 bar. **Competitive Edge** A full-service ski-in, ski-out resort in a picturesque village. **Rooms to Book** Fairmont Golds, on the renovated 7th floor, are worth the extra $120 for private check-in and concierge services. **Don't Miss** The surf and turf every Friday evening at the Windigo Restaurant. **Cost** Doubles from $. 800/441-1414 or 819/681-7000; www.fairmont.com

argentina
BARILOCHE
■ **Llao Llao Hotel & Resort** (86.54) Majestic 1940 cypress-and-stone resort; a new wing (42 suites) opens late 2006. **Stats** 162 rooms; 3 restaurants; 1 bar. **Competitive Edge** An unparalleled natural setting, surrounded by Patagonia's mountains and lakes. **Rooms to Book** Studios with lake views. **Don't Miss** A swim in the spectacular indoor-outdoor infinity pool. **Cost** Doubles from $$, including breakfast. 54-2944/448-530; www.llaollao.com

BUENOS AIRES
■ **Alvear Palace Hotel** (85.12) Landmark 1932 palace in Recoleta; a thorough renovation was completed last year. **Stats** 210 rooms; 2 restaurants; 1 bar. **Competitive Edge** The grandest, most elegant hotel in town. **Rooms to Book** Premiers, for their Jacuzzis and high-tech bathrooms. **Don't Miss** An all-Argentine wine tasting led by La Bourgogne's sommelier in the restaurant's wine cellar. **Cost** Doubles from $, including breakfast. 1891 Avda. Alvear; 800/223-6800 or 54-11/4808-2100; www.alvearpalace.com

BUENOS AIRES
■ **Caesar Park** (84.86) High-rise on a central, but quiet, Recoleta side street. **Stats** 173 rooms; 1 restaurant; 2 bars. **Competitive Edge** Fabulous location for shoppers—across the street is the city's poshest mall. **Rooms to Book** Garden-view rooms on floors 2–5, for their oasis-in-the-city feel. **Don't Miss** Chef Rodrigo Toso's haute Argentine menu at Agraz. **Cost** Doubles from $$, including breakfast. 1232 Posadas; 877/223-7272 or 54-11/4819-1100; www.caesar-park.com

belize
PLACENCIA
■ **Turtle Inn** (84.13) Francis Ford Coppola–owned, Balinese-inspired beach getaway on the Placencia Peninsula. **Stats** 19 cottages; 1 restaurant; 2 bars.

Competitive Edge High style combined with the best of Belize's ocean adventures. **Rooms to Book** Seafront Cottages with private gardens and easy ocean access. **Don't Miss** A tour of the mangrove estuaries in the lagoon. **Cost** Doubles from $$, including breakfast. *800/746-3743 or 011-501/824-4914; www.turtleinn.com*

SAN IGNACIO
■ **Blancaneaux Lodge** (86.19) 80-acre thatched-roof jungle resort; owned by Francis Ford Coppola. **Stats** 17 cabanas; 1 restaurant; 1 bar. **Competitive Edge** Exceptional luxury in the remote Mountain Pine Ridge Forest Reserve. **Rooms to Book** We like the 2-bedroom villas, for their spacious, open-air living rooms. **Don't Miss** Looking for monkeys on a walk through the reserve. **Cost** Doubles from $, including breakfast. *800/746-3743 or 011-501/824-4914; www. blancaneaux.com*

SAN IGNACIO
■ **Lodge at Chaa Creek** (82.05) Eco-friendly jungle retreat on the banks of the Macal River. **Stats** 34 cottages; 10 casitas; 1 restaurant; 1 bar. **Competitive Edge** Fantastic outdoor activities (hiking, horseback riding, mountain biking). **Rooms to Book** The Treetop Jacuzzi Suites. **Don't Miss** An expedition to the ruins of Tikal and Xunantunich. **Cost** Doubles from $$. *877/709-8708 or 011-501/824-2037; www. chaacreek.com*

chile
SANTIAGO
■ **Ritz-Carlton** (85.18) Multi-terraced building in the pedestrian-friendly El Golf neighborhood. **Stats** 205 rooms; 2 restaurants; 1 bar. **Competitive Edge** Refined Ritz style, plus all the service and amenities. **Rooms to Book** Club Level Rooms for great views and access to the lounge. **Don't Miss** Sampling a flight of Chilean wine at Wine 365. **Cost** Doubles from $. *15 Calle el Alcalde; 800/241-3333 or 56-2/470-8500 www.ritzcarlton.com*

costa rica
PENINSULA PAPAGAYO
■ **Four Seasons Resort** (85.00) Tranquil 45-acre resort set between 2 beaches. **Stats** 153 rooms; 4 restaurants; 1 bar. **Competitive Edge** The country's most luxurious hotel, with a design that conveys a strong sense of place. **Rooms to Book** Ground-floor Garden Views, for a tucked-into-the-jungle feel. **Don't Miss** The spa's decadent 2-hour Selva Verde Purification Ritual. **Cost** Doubles from $$$. *800/332-3442 or 506/696-0000; www.fourseasons.com*

mexico
ACAPULCO
■ **Las Brisas** (81.64) Retro-style bungalows, most with private pools, on a hill overlooking Acapulco Bay. **Stats** 263 casitas; 2 restaurants; 3 bars. **Competitive Edge** An isolated setting that feels a world away from touristy crowds of Acapulco. **Rooms to Book** Any of the 44 newly renovated casitas. **Don't Miss** Watching the sunset from Tres Palos Lagoon. **Cost** Doubles from $$, including breakfast. *866/427-2779 or 52-744/469-6900; www.brisas.com.mx*

BAJA
■ **One & Only Palmilla** (84.96) Legendary 1956 Spanish Mission–style retreat (reopened in 2004 after a complete overhaul), along a private stretch of coastline. **Stats** 172 rooms; 3 restaurants; 3 bars. **Competitive Edge** All the offerings of a large resort, combined with the atmosphere and intimacy of a small one. **Rooms to Book** Those with stone bathtubs from South Africa. **Don't Miss** Lounging on one of the 3 secluded beach coves, in a floating bed suspended above the water. **Cost** Doubles from $$. *San José del Cabo; 888/691-8081 or 52-624/146-7000; www.oneandonlyresorts.com*

BAJA
■ **Las Ventanas al Paraíso** (86.55) Exclusive clutch of stylish villas along a golden beach. **Stats** 61 suites; 2 restaurants; 2 bars. **Competitive Edge** Pitch-perfect style and an unbelievable attention to details, such as wireless TV's poolside. **Rooms to Book** Oceanview Rooftop Terrace Junior Suites for great views. **Don't Miss** A day trip driving along the coast in one of the hotel's Mini Coopers. **Cost** Doubles from $$$. *San José del Cabo; 888/767-3966 or 52-624/144-2800; www.rosewoodhotels.com*

CANCÚN
■ **JW Marriott Resort & Spa** (82.78) 14-story beachfront tower in the hotel zone. At press time, the hotel was closed because of damage from Hurricane Wilma; Marriott intends to reopen in early 2006. **Stats** 448 rooms; 2 restaurants; 1 bar. **Competitive Edge** Maintains an intimate ambience despite its size. **Rooms to Book** Ocean Views on the 5th and 6th floors. **Don't Miss** The 35,000-square-foot spa. **Cost** Doubles from $$. *800/228-9290 or 52-998/848-9600; www.marriott.com*

CANCÚN
■ **Le Méridien Resort & Spa** (82.23) 8-story tower with 3 pools, on the beach. At press time the hotel was operating at a limited capacity following Hurricane Wilma damage; Le Méridien plans to be fully operational by early 2006. **Stats** 213 rooms; 2 restaurants; 1 bar. **Competitive Edge** A quiet location off the main Cancún strip. **Rooms to Book** Deluxes with terraces. **Don't Miss** Nightly demonstrations by a Cuban cigar maker in the lobby. **Cost** Doubles from $$. *800/543-4300 or 52-998/881-2200; www.lemeridien.com*

CANCÚN
■ **Ritz-Carlton** (87.40) Hacienda-style resort in the hotel zone. At press time the hotel was closed because of damage from Hurricane Wilma but is scheduled to reopen in early 2006. **Stats** 355 rooms; 4 restaurants; 2 bars. **Competitive Edge** A refreshingly refined, adult-oriented atmosphere. **Rooms to Book** Oceanfronts with balconies. **Don't Miss** Renting one of the resort's new beach cabanas with an oversize sun bed. **Cost** Doubles from $$$. *800/241-3333 or 52-998/881-0808; www.ritzcarlton.com*

CUERNAVACA
■ **Las Mañanitas** (87.22) 1955 colonial-style property with the feeling of a private estate. **Stats** 27 suites; 1 restaurant; 1 bar. **Competitive Edge** An escape to another era, with traditional antiques and gorgeous formal gardens. **Rooms to Book** The 6 new suites. **Don't Miss** A dinner of escamoles (ant eggs), tortilla soup, and other regional dishes. **Cost** Doubles from $, including breakfast. *888/413-9199 or 52-777/362-0000; www.lasmananitas.com.mx*

MAYAN RIVIERA
■ **Maroma Resort & Spa** (83.75) White-stucco resort on the Yucatan Peninsula. At press time, the hotel was closed because of damage from Hurricane Wilma but was scheduled to reopen in early 2006. **Stats** 64 rooms; 2 restaurants; 2 bars. **Competitive Edge** An intoxicatingly romantic atmosphere. **Rooms to Book** Ocean Views, which are just steps from the beach. **Don't Miss** Traditional Mayan treatments at the new Kinan Spa. **Cost** Doubles from $$, including breakfast. *866/454-9351 or 52-998/872-8200 www.maromahotel.com*

MEXICO CITY
■ **Four Seasons Hotel** (88.44) Spanish colonial sanctuary on the city's foremost boulevard. **Stats** 240 rooms; 1 restaurant;

1 bar. **Competitive Edge** A prime location, just minutes from the capital's top attractions. **Rooms to Book** Premier Terraces with French doors and floor-to-ceiling windows. **Don't Miss** A tequila tasting at El Bar. **Cost** Doubles from $$. *500 Paseo de la Reforma; 800/332-3442 or 52-55/5230 1818; www.fourseasons.com*

OAXACA

■ **Camino Real** (82.82) Beautifully restored 16th-century convent near the main plaza. **Stats** 91 rooms; 1 restaurant; 2 bars. **Competitive Edge** A National Archaeological Treasure of Mexico, with stone fountains, original frescoes, and gardens. **Rooms to Book** Interior rooms are quieter than those facing the street. **Don't Miss** Excellent Oaxacan mole and other local delicacies in the restaurant. **Cost** Doubles from $$. *300 5 De Mayo; 800/722-6466 or 52-951/501-6100; www.caminoreal.com*

PUNTA MITA

■ **Four Seasons Resort** (86.67) Tiled-roof casitas and suites on a pristine private isthmus. **Stats** 140 rooms; 3 restaurants; 3 bars. **Competitive Edge** A real escape 45 minutes from Puerto Vallarta. **Rooms to Book** One-bedroom Garden View Suites (the bargain suites) are peaceful and have private plunge pools. **Don't Miss** Snorkeling with sea lions along Banderas Bay. **Cost** Doubles from $$. *800/332-3442 or 52-329/291-6000; www.fourseasons.com*

SAN MIGUEL DE ALLENDE

■ **Casa de Sierra Nevada** (81.63) Downtown hotel occupying five 16th- and 17th-century mansions. **Stats** 33 rooms; 2 restaurants; 2 bars. **Competitive Edge** Old-fashioned charm (stone doorways, tranquil courtyards, and canopy beds) in one of Mexico's most historic towns. **Rooms to Book** We like Casa Limón suites facing the pool. **Don't Miss** A traditional Mexican dinner with live music at the Park restaurant. **Cost** Doubles from $$. *46 Hospicio; 800/728-9098 or 52-415/152-7040; www.casadesierranevada.com*

ZIHUATANEJO

■ **La Casa Que Canta** (90.86) Cliff-hugging adobe hideaway, with a pair of pools and a new all-suite villa, overlooking Zihuatanejo Bay. **Stats** 33 suites; 1 restaurant; 1 bar. **Competitive Edge** All the romance that comes from a sophisticated, adult-oriented environment. **Rooms to Book** Private Pool Suites are the largest and have plunge

pools. **Don't Miss** A renewing cactus wrap treatment at the top-notch spa. **Cost** Doubles from $$. No guests under 16. *888/523-5050 or 52-755/555-7000; www.lacasaquecanta.com*

ZIHUATANEJO

■ **Hotel Villa del Sol** (85.48) Red tile–roofed casitas and tropical gardens on 6 beachfront acres. **Stats** 72 rooms; 2 restaurants; 3 bars. **Competitive Edge** A laid-back atmosphere and polished rooms. **Rooms to Book** All are unique; garden-facing Deluxes are especially intimate and private. **Don't Miss** Lunch in a secluded beachfront palapa. **Cost** Doubles from $$. *888/389-2645 or 52-755/555-5500; www.hotelvilladelsol.net*

peru

CUZCO

■ **Hotel Monasterio** (86.91) Restored 16th-century Spanish-colonial seminary with Baroque interiors. **Stats** 123 rooms; 2 restaurants; 1 bar. **Competitive Edge** The most luxurious hotel in vibrant Cuzco, with access to both Machu Picchu and downtown. **Rooms to Book** Deluxes that overlook the patio are also oxygen-enriched for the high altitude. **Don't Miss** A hotel-arranged weaving workshop with local artisans. **Cost** Doubles from $$, including breakfast. *800/223-6800 or 51-84/241-777; www.orient-express.com*

MACHU PICCHU VILLAGE

■ **Machu Picchu Pueblo Hotel** (81.51) Whitewashed cottages set into a lush hillside on the edge of Cuzco. **Stats** 83 rooms; 2 restaurants; 1 bar. **Competitive Edge** An exceptionally peaceful setting surrounded by gardens. **Rooms to Book** Junior Suites with views of the orchid gardens. **Don't Miss** A sauna in the bamboo-and-eucalyptus hut. **Cost** Doubles from $$, including all meals and excursions. *800/442-5042 or 51-84/211-122; www.inkaterra.com*

MACHU PICCHU VILLAGE

■ **Machu Picchu Sanctuary Lodge** (82.98) Eco-friendly Spanish colonial–style lodge, completely restored in 2001. **Stats** 31 rooms; 2 restaurants; 1 bar. **Competitive Edge** Prime location: it's the only hotel within the landmark Incan citadel. **Rooms to Book** Deluxes with terraces and mountain views. **Don't Miss** A hotel-arranged trek to the Temple of the Moon. **Cost** Doubles from $$$, including meals. *800/223-6800 or 51-84/211-039; www.orient-express.com*

ANGUILLA

■ **Cap Juluca** (86.44) Whitewashed Moorish-style villa resort on a crescent of alabaster sand. **Stats** 98 rooms; 3 restaurants; 2 bars. **Competitive Edge** The most romantic spot on the island with an emphasis on privacy throughout. **Rooms to Book** Junior Suites, with secluded sun terraces, are worth the premium. **Don't Miss** A Balinese massage in the comfort of your suite. **Cost** Doubles from $$$$, including breakfast. *888/858-5822 or 264/497-6666; www.capjuluca.com*

ANGUILLA

■ **CuisinArt Resort & Spa** (80.71) Mediterranean-style hideaway with a dramatic infinity pool, on a lovely beach. **Stats** 93 rooms; 2 restaurants; 2 bars. **Competitive Edge** The on-site gardens, which provide produce for the excellent restaurants and spa. **Rooms to Book** It's worth the upgrade to a suite with an ocean view. **Don't Miss** Daniel Orr's Caribbean cuisine (yellowfin tuna–and-coconut ceviche with garlic chives) at the Kitchen Stadium chef's table. **Cost** Doubles from $$$. *800/943-3210 or 264/498-2000; www.cuisinartresort.com*

ANTIGUA

■ **Curtain Bluff Resort** (87.20) Breezy 2-story buildings on a rise between 2 beaches. **Stats** 72 rooms; 2 restaurants; 2 bars. **Competitive Edge** An adult take on all-inclusive: everything from fishing and scuba diving to a personalized mini-bar is included. **Rooms to Book** The well-priced Junior Suites sit right on the sand. **Don't Miss** A tennis lesson with renowned head pro Rennie George. **Cost** Doubles from $$$$. *888/289-9898 or 268/462-8400; www.curtainbluff.com*

ANTIGUA

■ **Jumby Bay** (81.43) Colonial-style enclave on a private, 300-acre island. **Stats** 40 rooms; 15 houses for rent; 2

restaurants; 2 bars. **Competitive Edge** So exclusive and intimate that every staff member is guaranteed to know your name. **Rooms to Book** One of the 8 Rondavels, with wraparound terraces and outdoor showers. **Don't Miss** A reflexology session with legendary masseuse Su Hua. **Cost** Doubles from $$$$$, all-inclusive. *888/767-3966 or 268/462-6000; www.rosewoodhotels.com*

BAHAMAS

Four Seasons Great Exuma at Emerald Bay (83.93) 3-year-old resort on a quiet island with a white-sand beach. **Stats** 183 rooms; 3 restaurants; 1 bar. **Competitive Edge** The Greg Norman golf course—one of the region's most beautiful and challenging. **Rooms to Book** For privacy, take a Beachfront at either end of the resort. **Don't Miss** Exploring the island's fish-filled reefs. **Cost** Doubles from $$. *800/332-3442 or 242/336-6800; www.fourseasons.com*

BAHAMAS

■ **One & Only Ocean Club Paradise Island** (86.05) 1939 former Huntington estate overlooking a nice beach. **Stats** 105 rooms; 3 restaurants; 4 bars. **Competitive Edge** The exceptional spa with Balinese treatment villas. **Rooms to Book** For a traditional feel, standards in the original Hartford Wing. **Don't Miss** French-Asian fare at Jean-George Vongerichten's Dune. **Cost** Doubles from $$$$. *800/321-3000 or 242/363-2501; www.oneandonlyoceanclub.com*

BARBADOS

Coral Reef Club (81.34) Family-run retreat with coral-colored cottages along a tree-lined beach. **Stats** 88 rooms; 1 restaurant; 1 bar. **Competitive Edge** An especially relaxed and comfortable atmosphere thanks to the expert staff. **Rooms to Book** Vinca, Coleus, and Almond, 3 of the Luxury Junior Suites, are closest to the ocean. **Don't Miss** A lunch cruise on the hotel's catamaran. **Cost** Doubles from $$$. *800/223-1108 or 246/422-2372; www.coralreefbarbados.com*

BARBADOS

■ **Sandy Lane** (82.98) Classic Palladian-style beachfront resort with an exclusive, high-society feel. **Stats** 113 rooms; 3 restaurants; 3 bars. **Competitive Edge** Over-the-top glamour combined with plush, high-tech rooms. **Rooms to Book** From May to mid-December, an ocean view costs only $100 more and is worth every penny. **Don't Miss** An evening cocktail with panoramic views

at the clubhouse. **Cost** Doubles from $$$$$. *866/444-4080 or 246/444-2000; www.sandylane.com*

BERMUDA

■ **The Reefs** (86.40) Tranquil cliffside hideaway of pink stucco cottages above a private beach. **Stats** 65 rooms; 3 restaurants; 2 bars. **Competitive Edge** A renowned troika of restaurants, which are now a little more relaxed: jacket and tie are no longer required. **Rooms to Book** For privacy and views, the Point Suites and Windy Brae and Sandpiper Cottage Suites at either end of he resort. **Don't Miss** Snorkeling in the colorful Church Bay reefs. **Cost** Doubles from $$. *800/742-2008 or 441/238-0222; www.thereefs.com*

JAMAICA

■ **Half Moon** (80.81) Legendary 50-year-old estate on 400 acres overlooking the water. **Stats** 419 rooms; 4 restaurants; 7 bars. **Competitive Edge** Polished, attentive service in a resort that's chockablock with activities. **Rooms to Book** A Hibiscus Suite with a beachfront patio. **Don't Miss** A horseback ride on one of the hotel's thoroughbreds. **Cost** Doubles from $$. *800/626-0592 or 876/953-2211; www.halfmoon.com*

JAMAICA

■ **Jamaica Inn** (83.57) Quiet low-rise retreat with elegant interiors overlooking one of the island's best beaches. **Stats** 51 rooms; 1 restaurant; 2 bars. **Competitive Edge** One of Jamaica's most intimate and romantic spots. **Rooms to Book** Those in the Beach Wing, which sit on the sand. **Don't Miss** The restaurant's legendary breakfast. **Cost** Doubles from $$$. *800/837-4608 or 876/974-2514; www.jamaicainn.com*

JAMAICA

■ **Ritz-Carlton Golf & Spa Resort Rose Hall** (80.35) 5,000-acre property on a small beach; a beach club is a 5-minute shuttle ride away. **Stats** 427 rooms; 5 restaurants; 2 bars. **Competitive Edge** Some of the island's most beautiful grounds, including the White Witch golf course. **Rooms to Book** Among the Ocean Views, Nos. 1220,1245, 2220, and 2245 are the best. **Don't Miss** Jamaican dishes with an Asian twist at Jasmines. **Cost** Doubles from $$$. *800/241-3333 or 876/953-2800; www.ritzcarlton.com*

JAMAICA

Sandals Grande Ocho Rios Beach & Villa Resort (81.04) Couples-only mega-property on 110 acres on the island's

quiet northern end. **Stats** 529 rooms; 10 restaurants; 10 bars. **Competitive Edge** All-inclusive resort amenities, with the option of renting a villa for a more luxurious experience. **Rooms to Book** Those in the Riviera Building have the best views. **Don't Miss** A Blue Mountain coffee exfoliating scrub at the spa. **Cost** Doubles from $$$, all-inclusive. *800/726-3257 or 876/974-5691; www.sandals.com*

NEVIS

■ **Four Seasons Resort** (88.94) West Indian–style low-rise buildings with attractive plantation-inspired interiors along a pretty beach. **Stats** 196 rooms; 4 restaurants; 3 bars. **Competitive Edge** An unusually well-rounded resort with a terrific golf course and spa for adults—and activities aplenty for kids. **Rooms to Book** Although they don't overlook the water, Mountain Views are particularly quiet and affordable. **Don't Miss** The casual beach barbecue. **Cost** Doubles from $$$. *800/332-3442 or 869/469-1111; www.fourseasons.com*

PETER ISLAND

■ **Peter Island Resort** (82.19) Collection of cottages on a 1,300-acre private island with 5 beaches and prime diving sites. **Stats** 56 rooms; 2 restaurants; 1 bar. **Competitive Edge** Accessible only via boat or helicopter, it offers unparalleled exclusivity. **Rooms to Book** Any of the 20 newly renovated oceanfront suites with knockout views of Deadman's Bay Beach. **Don't Miss** A massage in one of the spa's ocean-view pavilions. **Cost** Doubles from $$$$$. *800/346-4451 or 284/495-2000; www.peterisland.com*

PUERTO RICO

Las Casitas Village & Golden Door Spa (82.50) Spanish colonial–style enclave—a hotel within a hotel at the massive El Conquistador resort—on a bluff overlooking both the Caribbean and the Atlantic. **Stats** 157 rooms; 13 restaurants; 8 bars. **Competitive Edge** A private, separately staffed retreat, with access to mega-resort amenities. **Rooms to Book** The new upper-level casitas with jaw-dropping views from floor-to-ceiling windows. **Don't Miss** A treatment at the renowned Golden Door Spa. **Cost** Doubles from $$$$. *800/996-3426 or 787/863-1000; www.luxuryresorts.com*

PUERTO RICO

■ **Horned Dorset Primavera** (85.18) Quiet colonial-style property on the island's west coast. Rooms in the original building will be closed through April 2006 for a full renovation. **Stats** 38 rooms; 2 restaurants; 1 bar. **Competitive Edge** Puerto Rico's most tranquil resort: no TV's, no phones, and no children under 12. **Rooms to Book** Spacious Primavera Suites, which cost nearly $300 less than usual throughout the renovation. **Don't Miss** Dinner at the elegant Primavera. **Cost** Doubles from $$$, including breakfast and dinner. *800/633-1857 or 787/823-4030; www.horneddorset.com*

ST. BART'S

Hôtel Guanahani & Spa (83.09) Breezy resort with new Clarins spa, set between a private beach and a lagoon. **Stats** 69 rooms; 2 restaurants; 2 bars. **Competitive Edge** Top-notch facilities, thanks to a recent redo, combined with a relaxed atmosphere. **Rooms to Book** Although they are slightly less private, we like those on the point for easy beach access. **Don't Miss** Taking a kite-surfing lesson. **Cost** Doubles from $$$. *800/223-6800 or 590-590/276-660; www.leguanahani.com*

ST. LUCIA

■ **Anse Chastanet Resort** (81.77) Cluster of villas with expansive views, tucked into the steep hills below the Piton mountains. A luxe, 22-room hilltop hotel within a hotel will open in May. **Stats** 49 rooms; 2 restaurants; 2 bars. **Competitive Edge** An exotic, laid-back atmosphere reminiscent of the South Pacific. **Rooms to Book** Those high on the hill for breathtaking views. **Don't Miss** A kayak tour of the island. **Cost** Doubles from $$, including breakfast and dinner. *800/223-1108 or 758/459-7000; www.ansechastanet.com*

ST. MARTIN

■ **La Samanna** (80.95) Whitewashed Mediterranean-style resort on 55 acres overlooking Baie Longue. **Stats** 81 rooms; 2 restaurants; 2 bars. **Competitive Edge** Set along the whitest, prettiest beach on St. Martin. **Rooms to Book** Any of the 6 new suites with private rooftop gazebos and pools. **Don't Miss** Renting a Midnight Cabana with telescope for an evening of champagne and stargazing, complete with butler service. **Cost** Doubles from $$$. *800/854-2252 or 590-590/876-400; www.lasamanna.com*

ST. THOMAS

■ **Ritz-Carlton** (81.80) Pink palazzo-style resort with marble arcades, ornate fountains, and 30 manicured acres, set along a 2-mile beach. **Stats** 152 rooms; 4 restaurants; 2 bars. **Competitive Edge** The plushest hotel in the easy-to-access, low-hassle U.S. Virgin Islands. **Rooms to**

Book Those in the Freesia Building have views of neighboring St. John Island. **Don't Miss** One of the resort's afternoon watercolor painting classes. **Cost** Doubles from $$$. *800/241-3333 or 340/775-3333; www.ritzcarlton.com*

TURKS AND CAICOS

■ **Grace Bay Club** (81.97) Intimate Spanish-style resort on one of the country's best beaches. Recently added a spa, gym, and family-friendly villas. **Stats** 59 suites; 3 restaurants; 2 bars. **Competitive Edge** A relaxed, but adult-oriented, atmosphere in a convenient location. **Rooms to Book** The 38 new suites are the freshest, but we like those in the main building. **Don't Miss** A meal at one of the beachside dining "pods." **Cost** Doubles from $$$. *800/946-5757 or 649/946-5757; www.gracebayclub.com*

TURKS AND CAICOS

■ **Parrot Cay Resort & Spa** (85.65) Trendsetting private-island resort on a long white-sand beach. **Stats** 60 rooms; 2 restaurants; 2 bars. **Competitive Edge** A refreshing Asian feel, from the pared-down aesthetics to the attentive service and excellent Shambala Spa. **Room to Book** No. 703 for technicolor sunsets seen from its private terrace. **Don't Miss** An exfoliating Javanese Royal Lulur Bath at the spa. **Cost** Doubles from $$$. *877/754-0726 or 649/946-7788; www.parrot-cay.como.bz*

VIRGIN GORDA

■ **Biras Creek Resort** (85.00) Hilltop cottages on a 140-acre peninsula with panoramic ocean views and a small, pretty beach. **Stats** 31 rooms; 1 restaurant; 1 bar. **Competitive Edge** Utter privacy and a relaxed, castaway feel. **Rooms to Book** Ocean Suites 9B and 11B: they're just steps from the pool and have knockout ocean views. **Don't Miss** Navigating a Boston Whaler along the coastline—even beginners can do it. **Cost** Doubles from $$$$. *800/223-1108 or 310/440-4225; www.biras.com*

VIRGIN GORDA

■ **Little Dix Bay Hotel** (84.35) Quiet, family-friendly resort (a former Rockefeller compound) on 500 beachside acres. **Stats** 100 rooms; 3 restaurants; 2 bars. **Competitive Edge** The island's most complete luxe services and amenities. **Rooms to Book** A junior suite with an outdoor living area. **Don't Miss** The couple's suite at the cliffside spa. **Cost** Doubles from $$$$. *888/767-3966 or 284/495-5555; www.rosewoodhotels.com*

world's best top 50 europe

austria

SALZBURG

■ **Hotel Goldener Hirsch** (85.83) Antiques-filled 15th-century building in the Old Town. **Stats** 69 rooms; 2 restaurants; 1 bar. **Competitive Edge** A Salzburg institution: it's the oldest hotel in town and a favorite among Austria's elite. **Rooms to Book** For views, one of the more expensive Festival Wing rooms; avoid 4th-floor rooms with lower ceilings. **Don't Miss** Wiener schnitzel in the main restaurant. **Cost** Doubles from $$$. *37 Getereidegasse; 800/325-3589 or 43-662/80840; www.goldenerhirsch.com*

VIENNA

■ **Hotel Bristol** (84.32) 1892 hotel with classic fin de siècle interiors, on the Ring opposite the opera house and Kärntnerstrasse shopping. **Stats** 140 rooms; 2 restaurants; 1 bar. **Competitive Edge** Historic grandeur, coupled with a welcoming atmosphere. **Rooms to Book** The 7 Classics that overlook the opera house. **Don't Miss** People-watching at Restaurant Korso, which just added sidewalk dining this year. **Cost** Doubles from $$. *1 Kärntner Ring; 800/228-3000 or 43-1/515-160; www.westin.com*

VIENNA

■ **Hotel Imperial** (86.25) 1863 former palace, on the Ring close to the Kärntnerstrasse and the opera house. **Stats** 138 rooms; 2 restaurants; 1 bar. **Competitive Edge** The most regal hotel in the city, from the public spaces to the chandeliered guest rooms. **Rooms to Book** The recently renovated ones on the 4th and 5th floors that have Ringstrasse views. **Don't Miss** A meal in Restaurant Imperial—like the décor, the dishes (goose-liver tart with sour cherries) are rich and traditional. **Cost** Doubles from $$$$. *16 Kärntner Ring; 800/325-3589 or 43-1/501-100; www.luxurycollection.com*

czech republic

PRAGUE

■ **Four Seasons Hotel** (89.24) 4 interconnected Old Town buildings with contemporary interiors, on the banks of the Vltava River near the Charles Bridge. **Stats** 161 rooms; 1 restaurant; 1 bar. **Competitive Edge** Prague's most luxurious quarters —plus a great location. **Rooms to Book** For only $48 more than Standards, one of the top-floor Superiors with a vaulted ceiling. **Don't Miss** Italian-meets-Bohemian cuisine at Allegra, widely considered to be the city's best restaurant. **Cost** Doubles from $$. *2A/1098 Veleslavinova; 800/332-3442 or 420-2/2142-7000; www.fourseasons.com*

england

HAMPSHIRE

■ **Chewton Glen** (87.39) Ivy-covered 18th-century retreat, set on 130 pristine acres at the edge of the New Forest. **Stats** 58 rooms; 1 restaurant; 1 bar. **Competitive Edge** The romance of a rambling historic house fused with top-notch modern facilities, including a world-class spa. **Rooms to Book** Those with balconies overlooking the gardens. **Don't Miss** An afternoon game of croquet or indoor tennis—two quintessentially English sports. **Cost** Doubles from $$. *New Milton; 800/344-5087 or 44-1425/275-341; www.chewtonglen.com*

LONDON

■ **Claridge's** (86.60) Landmark hotel with renowned Art Deco–style public spaces, in Mayfair close to New Bond Street's boutiques. **Stats** 203 rooms; 3 restaurants; 2 bars. **Competitive Edge** A high-wattage hotel famous for its Gordon Ramsay restaurant and beautifully updated rooms. **Rooms to Book** Rooms have either Art Deco or Victorian interiors; we prefer Art Deco. **Don't Miss** An Anne Sémonin jet-lag treatment at the spa. **Cost** Doubles from $$$. *Brook St.; 800/637-2869 or 44-207/629-8860; www.claridges.co.uk*

LONDON

■ **Dukes** (84.44) Thoroughly English 1908 property on a gaslit cul de sac near Green Park and St. James's Palace. **Stats** 90 rooms; 1 restaurant; 1 bar. **Competitive Edge** Residential seclusion and serenity in a central location. **Rooms to Book** The brightest standards are those ending in –04, which overlook the entrance. **Don't Miss** One of bartender Tony Micelotta's famous martinis. **Cost** Doubles from $$. *St. James's Place; 800/381-4702 or 44-207/491-4840; www.dukeshotel.co.uk*

LONDON

■ **The Goring** (87.30) Family-owned hotel with classic chintz- and leather-filled interiors, between Buckingham Palace and Victoria Station. **Stats** 71 rooms; 2 restaurants; 1 bar. **Competitive Edge** A bastion of old-school English hospitality that prides itself on getting to know guests. **Rooms to Book** Garden Views with king-sized beds. **Don't Miss** Lunch in the private garden, popular with Londoners on their way to Buckingham Palace. **Cost** Doubles from $$. *Beeston Place, Grosvenor Gardens; 800/987-7433 or 44-207/396-9000; www.goringhotel.co.uk*

france

CÔTE D'AZUR

■ **Château de la Chèvre d'Or** (85.64) Cliffside complex of historic stone buildings with panoramic views, in medieval village of Èze. **Stats** 32 rooms; 3 restaurants; 1 bar. **Competitive Edge** A secluded retreat high above the Riviera, yet within easy reach of all the action. **Rooms to Book** Each is unique; the new Salon Suite has a private terrace and Jacuzzi. **Don't Miss** A workout in the gym while looking out onto the sea. **Cost** Doubles from $$. *Èze; 800/735-2478 or 33-4/92-10-66-66; www.chevredor.com*

CÔTE D'AZUR

■ **Grand-Hôtel du Cap-Ferrat** (91.15) White Belle Époque palace set on 14 acres of gardens and forest. **Stats** 53 rooms; 2 restaurants; 1 bar. **Competitive Edge** Exclusive location at the tip of the Cap-Ferrat peninsula between Nice and Monaco. **Room to Book** No. 402, favored by heads of state, has great views. **Don't Miss** A swim in the Club Dauphin pool. **Cost** Doubles from $$$. *St.-Jean-Cap-Ferrat; 800/525-4800 or 33-4/93-76-50-50; www.grand-hotel-cap-ferrat.com*

CÔTE D'AZUR

■ **Hôtel Byblos** (84.35) St.-Tropez hot spot with colorful, interconnected buildings. **Stats** 96 rooms; 2 restaurants; 1 bar. **Competitive Edge** Exclusive atmosphere in the center of St.-Tropez, where the beautiful people come to party. **Rooms to Book** The remodeled Suites du Roy are ultra serene. **Don't Miss** Dinner at chef Alain Ducasse's Spoon Byblos, followed by dancing at Les Caves du Roy nightclub. **Cost** Doubles from $$$. *St.-Tropez; 800/223-6800 or 33-4/94-56-68-00; www.byblos.com*

CÔTE D'AZUR

■ **Hôtel du Cap Eden-Roc** (85.22) Secluded 1870 Napoleon III mansion with a 22-acre garden, at the tip of the Cap d'Antibes peninsula. **Stats** 130 rooms; 1 restaurant; 2 bars. **Competitive Edge** The ultimate in star-studded glamour: the hotel even has a pier for those arriving by yacht. **Rooms to Book** Those in the Eden Roc wing face the water and have private terraces. **Don't Miss** A drink at the waterside bar, with breathtaking sea views. **Cost** Doubles from $$$. *Antibes; 800/566-5356 or 33-4/93-61-39-01; www.edenroc-hotel.fr*

CÔTE D'AZUR

■ **La Réserve de Beaulieu** (86.30) Florentine Renaissance–style 1880 villa, in one of the Riviera's most attractive villages. **Stats** 39 rooms; 2 restaurants; 2 bars. **Competitive Edge** A $3 million spa, renovated bar, and Michelin 2-starred restaurant keep this landmark at the head of the class. **Rooms to Book** Those on the top floor have the best views from balconies. **Don't Miss** A stroll along the nearby pier. **Cost** Doubles from $$$. *Beaulieu-Sur-Mer; 800/223-6800 or 33-4/93-01-00-01; www.reservebeaulieu.com*

LOIRE VALLEY

■ **Domaine des Hauts de Loire** (87.74) Ivy-covered 19th-century country manor in a wooded park, halfway between Blois and Amboise. **Stats** 33 rooms; 1 restaurant. **Competitive Edge** A central base for exploring the area's castles—and one of the best restaurants in the region. **Rooms to Book** No. 27 has a small balcony; Nos. 2, 3, and 12 have views of the pond; No. 35 has floor-to-ceiling windows. **Don't Miss** A stroll through the surrounding deer-filled woods. **Cost** Doubles from $. *Onzain; 800/735-2478 or 33-2/54-20-72-57; www.domainehautsloire.com*

PARIS

■ **Four Seasons Hotel George V** (88.72) Ornate 1928 landmark with an excellent spa, newly renovated gym, and Michelin 3-starred restaurant. **Stats** 245 rooms; 2 restaurants; 1 bar. **Competitive Edge** Prime location near the Champs-Élysées, unbeatable views of the Eiffel Tower, and superb service. **Rooms to Book** All are big (minimum is 430 square feet); No. 824 has a terrace with sweeping views. **Don't Miss** The indoor pool surrounded by trompe l'oeil murals of the Versailles gardens. **Cost** Doubles from $$$$. *31 Ave. George V; 800/332-3442 or 33-1/49-52-70-00; www.fourseasons.com*

PARIS

■ **Hôtel de Crillon** (86.51) Gilded 18th-century Louis XV–style palace, in the heart of the city, steps from the

Tuileries Gardens and the Seine. **Stats** 147 rooms; 2 restaurants; 1 bar. **Competitive Edge** The most impressive architecture of the city's top hotels. **Rooms to Book** Nos. 409 and 511 have balconies and the best Eiffel Tower views. **Don't Miss** Alain Ducasse–protégé chef Jean-François Piège at Les Ambassadeurs. **Cost** Doubles from $$$. *10 Place de la Concorde; 800/223-6800 or 33-1/44-71-15-00; www.crillon.com*

PARIS
■ **Hôtel Plaza Athénée** (84.86) Historic palace in the midst of Paris's most exclusive boutiques. **Stats** 188 rooms; 4 restaurants; 1 bar. **Competitive Edge** An intimate palace hotel with a tony address and a Michelin 3-starred Alain Ducasse restaurant. **Rooms to Book** Those on the 7th and 8th floors have great Art Deco style. **Don't Miss** Taking home the hotel's signature red-leather slippers (available for purchase). **Cost** Doubles from $$$$. *25 Ave. Montaigne; 866/732-1106 or 33-1/53-67-66-65; www.plaza-athenee-paris.com*

PARIS
■ **The Ritz** (86.57) Legendary, turn-of-the-20th-century hotel built by César Ritz, on the Place Vendôme and near the Louvre and Musée d'Orsay. **Stats** 162 rooms; 1 restaurant; 2 bars. **Competitive Edge** The most venerable, iconic address in the city—Coco Chanel called it home for 37 years. **Rooms to Book** Those facing the interior are especially tranquil; suites have views of the Place Vendôme. **Don't Miss** Drinks poolside at the prettiest indoor piscine in town. **Cost** Doubles from $$$$. *15 Place Vendôme; 800/223-6800 or 33-1/43-16-30-30; www.ritzparis.com*

PROVENCE
■ **La Bastide de Moustiers** (87.68) Chef Alain Ducasse's 16th-century Provençal farmhouse, set on 10 pastoral acres in the French Alps. **Stats** 12 rooms; 1 restaurant; 1 bar. **Competitive Edge** Sophisticated Ducasse cuisine in a French country atmosphere. **Rooms to Book** Blanche is decorated in all white; Volière has a four-poster bed and claw-foot tub; Coquelicot has a private terrace. **Don't Miss** Helping chef Eric Santalucia prepare a gourmet lunch. **Cost** Doubles from $. *Moustiers-Ste.-Marie; 33-4/92-70-47-47; www.bastide-moustiers.com*

PROVENCE
■ **Hostellerie de Crillon le Brave** (84.85) 7 restored houses linked by cobblestoned alleys and gardens, in a quiet village 30 minutes from Avignon. **Stats** 32 rooms; 1 restaurant; 1 bar. **Competitive Edge** A secluded getaway offering a real flavor of French village life. **Rooms to Book** No. 33, in a 12th-century tower, for a view of Mont Ventoux from the bathtub; those in La Maison Berton de Balbe, Le Jas, and La Maison Reboul buildings are the largest. **Don't Miss** Spending an evening sampling vintages from nearby vineyards at Le Restaurant. **Cost** Doubles from $. *Crillon le Brave; 800/735-2478 or 33-4/90-65-61-61; www.crillonlebrave.com*

PROVENCE
■ **Hôtel d'Europe** (85.61) Historic 16th-century mansion once frequented by Dickens and Dalí, near the Palais des Papes. **Stats** 44 rooms; 1 restaurant; 1 bar. **Competitive Edge** Affordable comfort and tranquillity in a central location. **Room to Book** No. 115 has a lovely view of the interior courtyard and its stone fountain. **Don't Miss** A tasting-menu dinner from chef Bruno D'Angelis in the courtyard. **Cost** Doubles from $. *Avignon; 33-4/90-14-76-76; www.hotel-d-europe.fr*

PROVENCE
■ **Oustau de Baumanière** (88.18) Legendary 16th-century country house with formal gardens, near Les Baux-de-Provence. **Stats** 30 rooms; 1 restaurant. **Competitive Edge** An ideal location for touring the area's UNESCO World Heritage Sites. **Rooms to Book** Nos. 61, 62, and 63, which have been renovated in a contemporary style. **Don't Miss** A tour of the hotel's 100,000-bottle wine cellar. **Cost** Doubles from $$. *Les Baux-De-Provence; 800/735-2478 or 33-4/90-54-33-07; www.oustaudebaumaniere.com*

REIMS
■ **Château Les Crayères** (92.33) Turn-of-the-20th-century château (formerly Boyer Les Crayères) on a private 17-acre park, outside of town. **Stats** 20 rooms; 1 restaurant; 1 bar. **Competitive Edge** The exceptional Michelin 2-starred restaurant, headed up by chef Didier Elena. **Rooms to Book** The 6 Princess rooms, which overlook the park; the Princess Louise is the largest and has a terrace. **Don't Miss** Strolling the hotel's beautiful grounds. **Cost** Doubles from $$. *800/735-2478 or 33-3/26-82-80-80; www.gerardboyer.com*

germany
BERLIN
■ **Hotel Adlon Kempinski** (89.86) Contemporary re-creation of Berlin's most historic hotel, complete with brocade bedspreads and marble bathrooms. **Stats** 394 rooms; 3 restaurants; 1 bar. **Competitive Edge** An unbeatable central location, right beside the Brandenburg Gate. **Rooms to Book** One of the 69 new rooms with flat-screen TV's and DVD players. **Don't Miss** A dip in the large, Roman-style pool. **Cost** Doubles from $$. *77 Unter den Linden; 800/426-3135 or 49-30/22610; www.hotel-adlon.de*

ireland
COUNTY CLARE
■ **Dromoland Castle** (85.59) 1545 castle with crenellated turrets and suits of armor, 10 minutes from Shannon airport. **Stats** 100 rooms; 2 restaurants; 2 bars. **Competitive Edge** The quintessential Irish castle hotel, with a dramatic sense of history. **Rooms to Book** Nos. 308, 402, and 502 are the most romantic and have lake views. **Don't Miss** A round of golf on the championship-level course. **Cost** Doubles from $$$. *Newmarket-On-Fergus; 800/346-7007 or 353-61/368-144; www.dromoland.ie*

COUNTY KERRY
■ **Sheen Falls Lodge** (87.62) Waterside property with contemporary interiors and lots of outdoor activities. **Stats** 66 rooms; 3 cottages; 3 restaurants; 1 bar. **Competitive Edge** Set between the Sheen River and Kenmare Bay, it's the perfect gateway to the Ring of Kerry. **Rooms to Book** We like those overlooking Sheen Falls, which are illuminated at night. **Don't Miss** The smoked salmon at Oscar's Bar + Bistro—it comes straight from the lodge's own smokehouse. **Cost** Doubles from $$$. *Kenmare; 353-64/41600; www.sheenfallslodge.ie*

COUNTY MAYO
■ **Ashford Castle** (85.96) Sprawling 13th-century castle with 19th-century additions and baronial interiors, on a point surrounded by rivers on three sides. **Stats** 83 rooms; 2 restaurants; 2 bars. **Competitive Edge** An immense 350-acre estate that delivers all the romance of the Irish countryside. **Rooms to Book** A Standard with a lake view, or splurge on No. 430, in the old part of the castle, with a fireplace and four-poster bed. **Don't Miss** Retiring to the Dungeon Bar after a day of falconry or fishing. **Cost** Doubles from $$$. *Cong; 800/346-7007 or 353-94/954-6003; www.ashford.ie*

italy
AMALFI COAST
■ **Hotel Santa Caterina** (85.09) Cluster of 4 (soon to be 5) Belle Époque–style villas surrounded by Mediterranean gardens,

on a cliff near Amalfi. **Stats** 62 rooms; 2 restaurants; 2 bars. **Competitive Edge** The only luxury hotel in town with direct sea access—two elevators lead to a private beach. **Rooms to Book** Superiors with sea views and balconies (Nos. 21–24 were renovated last year). **Don't Miss** A lemon massage in the welcoming spa. **Cost** Doubles from $$, including breakfast. *Amalfi; 800/223-6800 or 39-089/871-012; www.hotelsantacaterina.it*

AMALFI COAST
■ **Il San Pietro** (88.71) Family-owned hotel just outside of Positano, with gardens and elevators that plunge down a seaside cliff. **Stats** 62 rooms; 1 restaurant; 3 bars. **Competitive Edge** An out-of-town location that delivers serenity and sweeping water views. **Rooms to Book** Deluxes are larger and **Cost** just slightly more. **Don't Miss** The 205-year-old on-site chapel. **Cost** Doubles from $$$, including breakfast. No guests under 10. *Positano; 39-089/875-455; www.ilsanpietro.it*

AMALFI COAST
■ **Le Sirenuse** (89.48) Serene, family-run 18th-century villa on a winding hillside street in the center of Positano. **Stats** 63 rooms; 1 restaurant; 3 bars. **Competitive Edge** One of the coast's most stylish properties, with a spa designed by Milan-based architect Gae Aulenti. **Rooms to Book** All Deluxes have sea views; Suites have vaulted ceilings and terraces. **Don't Miss** Champagne and oysters at the stunning terrace raw bar. **Cost** Doubles from $$$, including breakfast. No guests under 8. *Positano; 800/223-6800 or 39-089/875-066; www.sirenuse.it*

AMALFI COAST
■ **Palazzo Sasso** (89.80) Intimate 12th-century Moorish-style palazzo, set on a 1,000-foot cliff above the Mediterranean, steps from Ravello's main square. **Stats** 43 rooms; 2 restaurants; 1 bar. **Competitive Edge** Extremely attentive, personal service in a romantic location. **Rooms to Book** The 270-square-foot King Doubles on the 1st through 3rd floors have large French windows overlooking the Mediterranean. **Don't Miss** Updated local cuisine at Rossellinis restaurant. **Cost** Doubles from $$$$, including breakfast. *Ravello; 39-089/818-181; www.palazzosasso.com*

ASOLO
■ **Hotel Villa Cipriani** (85.06) Patrician cinquecento-style villa on a hill in the center of Asolo, an hour from Venice. **Stats** 31 rooms; 1 restaurant; 1 bar. **Competitive Edge** One of the few full-service properties in the Venetian hinterland; the hotel is an ideal base for visiting Palladian villas. **Rooms to Book** Nos. 101 and 102 have terraces overlooking the countryside. **Don't Miss** A walk through the hotel garden's pomegranate trees and olive groves. **Cost** Doubles from $, including breakfast. *800/325-3535 or 39-0423/523-411; www.sheraton.com*

CAPRI
■ **Capri Palace Hotel & Spa** (85.28) Whitewashed building with panoramic views of the Bay of Naples, in the quiet village of Anacapri. **Stats** 81 rooms; 2 restaurants; 1 bar. **Competitive Edge** The island's biggest spa and its only Michelin-starred restaurant. **Rooms to Book** For extra privacy, classic and Deluxe Doubles, which have private gardens and pools. **Don't Miss** The renowned anti-aging treatments at the spa. **Cost** Doubles from $$, including breakfast. *800/223-6800 or 39-081/978-0111; www.capripalace.com*

LAKE COMO
■ **Villa d'Este** (86.98) Grand, 25-acre Renaissance estate at Cernobbio on the Lake Como shore. **Stats** 158 rooms; 3 restaurants; 2 bars. **Competitive Edge** A superb lakeside location, stunning gardens, Zen-like spa, and jet-set atmosphere. **Rooms to Book** Most rooms in the smaller Queen's Pavilion are quieter and have lake views. **Don't Miss** A round of golf on the Peter Gannon–designed course, a half-hour away, said to be one of the best in Europe (guests get a discount). **Cost** Doubles from $$$$, including breakfast. *Cernobbio; 800/223-6800 or 39-031/3481; www.villadeste.it*

MILAN
■ **Four Seasons Hotel** (85.81) 15th-century former convent (with a popular, stylish bar scene) in the heart of the city's shopping area. **Stats** 118 rooms; 2 restaurants; 1 bar. **Competitive Edge** Attentive, highly personalized service in a fashionable location. **Rooms to Book** Deluxes on the 2nd and 3rd floors facing the main courtyard; suites 001, 014, and 114 have original frescoes. **Don't Miss** Sitting by the fire watching local fashionistas in Il Foyer lounge. **Cost** Doubles from $$$$. *6/8 Via Gesù; 800/332-3442 or 39-02/77088; www.fourseasons.com*

PORTOFINO
■ **Hotel Splendido** (86.38) 16th-century monastery on a hill above Portofino; Splendido Mare, its modern annex, is located on the main piazza. **Stats** 65 rooms (16 at Splendido Mare); 3 restaurants; 2 bars. **Competitive Edge** The most coveted address on the Italian Riviera, with spectacular views of the Ligurian coastline. **Rooms to Book** Sea Views at Splendido; rooms at Splendido Mare are more affordable. **Don't Miss** Housemade pasta with basil pesto served on the terrace of La Terrazza restaurant. **Cost** Doubles from $$$ (Splendido Mare) and $994 (Splendido). *800/223-6800 or 39-0185/267-801; www.hotelsplendido.com*

VENICE
■ **Bauer Il Palazzo** (89.07) Gothic mansion with its own Grand Canal boat dock, attached to the modern Bauer Hotel. **Stats** 82 rooms; 2 restaurants; 2 bars. **Competitive Edge** A quiet and exclusive hotel in a traditional, historical setting. **Rooms to Book** Palatial Views are larger than most in Venice and have views of the Grand Canal. **Don't Miss** A soak in the rooftop Jacuzzi—Venice's highest. **Cost** Doubles from $$$$. *1413/D San Marco; 800/223-6800 or 39-041/520-7022; www.ilpalazzovenezia.it*

VENICE
■ **Hotel Gritti Palace** (84.36) Late 15th-century Renaissance palace on the Grand Canal. **Stats** 91 rooms; 1 restaurant; 1 bar. **Competitive Edge** An opulent, intimate property that lets you play doge for the day. **Rooms to Book** Any overlooking the Grand Canal; of the rooms without views, those with pastel-colored boiserie walls are best. **Don't Miss** Enlisting a personal shopper for a tour of Venice's best boutiques. **Cost** Doubles from $$$. *2467 Campo Santa Maria del Giglio; 800/325-3589 or 39-041/794-611; www.luxurycollection.com*

monaco

MONTE CARLO
■ **Hôtel de Paris** (89.88) Legendary Beaux Arts landmark with an Alain Ducasse Michelin 3-starred restaurant, in Place du Casino. **Stats** 191 rooms; 3 restaurants; 1 bar. **Competitive Edge** Unparalleled glamour, plus a prime location virtually atop the casino. **Rooms to Book** For a view of both ocean and casino, Nos. 320, 420, or 520. **Don't Miss** A private tasting in the 600,000-bottle wine cellar. **Cost** Doubles from $$$. *Place du Casino; 800/223-6800 or 377/92-16-30-00; www.montecarloresort.com*

portugal

ALGARVE

■ **Hotel Quinta do Lago** (87.50) Family-friendly golf resort set on 1,700 acres in the Ria Formosa Nature Park. **Stats** 141 rooms; 2 restaurants; 2 bars. **Competitive Edge** One of Europe's most activity-filled resorts, in a peaceful setting. **Rooms to Book** Those with lagoon views also look out on the nature park. **Don't Miss** Excellent Portuguese cuisine served alfresco at the Brisa do Mar restaurant. **Cost** Doubles from $$. *Amancil; 800/223-6800 or 351-289/350-350; www.quintadolagohotel.com*

LISBON

■ **Lapa Palace** (86.39) Hilltop hotel, built in 1870 as a private residence, in the embassy district, a short drive from the city center. **Stats** 109 rooms; 2 restaurants; 2 bars. **Competitive Edge** A serene, residential setting, combined with authentic old-world ambience. **Rooms to Book** Garden Wings have balconies; those on the top 3 floors have views of the Tagus River. **Don't Miss** Beef tartare with a glass of Alentejo wine at Rio Tejo Bar. **Cost** Doubles from $$$, including breakfast. *4 Rua Do Pau de Bandeira; 800/237-1236 or 315-21/394-9494; www.lapapalace.com*

OBIDOS

■ **Pousada do Castelo** (85.36) Rustic turreted castle in a medieval walled village 50 miles north of Lisbon. **Stats** 9 rooms; 1 restaurant; 1 bar. **Competitive Edge** The ultimate chance to play king (or queen) for the night in your very own castle. **Rooms to Book** No. 203, a tower room with a king-size bed. **Don't Miss** Shopping for traditional ceramics in the small stores lining the town's cobblestoned streets. **Cost** Doubles from $$. *351-262/955-080; www.pousadasofportugal.com*

scotland

FORT WILLIAM

■ **Inverlochy Castle Hotel** (88.69) Stately Victorian castle with sumptuous interiors and a fantastic restaurant, at the foot of Scotland's highest mountain. **Stats** 17 rooms; 1 restaurant. **Competitive Edge** All the romance of staying among the glens and lochs in a historic Highland castle. **Room to Book** We like No. 23 for its quiet 3rd-floor location. **Don't Miss** Fishing for trout in the hotel's loch—the kitchen will cook your catch. **Cost** Doubles from $$$, including breakfast. *888/424-0106 or 44-1397/702-177; www.inverlochycastlehotel.com*

GLASGOW

■ **One Devonshire Gardens** (84.50) Five interconnected Victorian town houses with an intimate residential feel and a lovely terraced garden, in the West End. **Stats** 35 rooms; 2 restaurants; 1 bar. **Competitive Edge** Exquisite décor that manages to look modern and harmonize with 19th-century architectural details. **Room to Book** No. 2, for its four-poster bed and large windows. **Don't Miss** The monthly Pink Afternoon Tea, which benefits breast cancer research. **Cost** Doubles from $. *1 Devonshire Gardens; 44-141/339-2001; www.onedevonshiregardens.com*

switzerland

INTERLAKEN

■ **Victoria-Jungfrau Grand Hotel & Spa** (87.09) Classic 1864 Victorian resort with an excellent 60,000-square-foot spa, in the center of town below the Jungfrau mountain. **Stats** 222 rooms; 4 restaurants; 2 bars. **Competitive Edge** One of Europe's few true resorts, with hiking, tennis, great dining, and a kids' club, in a beautiful setting. **Rooms to Book** No. 302 has the best view of the Jungfrau; those in the Bel Air wing have a more modern feel. **Don't Miss** Pike fish and other local delicacies in the stylish Jungfrau Brasserie. **Cost** Doubles from $$$. *800/223-6800 or 41-33/828-2828; www.victoria-jungfrau.ch*

LAUSANNE

■ **Beau-Rivage Palace** (87.28) Historic 1861 Belle Époque hotel, on 10 landscaped acres next to Lake Geneva. The $9 million Cinq Mondes spa was added last fall. **Stats** 169 rooms; 2 restaurants; 2 bars. **Competitive Edge** Impeccable service: graduates of the city's famed hotel-management school often work here. **Rooms to Book** Nos. 155, 355, and 455 in the Palace wing have 10-foot ceilings and large lakefront balconies. **Don't Miss** A drink on the terrace at sunset, with spectacular views of the lake. **Cost** Doubles from $$$. *17–19 Place du Port; 800/223-6800 or 41-21/613-3333; www.brp.ch*

LUCERNE

■ **Palace Luzern** (85.48) Turn-of-the-20th-century carved-stone Neoclassical hotel with a grand lobby on the shores of Lake Lucerne, 5 minutes from town. **Stats** 136 rooms; 3 restaurants; 1 bar. **Competitive Edge** Superior lakefront setting that's peaceful yet not far from all the sights. **Rooms to Book** Any of the 40 newly renovated ones with lake views. **Don't Miss** A Time treatment customized to your personal needs, in the new spa. **Cost** Doubles from $$. *10 Haldenstrasse; 800/223-6800 or 41-41/416-1616; www.palace-luzern.com*

MONTREUX

■ **Raffles Le Montreux Palace** (87.13) Art-filled 1906 Belle Époque hotel on the shores of Lake Geneva. **Stats** 235 rooms; 3 restaurants; 2 bars. **Competitive Edge** The 21,500-square-foot spa and wellness center—one of the country's best. **Rooms to Book** No. 65, the Nabokov suite, where the author lived for the last 16 years of his life, has been restored in period style; Nos. 206 and 306 have their own winter gardens; of the more affordable categories, we prefer those overlooking the lake. **Don't Miss** French-Asian cuisine in the Jaan restaurant, recently awarded one Michelin star. **Cost** Doubles from $$. *800/637-9477 or 41-21/962-1212; www.montreux-palace.com*

turkey

ISTANBUL

■ **Çiragan Palace Hotel Kempinski** (89.62) Restored former sultan's palace with a modern annex, on the European shore of the Bosporus. **Stats** 304 rooms; 4 restaurants; 1 bar. **Competitive Edge** A peaceful waterfront location with a park in the rear and fantastic Bosporus views. **Rooms to Book** Sea Views have only partial Bosporus views; it's worth the upgrade to a Deluxe for straight-on vistas. For a more historic feel, book a suite in the original palace. **Don't Miss** An authentic Turkish bath at the mosaic-filled Ottoman-era hammam. **Cost** Doubles from $$. *32 Çiragan Caddesi; 800/426-3135 or 90-212/326-4646; www.ciraganpalace.com*

ISTANBUL

■ **Four Seasons Hotel** (91.74) Neoclassical former prison with Turkish-inspired interiors and a beautiful 4th-floor terrace, next to Hagia Sophia and the Topkapi Palace. **Stats** 65 rooms; 1 restaurant; 1 bar. **Competitive Edge** An unbeatable Old City location within walking distance of major sights, combined with Istanbul's most polished service. **Rooms to Book** Request one with a partial Blue Mosque view or upgrade to one of the 4th-floor Deluxes with a view from a private terrace. **Don't Miss** Lunch in the pretty garden courtyard at Seasons restaurant. **Cost** Doubles from $$. *1 Tevkifhane Sokak; 800/332-3442 or 90-212/638-8200; www.fourseasons.com*

world's best top 25
africa and the middle east

egypt

CAIRO

■ **Four Seasons Hotel at Nile Plaza** (86.09) 30-story hotel near Garden City on the east bank of the river. **Stats** 365 rooms; 5 restaurants; 2 bars. **Competitive Edge** An ideal urban location in the diplomatic and business district. **Rooms to Book** Any with a terrace overlooking the Nile. **Don't Miss** A swim in the hotel's 5th-floor pool. **Cost** Doubles from $$. *1089 Corniche el Nile; 800/332-3442 or 20-2/791-7000; www.fourseasons.com*

CAIRO

■ **Mena House Oberoi** (81.19) 1869 royal hunting lodge beside the Pyramids of Giza. **Stats** 523 rooms; 5 restaurants; 2 bars. **Competitive Edge** A jaw-dropping setting: the Sphinx is right next to the hotel's golf course. **Rooms to Book** It's worth the $110 extra for a balcony overlooking the Pyramids. **Don't Miss** The excellent Indian cuisine at the Moghul Room. **Cost** Doubles from $. *6 Pyramids Rd., Giza; 800/562-3764 or 20-2/377-3222; www.oberoihotels.com*

kenya

MASAI MARA

■ **Kichwa Tembo** (90.81) Luxe tented retreat with 2 stand-alone camps, both well-sited for watching the annual migration (June–October). **Stats** 49 tents; 2 restaurants; 2 bars. **Competitive Edge** A quiet location in the heart of one of Africa's most gorgeous landscapes. **Room to Book** Bateleur's No. 9, for great views of the plains. **Don't Miss** Cocktails on the Oloololo Escarpment. **Cost** Doubles from $$$, including meals. *888/882-3742 or 27-11/809-4300; www.ccafrica.com*

MASAI MARA

■ **Mara Serena Safari Lodge** (82.82) Domed huts modeled after a traditional Masai village, overlooking a migratory path. **Stats** 74 rooms; 1 restaurant; 1 bar. **Competitive Edge** A classic safari experience at an affordable price. **Room to Book** The suite facing the Masai Mara triangle has the best views. **Don't Miss** Seeing the Mara River hippo pools from a hot-air balloon. **Cost** Doubles from $$, including meals. *254-50/22253; www.serenahotels.com*

NANYUKI

■ **Mount Kenya Safari Club** (88.23) Country club–style resort with outlying cottages on 100 acres in the lower slopes of Mount Kenya. An extensive, modernizing room renovation is beginning this spring. **Stats** 116 rooms; 1 restaurant; 2 bars. **Competitive Edge** Clubby, genteel ambience in the African countryside. **Rooms to Book** Upgrade to a suite with a veranda. **Don't Miss** A trip to the on-site animal orphanage. **Cost** Doubles from $$, including meals. *800/845-3692 or 254-20/216-940; www.lonrhohotels.com*

SAMBURU GAME RESERVE

■ **Samburu Serena Safari Lodge** (81.56) Low-slung cottages amid a riverside forest on the banks of the Usao Nyiro. **Stats** 62 rooms; 1 restaurant; 1 bar. **Competitive Edge** A particularly lush setting on the fringes of Kenya's dry northern region. **Rooms to Book** Those farthest from the pool are the quietest. **Don't Miss** Watching the nightly crocodile feeding. **Cost** Doubles from $$, including meals. *254-64/30800; www.serenahotels.com*

SWEETWATERS GAME RESERVE

■ **Sweetwaters Tented Camp** (83.85) Cluster of thatched-roof tents in the heart of Big Five territory; home to the rare black rhino. **Stats** 30 tents; 2 restaurants; 2 bars. **Competitive Edge** A storybook setting, but easy to reach (just 2 1/2 hours by car from Nairobi). **Rooms to Book** Those in the first row have direct watering-hole views. **Don't Miss** Visiting the reserve's Chimpanzee Sanctuary, the only one in Kenya. **Cost** Doubles from $$, including meals. *254-62/31970; www.serenahotels.com*

morocco

FEZ

■ **Sofitel Palais Jamaï** (80.69) 19th-century palace with modern addition in the heart of the city. **Stats** 149 rooms; 3 restaurants; 1 bar. **Competitive Edge** Sits right above the ancient medina—a UNESCO World Heritage Site. **Rooms to Book** Those overlooking the medina. **Don't Miss** A thalasso treatment at the new spa. **Cost** Doubles from $$. *Bab Guissa; 800/763-4835 or 212-55/634-331; www.sofitel.com*

MARRAKESH

■ **La Mamounia** (80.87) Opulent 80-year-old palace with 18th-century gardens. Closing from May to December for a head-to-toe redesign. **Stats** 231 rooms; 5 restaurants; 5 bars. **Competitive Edge** A romantic ambience throughout. **Rooms to Book** Those facing the Koutoubia Mosque. **Don't Miss** Browsing the on-site boutiques. **Cost** Doubles from $$. *Ave. Bab Jdid; 800/223-6800 or 212-44/444-409; www.mamounia.com*

south africa

CAPE TOWN

■ **Cape Grace** (90.00) Distinguished hotel on its own quay at the Victoria & Alfred Waterfront. **Stats** 122 rooms; 1 restaurant; 1 bar. **Competitive Edge** A successful marriage of old (traditional décor) and new (innovative restaurant and spa). **Rooms to Book** Even-numbered rooms, for Table Mountain views. **Don't Miss** A 4-handed Thaba massage at the superb spa. **Cost** Doubles from $$$, including breakfast. *West Quay Rd.; 800/223-6800 or 27-21/410-7100; www.capegrace.com*

CAPE TOWN

■ **Mount Nelson Hotel** (83.40) Buttoned-up Victorian property in a quiet residential neighborhood. **Stats** 201 rooms; 2 restaurants; 1 bar. **Competitive Edge** One of the city's most historic properties, with lots of atmosphere. **Rooms to Book** The renovated Superiors that overlook the pool from the Oasis Wing. **Don't Miss** A glass of wine at Planet, the hotel's stylish bar. **Cost** Doubles from $$$$. *76 Orange St.; 800/223-6800 or 27-21/483-1000; www.mountnelson.co.za*

CAPE TOWN

■ **Table Bay Hotel** (87.29) Modern building with Victorian-style façade on the Victoria & Alfred Waterfront. **Stats** 329 rooms; 2 restaurants; 2 bars. **Competitive Edge** A harbor-front location linked to the main quay and the city's best shops, at the waterfront mall. **Rooms to Book** Those on the top floor have great views of Table Mountain. **Don't Miss** A harborside dinner at the Atlantic Restaurant. **Cost** Doubles from $$$. *Victoria & Alfred Waterfront; 800/223-6800 or 27-21/406-5000; www.suninternational.com*

JOHANNESBURG
■ **Park Hyatt** (80.65) Modern 9-story hotel connected to the Firs Shopping Centre in Rosebank. **Stats** 244 rooms; 1 restaurant; 1 bar. **Competitive Edge** Great amenities for business travelers, and a lovely neighborhood setting. **Rooms to Book** Regency Clubs, for free cocktails in the lounge. **Don't Miss** A swim in the rooftop pool at the Peak Health Club. **Cost** Doubles from $. *191 Oxford Rd.; 800/233-1234 or 27-11/280-1234; www.park.hyatt.com*

JOHANNESBURG
■ **Westcliff Hotel** (83.33) Mediterranean-style villas above the Zoological Gardens in the Westcliff suburb. **Stats** 115 rooms; 2 restaurants; 1 bar. **Competitive Edge** Glamorous outdoor spaces, including an infinity pool overlooking the zoo. **Room to Book** Of the entry-level rooms, No. 405 has a balcony and a skylight. **Don't Miss** A cocktail among the city's elite at the Polo Lounge. **Cost** Doubles from $$. *67 Jan Smuts Ave.; 800/223-6800 or 27-11/481-6000; www.westcliff.co.za*

KRUGER NATIONAL PARK AREA
■ **Londolozi Private Game Reserve** (86.34) Exclusive camp of thatched-roof chalets and bush suites, in the Sabi Sand Game Reserve bordering Kruger. **Stats** 36 rooms; 6 restaurants; 5 bars. **Competitive Edge** A model safari camp, both for its game viewing and its wildlife conservation. **Rooms to Book** The Bateleur Camp suites along the Sand River. **Don't Miss** A visit to the nearby staff village to find out what it's like to live in the bush. **Cost** Doubles from $$$$$, including meals and drinks. *888/882-3742 or 27-11/809-4300; www.ccafrica.com*

KRUGER NATIONAL PARK AREA
■ **MalaMala Game Reserve** (87.86) Trio of renowned camps (the residential-style Rattray's opened last fall) overlooking the Sand River. **Stats** 33 rooms; 3 restaurants; 3 bars. **Competitive Edge** Some of the best guides in the business. **Rooms to Book** Nos. 1–4 at MalaMala have prime river views. **Don't Miss** Spotting nocturnal wildlife on a nighttime "spotlight" safari. **Cost** Doubles from $$$$$, including meals. *27-11/442-2267; www.malamala.com*

KRUGER NATIONAL PARK AREA
■ **Sabi Sabi Private Game Reserve** (89.41) Three diverse lodges next to Kruger. The 6-room Little Bush Camp opens in March. **Stats** 46 rooms; 3 restaurants; 3 bars. **Competitive Edge** A classic bush experience with a lodge to suit any mood. **Rooms to Book** Those at the dramatic and natural Earth Lodge. **Don't Miss** Sampling South African wines from the underground cellar. **Cost** Doubles from $$$$$, including meals and drinks. *27-11/483-3939; www. sabisabi.com*

KRUGER NATIONAL PARK AREA
■ **Singita** (94.57) Quartet of chic lodges (expanding this year), ranging in style from mod-colonial to ultramodern. **Stats** 39 rooms; 4 restaurants; 4 bars. **Competitive Edge** Hollywood in the bush: modern architecture, top-notch service, and luxe amenities. **Rooms to Book** Those in the intimate and secluded riverside Sweni Lodge. **Don't Miss** Picking up the best South African vintages at Lebombo's wine boutique. **Cost** Doubles from $2,170, including meals and drinks. *27-21/683-3424; www.singita.com*

SUN CITY
■ **Palace of the Lost City** (81.41) The top hotel in the mammoth Sun City resort. **Stats** 338 rooms; 2 restaurants; 1 bar. **Competitive Edge** It's Vegas in the bush—plus safaris. **Rooms to Book** Ground-floor rooms, for garden access. **Don't Miss** A dinner of fresh game (springbok or ostrich) at Crystal Court restaurant. **Cost** Doubles from $$$. *800/223-6800 or 27-14/557-1000; www.suninternational.com*

tanzania

NGORONGORO CRATER
■ **Ngorongoro Crater Lodge** (86.95) Magnificently designed stilted huts beside the 3 million–year-old crater. **Stats** 30 suites; 3 restaurants; 3 bars. **Competitive Edge** Unique architecture and over-the-top interiors in an awe-inspiring setting. **Room to Book** No. 22 is the highest stilted room and has the most dramatic view of the crater. **Don't Miss** A gourmet picnic on the crater floor. **Cost** Doubles from $$$, including meals and drinks. *888/882-3742 or 27-11/809-4300; www.ccafrica.com*

NGORONGORO CRATER
■ **Ngorongoro Serena Safari Lodge** (83.33) Masai-inspired lodge on the crater's edge. **Stats** 76 rooms; 1 restaurant; 1 bar. **Competitive Edge** The skilled service of safari experts in an unparalleled location. **Rooms to Book** Those on the top floors, for the best views. **Don't Miss** A guided visit to a traditional Masai cattle market. **Cost** Doubles from $$, including meals. *255-272/537-052; www.serenahotels.com*

NGORONGORO CRATER
■ **Ngorongoro Sopa Lodge** (85.00) Thatched-roof suites overlooking the crater. **Stats** 96 suites; 1 restaurant; 2 bars. **Competitive Edge** A comfortable and affordable way to see the crater. **Room to Book** The suite closest to the main building is the most convenient. **Don't Miss** Evening cocktails on the terrace. **Cost** Doubles from $$, including meals. *800/806-9565 or 255-272/500-630; www.sopalodges.com*

SERENGETI NATIONAL PARK
■ **Serengeti Sopa Lodge** (84.23) Secluded lodge with verandas overlooking acacia woodlands and the plain. **Stats** 78 suites; 1 restaurant; 2 bars. **Competitive Edge** Well situated for animal sightings, with year-round water holes. **Rooms to Book** Any of the recently renovated ones. **Don't Miss** Checking out locally made jewelry at the on-site boutique. **Cost** Doubles from $$, including meals. *800/806-9565 or 255-272/500-630; www.sopalodges.com*

united arab emirates

DUBAI
■ **Jumeirah Beach Hotel** (83.13) Wave-shaped property on the Persian Gulf, near the city's financial center. **Stats** 618 rooms; 16 restaurants; 5 bars. **Competitive Edge** All the facilities of a complete beach resort, in a convenient location. **Rooms to Book** Those with views of the Burj al Arab tower. **Don't Miss** The nearby Wild Wadi water park—guests have unlimited access to it. **Cost** Doubles from $$$. *971-4/348-0000; www.jumeirah.com*

zambia

LIVINGSTONE
■ **Royal Livingstone** (85.00) Modern colonial-style buildings on the banks of the Zambezi River. **Stats** 173 rooms; 2 restaurants; 1 bar. **Competitive Edge** An outstanding location on the lip of Victoria Falls. **Rooms to Book** Well-priced standards have the same views as suites. **Don't Miss** Ukuchina, a traditional Zambian massage, at the riverside cabana. **Cost** Doubles from $$$, including breakfast. *800/223-6800 or 260-3/321-122; www.suninternational.com*

world's best top 25 asia

cambodia

SIEM REAP

■ **Raffles Grand Hotel d'Angkor** (86.20)
1932 landmark, artfully restored
and expanded, with formal gardens
near Angkor Wat. **Stats** 131 rooms;
3 restaurants; 2 bars. **Competitive
Edge** Historical ambience in a
tradition-rich location. **Rooms to Book**
Those in the original building, which
have four-poster beds. **Don't Miss**
Traditional Cambodian cuisine at
Restaurant Le Grand. **Cost** Doubles
from $$. *800/637-9477 or 855-63/963-888;
www.raffles.com*

china

BEIJING

■ **St. Regis** (85.97) Modern tower with
residential décor; convenient to the
Jian Guo Men Wai business district. **Stats**
273 rooms; 5 restaurants; 4 bars.
Competitive Edge The most personalized
service in the city, with butlers on
every floor. **Rooms to Book** Those facing
east overlook the diplomatic gardens.
Don't Miss A natural hot-springs
bath in the 16,000-square-foot spa. **Cost**
Doubles from $$. *21 Jian Guo Men
Wai Rd.; 877/787-3447 or 86-10/6460-6688;
www.stregis.com*

HONG KONG

■ **Peninsula Hong Kong** (89.84)
77-year-old grande dame with a modern
30-floor tower facing the harbor in
Kowloon. **Stats** 300 rooms; 7 restaurants;
1 bar. **Competitive Edge** A balance
of old-world style (vintage Rolls-Royce
fleet) and modern energy (the Felix
restaurant, designed by Philippe Starck).
Rooms to Book Those ending in -11
and -12 in the original building are
plush yet affordable. **Don't Miss** The
36,000-square-foot spa, set to open early
this year. **Cost** Doubles from $$.
*Salisbury Rd.; 800/223-6800 or 852/2920
2888; www.peninsula.com*

india

AGRA

■ **Oberoi Amarvilas** (90.11)
Serene Moghul palace–style hotel with
colonnaded pools and elaborate
gardens, facing the Taj Mahal. **Stats** 102
rooms; 2 restaurants; 1 bar. **Competitive
Edge** Views from every room (and most
public spaces) of one of the world's
greatest monuments. **Rooms to Book**
Higher-floor Deluxes with terraces. **Don't
Miss** Ayurvedic therapies by Banyan
Tree at the top-notch spa. **Cost** Doubles
from $$$. *800/562-3764 or 91-562/233-1515;
www.oberoihotels.com*

JAIPUR

■ **Oberoi Rajvilas** (94.00) Standard-setting
property (arches, courtyards, pools) on
32 manicured acres just outside the city.
Stats 71 rooms; 1 restaurant; 1 bar.
Competitive Edge Lavish architecture
and pampering service let you live out
a maharaja fantasy. **Rooms to Book**
Luxury Tents, with Burmese teak floors,
Edwardian claw-footed bathtubs,
and embroidered canopies. **Don't Miss**
A private session with the on-site yogi.
Cost Doubles from $$$. *800/562-3764 or
91-141/268-0101; www.oberoihotels.com*

indonesia

BALI

■ **Amandari** (91.02) Balinese-style village
along the Ayung River near Ubud. **Stats**
31 suites; 1 restaurant; 1 bar. **Competitive
Edge** Pitch-perfect design, from the stone
walls and teak pavilions to the Javanese
marble floors. **Rooms to Book** Valley
Suites have outdoor sunken bath tubs
and overlook rice paddies. **Don't Miss**
Traditional Balinese dance lessons,
arranged by the cultural concierge. **Cost**
Doubles from $$$. *Ubud; 800/477-9180 or
62-361/975-333; www.amanresorts.com*

BALI

■ **Amankila** (90.44) Collection of alang-
alang–roofed villas in the verdant hills of
East Bali, near Lombok Strait. **Stats** 34
suites; 3 restaurants; 1 bar. **Competitive
Edge** A peaceful location, away from
other resorts and above a small (but nice)
beach. **Rooms to Book** For a sybaritic
stay, a Pool Suite with a private, stone-
walled plunge pool. **Don't Miss** Guided
tours of the nearby palaces. **Cost** Doubles
from $$$. *Manggis; 800/477-9180 or
62-363/41333 www.amanresorts.com*

BALI

■ **Four Seasons Resort at Jimbaran Bay**
(91.85) Thatched-roof villas with private
plunge pools on 35 acres above a lovely
southern beach. **Stats** 147 villas; 4
restaurants; 2 bars. **Competitive Edge**
The atmosphere of a tranquil, intimate
property, with the more extensive
amenities of a larger resort. **Rooms to
Book** Villas 101–109 are closest to the
beach. **Don't Miss** Traditional Indonesian
cooking classes at the on-site school.
Cost Doubles from $$$. *800/332-3442 or
62-361/701-010; www.fourseasons.com*

BALI

■ **Four Seasons Resort at Sayan** (95.00)
Authentic thatched villas with modern
indoor-outdoor interiors and lotus
pools, in the breathtaking Ayung River
Valley. **Stats** 60 suites; 2 restaurants; 1
bar. **Competitive Edge** The private jungle
setting and stunning contemporary
architecture make for pure romance.
Rooms to Book Elevated Riverfront Villas
are especially serene. **Don't Miss**
Sunset yoga with panoramic views
beside the rooftop lily pool. **Cost** Doubles
from $$. *Ubud; 800/332-3442 or 62-
361/977-577; www.fourseasons.com*

BALI

■ **Ritz-Carlton Bali Resort & Spa** (88.03)
Cliffside resort with a private Jimbaran
jetty. **Stats** 374 rooms; 9 restaurants; 3
bars. **Competitive Edge** Ritz-Carlton
luxury at an unbeatable price. **Rooms
to Book** Club rooms (an extra $80) for
great views and free snacks and drinks.
Don't Miss 180-degree ocean views
at the sleek Martini Club. **Cost** Doubles
from $$. *Jimbaran; 800/241-3333 or
62-361/702-222; www.ritzcarlton.com*

japan

OSAKA

■ **Ritz-Carlton** (86.25) Quiet high-rise
hotel with European-style interiors in
the Nishi-Imeda district. **Stats** 292 rooms;
4 restaurants; 2 bars. **Competitive
Edge** Unparalleled views of Osaka Bay
and the mountains. **Rooms to Book**
Japanese Suites with tatami mats and
shoji screens. **Don't Miss** The tea
sommelier at Xiang Tao restaurant.
Cost Doubles from $$. *2-5-25 Umeda,
Kita-Ku; 800/241-3333 or 81-6/6343-7000;
www.ritzcarlton.com*

TOKYO

■ **Park Hyatt** (85.94) Urbane property on
the top 14 floors of a Kenzo Tange–
designed Shinjuku tower. **Stats** 177
rooms; 3 restaurants; 2 bars. **Competitive
Edge** Super-attentive service in a
superbly designed space. **Rooms to Book**
A corner Park View overlooking Mount
Fuji. **Don't Miss** A see-and-be-seen

268

dinner at the New York Grill. **Cost** Doubles from $$$. *3-7-1-2 Nishi-Shinjuku; 800/223-1234 or 81-3/5322-1234; www.park.hyatt.com*

singapore

SINGAPORE

■ **Four Seasons Hotel** (88.89) 20-story tower surrounded by gardens, near shopping on Orchard Road. **Stats** 254 rooms; 2 restaurants; 1 bar. **Competitive Edge** A private, residential-style setting, just minutes from the city center. **Rooms to Book** Corner Premiers, which have bay windows and Orchard Road views. **Don't Miss** Creative dim sum at Jiang Nan Chun. **Cost** Doubles from $$. *190 Orchard Blvd.; 800/332-3442 or 65/6734-1110; www.fourseasons.com*

SINGAPORE

■ **Raffles Hotel** (86.92) 1887 colonial-style hotel with English-inspired gardens, in the business district. **Stats** 103 rooms; 13 restaurants; 5 bars. **Competitive Edge** As city's most historic and iconic hotel, it delivers unparalleled atmosphere; it even has its own museum. **Rooms to Book** Any away from the busy shopping arcade. **Don't Miss** Afternoon tea among an A-list crowd. **Cost** Doubles from $$. *1 Beach Rd.; 800/637-9477 or 65/6337-1886; www.raffles.com*

SINGAPORE

■ **Ritz-Carlton Millenia** (87.90) 32-story sleek tower with a spectacular art collection, in Marina Centre. **Stats** 608 rooms; 3 restaurants; 1 bar. **Competitive Edge** A great location and the largest standard rooms among the city's top hotels. **Rooms to Book** For great views, premier suites overlooking Marina Bay and CBD skyscrapers. **Don't Miss** The hotel's superb 4,200-piece art collection. **Cost** Doubles from $$. *7 Raffles Ave.; 800/241-3333 or 65/6337-8888; www.ritzcarlton.com*

thailand

BANGKOK

■ **Four Seasons Hotel** (87.30) Understated low-rise (the former Regent) with tropical gardens and a large, lovely pool. **Stats** 340 rooms; 6 restaurants; 2 bars. **Competitive Edge** A hub for Thai high society, thanks to the buzzing restaurants Biscotti and Shintori. **Rooms to Book** The private cabana rooms with gardens and skylit bathrooms are worth the upgrade. **Don't Miss** Watching the tai chi practitioners in Lumpini Park nearby. **Cost** Doubles from $$. *155 Rajadamri Rd.; 800/332-3442 or 66-2/250-1000; www.fourseasons.com*

BANGKOK

■ **Oriental Bangkok** (91.71) Legendary 130-year-old property on the banks of the Chao Phraya. **Stats** 393 rooms; 9 restaurants; 2 bars. **Competitive Edge** With doting service and one of the world's best spas, it's a destination in itself. **Rooms to Book** Split-level Garden rooms in the historic Old Wing are recently renovated. **Don't Miss** A Thai massage at the Oriental Spa, across the river. **Cost** Doubles from $$. *48 Oriental Ave.; 800/526-6566 or 66-2/659-9000; www.mandarinoriental.com*

BANGKOK

■ **Peninsula Bangkok** (92.10) 39-floor tower with serene Asian-influenced interiors on the quiet Thonburi side of the Chao Phraya River. **Stats** 370 rooms; 5 restaurants; 1 bar. **Competitive Edge** A fusion of old-world service with information-age technology. **Rooms to Book** Those ending in -08 and -12 overlook some of the city's oldest Buddhist temples. **Don't Miss** A private canal tour arranged by the concierge. **Cost** Doubles from $$. *333 Charoen Nakorn Rd.; 800/223-6800 or 66-2/861-2888; www.peninsula.com*

BANGKOK

■ **Shangri-La Hotel** (86.58) Two-tower riverside complex with palm-fringed terraces and fine gardens. **Stats** 799 rooms; 8 restaurants; 1 bar. **Competitive Edge** Light-filled public spaces make for a relaxed beach-resort-in-the-city feel. **Rooms to Book** Those ending in -25 on the high floors have balconies and river views. **Don't Miss** A holistic treatment at the 2-year-old Tibetan-influenced Chi Spa. **Cost** Doubles from $$. *Charoen Krung Rd.; 800/942-5050 or 66-2/236-7777; www.shangri-la.com*

BANGKOK

■ **Sukhothai** (88.48) Cluster of low-rises surrounded by gardens and lotus pools, in the business district. **Stats** 210 rooms; 3 restaurants; 1 bar. **Competitive Edge** Ed Tuttle's renowned design combined with superb service. **Rooms to Book** Large Garden Suites with lily-pond views. **Don't Miss** Cocktails in the newly refurbished Zuk Bar. **Cost** Doubles from $$. *13/3 S. Sathorn Rd.; 800/223-6800 or 66-2/344-8888; www.sukhothai.com*

CHIANG MAI

■ **Four Seasons Resort** (92.84) Thai pavilions and a great spa surrounded by rice paddies and tropical gardens, in the Mae Rim Valley. **Stats** 80 rooms; 2 restaurants; 2 bars. **Competitive Edge**

World-class design delivers an authentic Siamese up-country atmosphere. **Rooms to Book** Upper-level Pavilions, with decks and views of rice paddies. **Don't Miss** An elephant trek in the jungle. **Cost** Doubles from $$. *800/332-3442 or 66-53/298-181; www.fourseasons.com*

PHUKET

■ **Amanpuri** (87.26) Former coconut plantation with teak pavilions on 77 acres of jungle headlands above a secluded beach. **Stats** 40 rooms; 30 villas; 3 restaurants; 1 bar. **Competitive Edge** The original Aman resort is still a standard-setter for luxe minimalism and pampering service. **Rooms to Book** Nos. 103 and 105 have dramatic views. **Don't Miss** The spa treatment rooms with steam showers and patios. **Cost** Doubles from $$$. *800/477-9180 or 66-76/324-333; www.amanresorts.com*

PHUKET

■ **Banyan Tree** (89.00) Cluster of Asian-style villas, each with a private garden, among the lagoons on Bang Tao Bay. **Stats** 115 villas; 4 restaurants; 1 bar. **Competitive Edge** The romance of a small resort, combined with large-scale amenities and programs. **Rooms to Book** Splurge on an extra-large Spa Pool Villa with a private plunge pool. **Don't Miss** An Andaman Sea sunset cruise on the resort's long-tail boat. **Cost** Doubles from $$$. *800/745-8883 or 66-76/324-374; www.banyantree.com*

PHUKET

■ **JW Marriott Resort & Spa** (88.50) Low-rise resort with 27 acres of tropical gardens. **Stats** 265 rooms; 5 restaurants; 3 bars. **Competitive Edge** Set on Mai Khao Beach—the quietest stretch of sand on the island. **Rooms to Book** Standards on the ground floor have private garden terraces. **Don't Miss** The resort's weekly batik-making class. **Cost** Doubles from $$$. *800/228-9290 or 66-76/338-000; www.marriott.com*

vietnam

NHA TRANG

■ **Ana Mandara Resort** (86.09) Relaxed traditional Vietnamese-style property on a southern coast beach. **Stats** 74 rooms; 2 restaurants; 2 bars. **Competitive Edge** Down-to-earth stylishness, combined with a terrific spa and a great price. **Rooms to Book** A tranquil Deluxe Seaview room with direct beach access. **Don't Miss** Renting a mountain bike for a countryside tour. **Cost** Doubles from $. *84-58/522-222; www.sixsenses.com*

australia

BLUE MOUNTAINS

■ **Lilianfels Blue Mountains Resort & Spa** (79.84) Clifftop hotel, with an excellent restaurant, a 90-minute drive from Sydney. **Stats** 89 rooms; 2 restaurants; 1 bar. **Competitive Edge** The most luxurious property in Australia's Blue Mountains, a World Heritage Site. **Rooms to Book** Nos. 227 and 228 have large windows on two sides and spectacular views of the Jamison Valley. **Don't Miss** Exploring the area's Aboriginal sites with an in-house guide. **Cost** Doubles from $$. *Katoomba; 800/237-1236 or 61-2/4780-1200; www.lilianfels.com.au*

CAIRNS

■ **Kewarra Beach Resort** (82.58) Laid-back property with bungalows set between the rain forest and beach. **Stats** 75 rooms; 1 restaurant; 1 bar. **Competitive Edge** An intimate, authentically tropical resort that won't break the bank. **Rooms to Book** Those in the Pipi Moud bungalows, set on the beach. **Don't Miss** A nature walk and bird-watching tour led by the resort's gardener. **Cost** Doubles from $. *61-7/4057-6666; www.kewarra.com*

GREAT BARRIER REEF

■ **Hayman Island** (83.71) Refined private-island resort with beautiful pools, on a picture-perfect Coral Sea beach. **Stats** 244 rooms; 4 restaurants; 3 bars. **Competitive Edge** An extensive activities program, including trips to the reef. **Rooms to Book** Lagoon Rooms on levels 3 and 4 have great views of Hook Island. **Don't Miss** A Guerlain facial at the brand-new Spa Chakra. **Cost** Doubles from $$$. *800/223-6800 or 61-2/9268-1888; www.hayman.com.au*

GREAT BARRIER REEF

■ **Lizard Island** (91.82) Exclusive private-island retreat of colorful clapboard buildings with modern interiors on 400 acres of national park. **Stats** 40 rooms; 1 restaurant; 1 bar. **Competitive Edge** Urbane, romantic setting with great snorkeling and diving. **Rooms to Book** Villas on Sunset Point for tranquillity and Coral Sea views. **Don't Miss** A guided nature walk. **Cost** Doubles from $$$$$, including meals and most activities. *800/225-9849 or 61-2/8296-8010; www.lizardisland.com.au*

GREAT BARRIER REEF

■ **Sebel Reef House & Spa** (77.32) Intimate colonial-style hotel surrounded by lush grounds, in an oceanside village 20 minutes from Cairns. **Stats** 69 rooms; 2 restaurants; 2 bars. **Competitive Edge** A sophisticated property with a low-key ambience to match its beach setting. **Rooms to Book** The new Brigadier Beachfront Spa Rooms—worth the $80 premium for extra-large baths and ocean views from every window. **Don't Miss** A glass of the hotel's signature sangria during the candlelit cocktail hour. **Cost** Doubles from $$. *Palm Cove; 61-7/4055-3633; www.reefhouse.com.au*

MELBOURNE

■ **Crown Towers** (82.04) Contemporary high-rise on the banks of the Yarra River. **Stats** 482 rooms; 5 restaurants; 1 bar. **Competitive Edge** Attached to the massive Crown Entertainment complex (casino, cinema, 40-plus restaurants and bars). **Rooms to Book** Crystal Clubs, for access to the 24-hour lounge. **Don't Miss** The skyline views from the rooftop garden. **Cost** Doubles from $$. *8 Whitman St.; 61-3/9292-6868; www.crowntowers.com.au*

MELBOURNE

■ **Grand Hyatt** (77.13) Curving 33-story tower with Art Deco–inspired interiors, steps from downtown businesses and shopping. **Stats** 548 rooms; 1 restaurant; 2 bars. **Competitive Edge** One of the city's first luxury hotels is still one of its finest—and in an exceptionally convenient location. **Rooms to Book** Those ending in -07 above the 25th floor, for 180-degree views of the Yarra River. **Don't Miss** Cocktails in clubby Bar Deco. **Cost** Doubles from $$. *123 Collins St.; 800/233-1234 or 61-3/9657-1234; www.grand.hyatt.com*

MELBOURNE

■ **Langham Hotel** (82.84) 24-story hotel (formerly Sheraton Towers Southgate) on the south bank of the river. **Stats** 387 rooms; 1 restaurant; 1 bar. **Competitive Edge** Dramatic views throughout, combined with the excellent Chuan Spa. **Rooms to Book** Corner Deluxes, which have sweeping river views. **Don't Miss** The 9th-floor infinity-edge whirlpool. **Cost** Doubles from $$. *1 Southgate Ave., Southbank; 61-3/8696-8888; www.langhamhotels.com*

MELBOURNE

■ **Park Hyatt** (83.95) Discreet low-rise hotel with marble lobby, next to the Fitzroy Gardens downtown. **Stats** 240 rooms; 2 restaurants; 1 bar. **Competitive Edge** The most stylish and residential-feeling of the city's top hotels. **Rooms to Book** Those in the new wing. **Don't Miss** Checking out the multi-story Radii restaurant, for eclectic design and innovative cuisine. **Cost** Doubles from $$$. *1 Parliament Square; 800/233-1234 or 61-3/9224-1234; www.park.hyatt.com*

MELBOURNE

■ **Sofitel** (79.39) Residential-style property occupying floors 35–50 of a downtown tower above the Collins Place mall. **Stats** 363 rooms; 1 restaurant; 3 bars. **Competitive Edge** Melbourne's tallest hotel delivers fabulous views from every room. **Rooms to Book** Those on the south side for a sweeping panorama to Port Phillip Bay. **Don't Miss** The curated contemporary art exhibitions in the hotel's public spaces. **Cost** Doubles from $$$. *25 Collins Street; 800/763-4835 or 61-3/9653-0000; www.sofitel.com*

SYDNEY

■ **Crowne Plaza Darling Harbour** (77.86) 10-story hotel with simple, contemporary décor, a quick walk from the convention center and the heart of the business district. **Stats** 345 rooms; 1 restaurant; 2 bars. **Competitive Edge** A great location for business travelers and families (near the aquarium, IMAX, and museums). **Rooms to Book** Splurge for the Club Floor (an extra $55), for express check-in and access to the lounge. **Don't Miss** Checking out the restaurants, cafés, and bars at nearby Cockle Bay Wharf. **Cost** Doubles from $. *150 Day St.; 800/327-0200 or 61-2/9261-1188; www.crowneplaza.com*

SYDNEY

■ **Four Seasons Hotel** (86.28) 34-story building in the Rocks district, overlooking the harbor and the opera house. **Stats** 531 rooms; 2 restaurants; 1 bar. **Competitive Edge** All-around polish, from the business amenities to the excellent spa. **Rooms to Book** Harbor-facing rooms above the 20th floor, for the best views. **Don't Miss** A poolside lunch at the Cabana restaurant.

Cost Doubles from $$. *199 George St.; 800/332-3442 or 61-2/9238-0000; www. fourseasons.com*

SYDNEY
■ The InterContinental (80.95)
Neoclassical former Treasury Building near the Circular Quay. **Stats** 509 rooms; 3 restaurants; 2 bars. **Competitive Edge** A location between the business district and the botanical gardens. **Rooms to Book** Club rooms, for personal concierge service. **Don't Miss** Afternoon tea in the Cortile. **Cost** Doubles from $$. *Bridge and Phillip Sts.; 800/327-0200 or 61-2/9253-9000; www.intercontinental.com*

SYDNEY
■ Observatory Hotel (84.41)
Sophisticated hotel with personalized service on a quiet backstreet near the Circular Quay. **Stats** 100 rooms; 1 restaurant; 1 bar. **Competitive Edge** An intimate, residential feel throughout. **Rooms to Book** Those with Walsh Bay views. **Don't Miss** The indoor pool, with a ceiling painted to look like the night sky. **Cost** Doubles from $$$. *89–113 Kent St.; 800/745-8883 or 61-2/9256-2222; www. observatoryhotel.com.au*

SYDNEY
■ Park Hyatt (83.41)
Refined, art-filled low-rise on its own harbor jetty in the Rocks district. **Stats** 158 rooms; 1 restaurant; 2 bars. **Competitive Edge** Superb, modern style meets excellent service. **Rooms to Book** Any of the 3rd-floor Opera Views. **Don't Miss** Sunset cocktails beside the rooftop pool. **Cost** Doubles from $$$. *7 Hickson Rd.; 800/233-1234 or 61-2/9241-1234; www.park.hyatt.com*

SYDNEY
■ Sheraton on the Park Hotel (79.91)
22-story sandstone tower on Hyde Park, in the city center; it recently completed a $14.5 million redo. **Stats** 557 rooms; 3 restaurants; 1 bar. **Competitive Edge** All the urban conveniences, steps from one of the city's prettiest parks. **Rooms to Book** Northeast corner rooms on the upper floors, for views of the park and the Royal Botanic Garden. **Don't Miss** A massage in the rooftop spa. **Cost** Doubles from $$. *161 Elizabeth St.; 800/325-3535 or 61-2/9286-6000; www.sheraton.com*

SYDNEY
■ W (78.89)
Stylish property in a converted warehouse on a historic downtown wharf, near restaurants and nightlife. **Stats** 100 rooms; 1 restaurant; 1 bar. **Competitive Edge** Cutting-edge design and loft-like public spaces make for one of the city's liveliest hotel scenes. **Rooms to Book** Splurge on the airy Marina Rooms (an extra $74) for stunning skyline views. **Don't Miss** Taking advantage of the hotel's attentive 24-hour concierge and room service. **Cost** Doubles from $$. *The Wharf at Woolloomooloo; 877/946-8357 or 61-2/9331-9000; www.whotels.com*

SYDNEY
■ The Westin (77.59)
Contemporary city-center hotel, set in the historic General Post Office building with a modern tower attached. **Stats** 416 rooms; 1 restaurant; 2 bars. **Competitive Edge** The No. 1 Martin Place complex, which fills the rest of the post office, has some of the city's best restaurants and shops. **Rooms to book** Heritage Rooms in the old building, for their historic charm. **Don't Miss** Mosaic restaurant's sophisticated, bento box–style lunch. **Cost** Doubles from $$. *No. 1 Martin Place; 800/228-3000 or 61-2/8223-1111; www.westin.com*

fiji
NADI
■ Westin Denarau Island Resort & Spa (formerly the Sheraton Royal Denarau) (77.58)
Low-rise resort surrounded by 25 lush acres along a stretch of prime Nadi Bay Beach; a full room renovation, as well as a new spa and pool, will be complete in August. **Stats** 274 rooms; 3 restaurants; 3 bars. **Competitive Edge** The island's most up-to-date facilities, following the redo. **Rooms to Book** Those in the 300 and 400 blocks are close to the pool and the beach; the 600 block is most secluded. **Don't Miss** Meke dance performances and fire-walking ceremonies at the on-site arts complex. **Cost** Doubles from $$. *800/228-3000 or 679/675-0000; www.westin.com*

french polynesia
BORA-BORA
■ Bora Bora Lagoon Resort & Spa (82.37)
Rustic bungalows on the private island of Motu Toopua. **Stats** 79 rooms; 2 restaurants; 2 bars. **Competitive Edge** The Marü Spa, which has the region's best couples treatments. **Rooms to Book** End-of-pontoon rooms, for unobstructed views. **Don't Miss** Chartering a luxury yacht to ply the lagoon. **Cost** Doubles from $$$. *Vaitape; 800/237-1236 or 689/604-000; www.orient-expresshotels.com*

BORA-BORA
■ Bora Bora Pearl Beach Resort & Spa (80.87)
Thatched-roof suites surrounded by tropical gardens. A new spa is opening soon. **Stats** 80 rooms; 2 restaurants; 2 bars. **Competitive Edge** Top-notch snorkeling and diving facilities. **Rooms to Book** Premium Overwater bungalows, for views and privacy. **Don't Miss** A catamaran cruise at dusk. **Cost** Doubles from $$$. *Vaitape; 689/508-452; www.pearlresorts.com*

BORA-BORA
■ Hotel Bora Bora (83.50)
Exclusive cluster of Polynesian-style bungalows set among beaches and lagoons. **Stats** 54 rooms; 1 restaurant; 2 bars. **Competitive Edge** Bora-Bora's most stylish resort (claw-foot tubs, exotic woods), thanks to the Aman touch. **Rooms to Book** Pool Farés, for their intimate setting and private pools. **Don't Miss** Horseback riding on abandoned islets. **Cost** Doubles from $$$. *Point Raititi; 800/477-9180 or 689/604-411; www.amanresorts.com*

BORA-BORA
■ InterContinental Le Moana Resort (80.24)
Peaceful collection of bungalows (formerly the Bora Bora Beachcomber InterContinental Resort) at beautiful Matira Point. Closed through June 2006 for repairs from a storm surge. **Stats** 64 rooms; 2 restaurants; 2 bars. *Point Matira; 800/327-0200 or 689/604-900; www.intercontinental.com*

new zealand
CHRISTCHURCH
■ The George (77.31)
Intimate hotel in the heart of the city, steps from 450-acre Hagley Park. **Stats** 55 rooms; 2 restaurants; 1 bar. **Competitive Edge** Pescatore and 50 on Park, two of the city's best restaurants. **Rooms to Book** 3rd-floor Kings, for peaceful garden views and private balconies. **Don't Miss** Touring the banks of the Avon River on one of the hotel's bikes. **Cost** Doubles from $$. *50 Park Terrace; 800/525-4800 or 64-3/379-4560; www.thegeorge.com*

TAUPO
■ Huka Lodge (91.00)
Standard-setting, ultra-luxe North Island lodge on 17 wooded acres above the trout-filled Waikato River. **Stats** 24 rooms; 1 restaurant; 1 bar. **Competitive Edge** Bewitching mix of escapist luxury and a rustic setting. **Rooms to Book** Nos. 4, 13, 16, and 19 have their own fireplaces. **Don't Miss** The nightly tasting menus—ask for the table beside the outdoor fireplace. **Cost** Doubles from $$$$$, including breakfast, pre-dinner drinks, and dinner. *800/525-4800 or 64-7/378-5791; www.hukalodge.co.nz*

The St. Regis Hotel, New York City.

index

index

credits

contributors

Lisa Abend	Michael Hannwacker	Shane Mitchell
Paul Alexander	Farhad Heydari	Bridget Moriarity
Richard Alleman	Kendall Hill	Clara Ogden
Tom Austin	Bill Hinchberger	Aoife O'Riordain
Anna Bakola	Kristin Hohenadel	Christopher Petkanas
Aaron Barker	Catherine Hong	Kevin Raub
Andrea Bennett	Jen Howze	Douglas Rogers
Elena Bowes	Peter Hyman	Sarah Rose
Anya von Bremzen	H. Scott Jolley	Seth Sherwood
Robin Cherry	Lisa Kalis	Mireille Silcoff
Victoria DiSilverio	Xander Kaplan	Rachel Snyder
Julie Earle-Levine	David Kaufman	Anya Strzemien
Mark Ellwood	David A. Keeps	Rima Suqi
Amy Farley	Leanne Kitchen	Guy Trebay
Carrie Fisher	Liz Krieger	Joanne Trestrail
Sarah Forrest	Sarah Raper Larenaudie	Meeghan Truelove
Martin Forstenzer	Matt Lee	Vicki Vasilopoulos
Howard W. French	Ted Lee	Hannah Wallace
Eleni N. Gage	Peter Jon Lindberg	Valerie Waterhouse
Hillary Geronemus	Robert Maniaci	Susan Welsh
Sascha de Gersdorff	Jane Margolies	Amy Westervelt
Peter S. Green	Connie McCabe	Stephen Whitlock
Granville Greene	Rob McKeown	Elizabeth Woodson
Jaime Gross	Jessica Merrill	Kristine Ziwica
Michael Gross	Charles Michener	
	Clark Mitchell	
	Heidi Sherman Mitchell	

photographers

For 35 years, *Travel + Leisure* magazine has been the leading authority for the discerning traveler, guiding readers through its comprehensive coverage of hotels, restaurants, and shopping around the world. In addition, it has provided insightful articles on the places, ideas, and trends that define modern global culture. With award-winning writing, photography, and design, T+L is the world's leading travel magazine. Visit us at www.travelandleisure.com.